# ALVAR AALTO AND THE FUTURE OF ARCHITECTURE

In the contemporary practice of architecture, digital design and fabrication are emergent technologies in transforming how architects present a design and form a material strategy that is responsible, equitable, sustainable, resilient, and forward-looking. This book exposes dialogue between history, theory, design, construction, technology, and sensory experience by means of digital simulations that enhance the assessment and values of our material choices. It offers a critical look to the past to inspire the future.

This new edition looks to Alvar Aalto as the primary protagonist for channeling discussions related to these topics. Architects like ALA, Shigeru Ban, 3XN, Peter Zumthor, and others also play the role of contemporary guides in this review. The work of Aalto and selected contemporary architects, along with computer modeling software, showcase the importance of comprehensive design. Organized by the Five Ts of contemporary architectural discourse—Typology, Topology, Tectonics, Technic, Thermodynamics—each chapter is used to connect history through Aalto and develop conversations concerning historical and contemporary models, digital simulations, ecological and passive/active material concerns, construction and fabrications, and healthy sensorial environments.

Written for students and academics, this book bridges knowledge from academia into practice and vice versa to help architects become better stewards of the environment, make healthier and more accountable buildings, and find ways to introduce policy to make technology a critical component in thinking about and making architecture.

**Robert Cody**, AIA, NCARB, LEED AP, is Partner at Amoia Cody Architecture, Professor of Practice, and Former Associate Dean and Chair at the New York Institute of Technology School of Architecture and Design. For over 30 years, he has worked on projects from wood-frame houses to precast concrete office buildings, interior renovations to freestanding towers, design competitions to physical construction, and ecological design, to The Museum of Modern Art. Cody has practiced and taught architectural design theory, building construction, and architecture studios with particular concentration in the comprehensive design studio. He has coordinated and taught travel studios in Italy and Scandinavia. He has also been the New York Tech NCARB AXP Coordinator and AIAS Faculty Advisor since 2012.

**Angela Amoia** is Partner at Amoia Cody Architecture and Adjunct Associate Professor of Architecture at the New York Institute of Technology School of Architecture and Design. Amoia has practiced and taught history, theory, architecture studios, including the comprehensive design studio, and study abroad in Italy since graduating from Columbia University with a Master's degree in Advanced Architectural Design. Her role as project manager ranged in scale from skyscrapers to large-scale academic facilities and residential houses and loft buildings.

# ALVAR AALTO AND THE FUTURE OF ARCHITECTURE

*Robert Cody and Angela Amoia*

Routledge
Taylor & Francis Group

NEW YORK AND LONDON

Cover image: The Swatch Headquarters in Construction, Switzerland, Shigeru Ban Architects, 2019 (Credit: Blumer-Lehmann AG)

First published 2023
by Routledge
605 Third Avenue, New York, NY 10158

and by Routledge
4 Park Square, Milton Park, Abingdon, Oxon, OX14 4RN

*Routledge is an imprint of the Taylor & Francis Group, an informa business*

© 2023 Robert Cody and Angela Amoia

*Library of Congress Cataloging-in-Publication Data*
A catalog record for this book has been requested

ISBN: 978-0-367-74972-9 (hbk)
ISBN: 978-0-367-74973-6 (pbk)
ISBN: 978-1-003-16057-1 (ebk)

DOI: 10.4324/9781003160571

Typeset in Bembo
by Apex CoVantage, LLC

# CONTENTS

# ILLUSTRATIONS

## Illustrators

# ACKNOWLEDGMENTS

We want to thank NYIT, the Dean of the School of Architecture and Design, Maria Perbellini, and the SoAD administrative team for their support. For their time and wisdom, Director David Diamond, Professors Matthias Altwicker and Farzana Gandhi, and Librarian Vanessa Viola. To our students, past, present, and future. Steven Sculco for his copyedit, illustrations, and imagination. For our shared world and our families' future: Katarina & Gabriella, Gianluca, Brianna & London, Victoria, Mikey, and Frankie. Special thanks to Professor Paul Amatuzzo for introducing us to Aalto's work in Italy as traveling students. We have been most thankful to each other for our continuous collaboration ever since.

# INTRODUCTION—ALVAR AALTO AND THE FUTURE OF ARCHITECTURE

We started this book with a question: *Can architecture be made more responsive to its future?* To help answer our question and find direction, we look to a mentor— Alvar Aalto. Along with his collaborators, Aalto researched planning and materials, incorporated data through experimentation, developed novel fabrication techniques, and provided intellectual discourse on the future through his writings and speeches. He identified the differences between social, technical, and behavioral types of progress. In addition, his practice and experimental methodology mirror contemporary architectural thinking and working models.

Aalto and his Atelier established an approach to design that integrated art and technology in a comprehensive, flexible, and empathetic way. With Aalto's guidance, we work to position a point of view that accommodates ecological circumstances and social equity. By reviewing architecture, not for its appearance but its *affect*, we realize a fundamental analysis of Aalto that remains critically relevant today.

Our motive is to expose and enhance the values of integrating history, theory, science, and technology in design. As architects, we negotiate countless conditions to connect ideas with physical reality. We engage in research and inquire about the past to move forward through the present. We explore the nature of materiality and its agency in making buildings equitable and responsible. Finally, we develop comprehensive strategies that incorporate optimal uses of materials, fabrication options, and conditioning systems that are efficient and advance the health and well-being of the people who occupy our buildings.

We discuss history, past and current practices, and digital tools; all used to make informed decisions. This book is not a history volume, textbook, or guidebook on using digital tools, nor is it expressly about Alvar Aalto. Instead, it is an

DOI: 10.4324/9781003160571-1

appraisal that moves us closer to building design as a synthetic body, built considering people and environments.

Through our writings and examples, we emphasize that to accomplish this goal, students, educators, and practitioners must utilize and advance digital tools and requisite simulative representative environments as a future working method. Of course, we do not suggest that every class or practice convert its entire working method into a digital design procedure. Still, we should all ask how digital analysis, simulation tools, fabrication methods, and sensor systems might enact a more comprehensive architecture as imminent praxis.

## Alvar Aalto and the Future?

The unparalleled design sensitivity and comprehensive integration of place, history, and technology make Hugo Alvar Henrik Aalto (1898–1976), the architect from Finland, a model figure to help us assess contemporary architecture. We study the work of Aalto to look to the future, not because his work is intellectually superior or more historically significant, but because his concepts are comprehensive—a body of form and material, made with flexible standards and a sensitive attitude towards people and their environment.

In the second edition of *Space, Time and Architecture*, published in 1949, Sigfried Giedion named "three institutional buildings inseparably linked to the rise of contemporary architecture"; Le Corbusier's League of Nations Palace planned in Geneva, Switzerland; Walter Gropius' Bauhaus at Dessau in Germany; and Alvar Aalto's Sanatorium in Paimio, Finland. These three projects set new typologies that expressed new forms for gathering and working. They also demonstrated the promise of healthy environments, encouraged standardized production, and applied new construction methods.

The Paimio Sanatorium, conceived as a total work of architecture, remains a model for understanding architecture made for the human experience. It harmonizes form and material in service of function—the care of those stricken by tuberculosis—which plagued the first half of the 20th century. As Juhani Pallasmaa described, "Alvar Aalto's Paimio Sanatorium is heartbreaking in its radiant belief in a humane future and the success of the societal."[1] Although the building's original function has gone away with proper treatment and proliferate vaccination against TB, its humanist spirit lives on.

Aalto was an architect, artist, and technician. An author with many collaborators and editors, he understood that a team of experts is required to make sophisticated buildings. In 1940, Aalto wrote,

> The problems of architecture cannot usually be solved at all using technical methods . . . architecture is a super-technical form of creation in which this harmonizing of various forms of function plays a key role . . . A building is not a technical problem at all—it is an *archi-technical problem*.[2]

Aalto's first wife, Aino Maria Marsio-Aalto (1894–1949)—who passed away at a young age—and his second wife, Elissa Aalto (1922–94), were significant contributors to his work and practice. As the first creative director of Artek (founded in 1935), Aino helped develop interrelationships between architecture, interiors, furniture, glassware, and landscapes. She also acted as Alvar's manager and was his collaborator in the most vital projects, Paimio Sanatorium (1932), Viipuri Library (1935), the Finnish Pavilion of the New York World's Fair (1939), and Villa Mairea (1939). Elissa also managed Aalto and was a crucial figure in the Aalto Atelier. In addition, she completed renowned later works, including the Santa Maria Assunta Church in Riola di Vergato, Italy (1978, the campanile completed in 1993), and the Essen Opera House in Germany (1988).

The Aaltos' experiments at Artek and in the Aalto Atelier fostered innovation: their use of *flexible standardization* enabled an innovative approach that resisted convention. Moreover, Aalto engrained a deep understanding of *materia* in the studio culture. As a result, the works, crafted with the percept of material culture and history, transcend type and traditional tectonic order. Structure and material were associative technics that responded to modern construction and vernacular sensibility. Last, a respect for the "little man" resulted in an empathetic architecture for the human environment and thermodynamic reception.

In his writings and lectures, Aalto accentuated the importance of comprehensive and human-centric thinking, often using metaphor. In 'The White Table,' he tells us that formative experiences may guide the entirety of our life and legacy. Accordingly, we have selected texts that are vital to that understanding. In 'The Trout and the Stream,' Aalto discusses the *universal substance* of art and nature, which is advanced further in 'The Relationship between Architecture, Painting, and Sculpture,' where we learn about *materia,* the essence of architecture and design. 'From Doorstep to Living Room' delivers a discourse on model form and adaptation to climate. 'The Humanizing of Architecture' is a seminal text on human concerns and how architecture must include the *psychophysical* realm to advance into a new stage. In 'The Human Factor,' we find questions concerning technology. Finally, 'The Reconstruction of Europe Is the Key Problem for the Architecture of Our Time' concerns the future of architecture.

In 2021, the Council of Europe added Alvar Aalto to its Cultural Routes as his life and buildings "contribute to the well-being, equality and peaceful living in societies,"[3] and UNESCO[4] has tentatively listed the works in Finland acknowledging their authentic and outstanding universal value.

Previously, we visited Aalto buildings with students in Finland, Denmark, Germany, Italy, and the USA (Figure 0.1). We experienced his thoughtful assimilation and effect of light and material. We observed repeating organizational and detail strategies and flexible accommodation to both location and function. In addition, Aalto's materials, colors, and textures heighten sensitivities and intensify relationships to the landscape. For Aalto, the topical dimension of architecture is a measured *form-system-material* triad situated in place for people.

**FIGURE 0.1**  NYIT 2019 SoAD Thesis Students visit the Villa Mairea. Left to Right: Alexandra Panichella, Matthew Acer, Robert Cody, Golda Hoorizadeh, Jacqueline Ras, Steven Sculco, Trey Graham, Candy Salinas, Siobhan O'Gorman, Kazi Tabassum.

Photo by Angela Amoia.

Furthering our consideration of Aalto, Kenneth Frampton has said that

> Aalto is the most important architect of the twentieth and now even the twenty-first century. He is still one of the very few architects who have been able to conceive of an architecture capable of providing a certain level of security for ordinary people through his subtle use of form and material.[5]

The skylights, ceilings, material, and formations with light and nature situate Aalto's buildings in their places. The plans, stairs, metamorphic masses, and curvilinear forms introduce pattern and variation. Material elements, their positions, and the memories evoke an atmosphere, or a sense of mood. In the work of Aalto, we see how elements become interrelated arrangements, both associative and elastic. In today's context, studying these interrelationships prompts a working method that anticipates optimization and the mass–customization now possible with computer-aided design and fabrication tools.

Most importantly, we look to Aalto's *super-technical* approach to postulate that architecture could not only be more efficient, but more thermodynamically active and experientially powerful. This review of Aalto's works and writings provides working parameters that seek to advance the making of reactive environments using the tools and techniques of today.

**Five Meme Methodology**—Topology—Typology—Tectonic—Technic—Thermodynamic

Michel Foucault uses *heterotopia* to describe discursive spaces with layers of meaning or relationships beyond what immediately meets the eye. Likewise, some have used this term to describe Aalto's utopic vision of interrelating boundaries of matter and sensation. This book looks to outline these interrelationships using a Five Meme Methodology.

We are all familiar with the Five Ws + H: the *who, what, where, when, why*, and *how* of information gathering and problem-solving.

Keep in mind that design is not for *me*; it is for people *who* use the buildings you create. Buildings and projects you review must assist in this discovery. After you know *who* you design for, *what* you choose to make is answered by finding what is best for people, place, and the world around us. *Where* you build has consequences. History and analysis can help tell us *when* something was, what it is, and what it can or should be. *How* we choose to design is significant. Our choices can damage or enhance our environments. *Why* we design is vital. We must be committed to making things better, using less energy, crafting responsibly, and always putting the environment and the body of humanity first.

This book introduces Five Ts that embody the essence of architecture: *Topology, Typology, Tectonic, Technic, and Thermodynamic*. The Five Ts are memes that span the history of building construction and architectural discourse.

A meme is an idea, behavior, or style that spreads through imitation from person to person within a culture, often carrying a symbolic meaning that represents a particular phenomenon or theme. In his book, *The Selfish Gene*, evolutionary biologist Richard Dawkins suggests that "an idea-meme" might be defined as an entity capable of being transmitted from one brain to another.[6]

The Five Ts are parts of an existential discourse necessary to confront the climate of our changing world. As talking points in a package of responsive architectural design strategies, the Five Ts provide a framework for evaluating comprehensive concepts and models that commit materials and values towards human comfort ahead of prescriptive means and methods.

Alongside the works and writings of Aalto is our discussion of the Five Ts as they relate to his works and to other historic and contemporary buildings that exemplify these ideals. Diagrams, citations, and a working vocabulary in the text enable further encounters, establish a broader point of view, and bind the many subjects encompassed. Finally, we advance this review by suggesting how digital design and fabrication, when used responsibly, are essential tools for delivering an ecologically informed, 21st-century architecture.

**Topology**—Place | Situation | Position | Surroundings| Interrelationship | Form | Ecology | Spirit

Topology is defined by layered surfaces and elastic boundaries of possibilities, judgments, and accommodations. In architecture, topology is obtainable, not as a mathematical construct, but as an interrelationship of form to its location, responding to places and situating to the surrounding world.

Topological formation in architecture should be dynamic variation, facilitated by information technology, informed by its surroundings. Morphological structures that are derivatives of an ecological topology become manifestations in service of dwelling in our world, not formal operations that are self-intrinsic manifestations acting against the natural world.

Alvar Aalto used variable, flexible design methods to make buildings contoured and grounded to a location. His buildings empathically draw in the landscape, material, and context. They are positioned within and around the specific spaces and circumstances of place for dwelling.

Contemporary technologies allow us to measure the environment and position ourselves to view our work in novel ways. Reviewing Aalto's topological form-system provides an opportunity to speculate on how the use of new technologies can help us make more responsive buildings than ever before.

In topology, we study the measure of a building's position, orientation, and interrelationship to its surrounding environment. The morphology of a place, its ecology, climate, and social structure provide specific parameters for measuring a building's performance.

**Typology**—History | Culture | Function | Space | Order | Organization | Orientation | Boundaries

Analyzing architectural forms can help us understand more about a place, its traditions and customs, materials, technologies, and fabrications. Unpacking type in architecture allows us to read and discover adaptations and strategies needed to bring forward new typologies.

Aalto looked to the past, not to imitate, but to create a new architecture that unified tradition and modernity towards new type-forms. His working method, infused with the memory of history and cultural experience, responses to nature, and technical syntheses, allowed him to make typologically flexible buildings. We gain inspiration to help define an ecological type and a new typology through Aalto. Today, digital tools enable us to design novel type-form and accurately build a comprehensive body and envelope. Knowledge surrounding the discipline of architecture provides opportunities to discover its ecological potential.

In typology, we study the measure of order and organizations to position spaces to be more wholly related to our environment. The parameters classify arrangements in response to how a building performs for the human body. Function is linked to form, not only by order, but also by bodily motions and the experiences those movements provide. Moving from one space to the next involves a series of thresholds and boundaries. These zones are sometimes open, sometimes closed, but are always set up around experience.

**Tectonic**—Elements | Material | Structure | Atmosphere | Agency | Expression | Embodiment

Architectural tectonics has been rooted in cultural matters, form to force material strategies, and poetic interpretation. In recent years, information processing with computational design and fabrication has made tectonics in architecture more elastic and less rooted in formal characterizations.

Aalto did not recognize tectonics in the traditional sense. He instead used the agency of materials to interrelate form, structure, and environment. Aalto used the term *materia* to advance this position; unity between art, technology, and nature. Aalto's work manifests a form-system-material triad that he called "technical functionalism." We recognize this most in his use of wood, a material used for its atmospheric qualities, elemental properties, and ecological parameters. We can imagine Aalto's work as an embodiment of principles that make him a forerunner of *ecological tectonics*, a new tectonic of form and material calculated to function with a smaller environmental footprint while maximizing the physical, perceptual experience.

In Tectonics, we study the measure of material. The choice of material in architecture is about history, structural characteristics, poetic interpretation, and ecological accountability. Material matters in contemporary practice are performative and embody energy and health. We measure energy efficiencies in operation as well as energies expended in extraction, material processing, and pollutants. It is no longer about 'less is more' but 'doing more with less' and making better decisions.

Together, these focus points form a synergistic structure of the interrelationships of form, space, matter, sensation, and responsiveness. This expanded definition of material, through the lens of ecology, may help us better account for energy, empathy, and aesthetic performance.

**Technic**—Standards | Compliance | Efficiency | Construction | Flexibility | Fabrication

Technic involves the art and craft of a discipline. In architecture, the tools of designing and fabricating buildings have fundamentally changed. Today, computational analysis and novel fabrication technologies have disrupted traditional standard practices.

Alvar Aalto, through his notion of *flexible standardization*, presents a model for emergent design solutions that include nature and humanism in a holistic, synthetic, artful, technological environment. Aalto developed universal standards, and with his open imagination, he found new forms of production and elastic planning strategies. Aalto called this *viable variety*, which he deemed natural standardization.

Buildings are subject to innumerable circumstances that have made simultaneous analyses difficult until now. We can define a more informed ecological standard through material intelligence with environmental performance built into model codes and the variable input parameters in our digital tools.

In Technic, we study measures of efficiency, elasticity, and adaptability. For example, choices concerning building fabrication have as much to do with energy consumption during construction as the building's life-cycle cost. Fostering experiments to review networks of orientation, organization, material, and acclimatizing features will allow us to deliver a promising spatially and formally compelling form of architecture that is efficient and sensual. Performance measures energy efficiency and accounts for comfort and experience of the body. The final measure of architecture is its performance.

**Thermodynamic**—Sensation | Experience | Comfort | Health | Psychophysical | Phenomenal

Thermodynamics in architecture includes material systems related to heat and energy that interact with our human sensory systems. Physical sensation and mental perception overlap literal and phenomenal boundaries surrounding what we see, feel, and imagine.

Aalto understood that to humanize architecture, one must incorporate the psychophysical realm of experience. He did this most notably in the Paimio Sanatorium, with all design aspects focused on the body. He used materials to guide our experience and incorporate nature to arouse sensory perception and memory. As a sensory material environment, the building includes active systems used to enhance, or augment, this natural form-system-material approach. Aalto described this as the "supra-technical" creation that is architecture—a synthetic integration of dynamic forces made to condition the mind and body through the conditions of building.

Contemporary simulation technologies and sensors can improve our health and expand an atmosphere of sensation. Our future will be built using these tools, perhaps eventually incorporating neuroscience as the ultimate measure of comfort and experience.

## Five Meme Interrelationships

At the end of each chapter, we present two recent projects that comprise the Five Ts. They provide a current point of view and are accompanied by diagrams, offering insight into the reading of this text.

The Zollverein School of Management in Essen, Germany and the Central Library Oodi in Helsinki, Finland provide examples of the use of digital tools for accommodating particular site conditions, thus situating buildings in light of place.

The Perez Art Museum situates building form, internal organization, and material strategies to propose an ecological model type. The W.I.N.D. House by UNStudio delivers new standards for contemporary typology.

The Kunsthaus Bregenz in Austria by Peter Zumthor, by using a thermally active material system, exemplifies a tectonic crossover. Likewise, the Maggie's Center in Leeds, UK by Heatherwick Studio embodies ecological tectonics in its material structure.

In the Swatch Headquarters by Shigeru Ban we see an ecological material technic. In the Olympic House by 3XN we see a model of flexible planning and fabrication that is empathetic and performative.

The Löyly Sauna in Helsinki incorporates *literal* thermodynamical systems as bodily experience, while the Gifu Media Cosmos by Toyo Ito offers a *phenomenal* approach towards the linking of material with light and sensation.

## Thoughts for the Future

How we make and inhabit space in the world is changing. To gain further familiarity with the pressures of our changing world, we encourage our students to review the United Nations Climate Action Fast Facts.[7] Throughout our existence as a species, human impacts have altered the surface of our planet. In the past, changes were slow and primarily local. Now, these changes produce more significant effects globally, impacting us all indiscriminately.

The Unites States National Oceanic and Atmospheric Administration (NOAA) report, published in the *Bulletin of the American Meteorological Society*, confirms that in 2020, despite a 6 to 7 percent drop in emissions from reduced activity amid the COVID-19 pandemic, the concentration of greenhouse gases in our atmosphere still hit the highest level ever recorded.

While a growing coalition of countries has committed to net zero emissions by 2050, about half of emissions cuts must be in place by 2030 to keep warming below 1.5 °C. In addition, fossil fuel production must decline by roughly 6 percent per year between 2020 and 2030. Since nearly half of all emissions are due to building occupancy, construction, and transportation or material processing activity, architects play a crucial role in mitigating climate change.

Since the 1980s, model codes, better materials, accurate specifications, and economic strategies have reduced energy consumption in buildings by 20 percent. Specifying an additional 20 percent reduction through contemporary modeling and construction technologies is not only plausible but imperative.

In architectural education, it is essential to understand the impacts of technology on design. Students, educators, and practitioners alike must work through analytical methods that incorporate the lessons of history and innovation in order to adopt and adapt technologies for responsive environments.

As students, much of what we do in a design studio is speculative, not accountable to performative metrics. However, using computational tools, the studio can make accurate measures to be more generative and novel as we approach a new paradigm in ecological design.

The Five Ts can be used as theoretical and applied research methodology for design studio practice. In this way, we can evaluate and demonstrate skills of making integrated decisions with considerations of historical precedent, environmental stewardship, technical documentation, accessibility, site conditions, life-safety, environmental systems, structural systems, building envelope systems and assemblies, and concerns of social equity and material resources.

In practice, qualified building performance analysis is essential. Therefore, integrating simulation as part of the design process is critical to maintaining the relevancy of architecture. This is important, not only for the responsible modeling of form and the accurate predicting of building performance, but also for simulating architecture's emotive force.

## Notes

1 Pallasmaa, Juhani. *The Eyes of the Skin: Architecture and the Senses.* Wiley-Academy, 2005.
2 Aalto, Alvar. 'The Reconstruction of Europe,' in *Alvar Aalto in His Own Words.* Ed. Schildt, Göran. Otava, 1997, p.154.
3 https://www.coe.int/en/web/cultural-routes/alvar-aalto-route (Accessed 05 March 2022).
4 https://whc.unesco.org/en/tentativelists/6509/ (Accessed 05 March 2022).
5 Cultural Sustainability. *An Interview with Kenneth Frampton.* Architecture Norway, An Online Review of Architecture, 05 September 2006.
6 Dawkins, Richard. *The Selfish Gene.* Oxford University Press, 1989, p.196.
7 https://www.un.org/en/climatechange/science/key-findings (Accessed 05 March 2022).

# 1
# TOPOLOGY—DESIGN IN *LIGHT* OF PLACE

**Topology** = the way in which constituent parts are interrelated or arranged. (*Tópos*: "place")

All places are unique, nested within a *topos* or place. For Aristotle, *topos* is rooted in rhetoric, as the place or location to begin one's argument. Place and location are the foundational discursive terms in making architecture. An association with your location forms these *topoi* amidst successive places. Places are situated in our memory and thus create an understanding of location.

Logos is the reasoned discourse that accounts for the topics of our world. Topo- (*topos*), as a combining form prefix, commonly understood as meaning *place*, combined with -ology (*logos*), forms the branch of knowledge about the study of *place* that accounts for the substances of our universe.

Our world is a continuous surface, comprised of many deformations, textures, substances, and living things that inhabit it. When *Topo-* is combined with *-graphy*, which denotes representing, we understand place as a description that is drawn out upon a surface.

It is essential to distinguish between *topography*, and *topology*. Topology can be historically defined as "the art or method of assisting memory by associating the thing, or subject, to be remembered with some place."[1] It subjects a relationship between land and memory, our sense of place. On the other hand, topography represents the natural features, surface reliefs, and elevations as graphical depictions on a map. It is quite literally the writing and drawing out of place.

DOI: 10.4324/9781003160571-2

"Topology does not know the straight line, but it forms a part of the projective and Euclidean systems."[2] Topographical surveying and mapping have relied on a Cartesian coordinate system—a tri-dimensional or set of numerical coordinates—with signed distances to the point from fixed perpendicular lines, measured in the same unit of length. This system, defined by vectors, consists of straight lines connecting point to point.

Greek town planning generally relied on the terrain or *topos* to form towns and structures. The Greek temple stood in contrast to the ground; however, it remained developed with the earth, whereas the Roman system imposed an order against the earth. Between then and now, much has changed. Therefore, we need to contour our point of view towards a new strategy. In many non-Western and pre-Cartesian societies, topology is not only morphological but also a joining of topography and culture, formed and preserved through communion.

Topology is an analytical study of the morphology of elements representing the relief present in a place with the ecological system served by deformation in the earth's surface. This reading is critical to view our world as quantitative and qualitative. The climate of a region is often shaped by the changing surface features, as are the boundaries of cultures. Mountain ranges or bodies of water are topographical conditions that often present political boundaries. Yet, they are no more than unbiased deformations on the natural surface. As two-dimensional representations, our mappings often incite artificial boundaries and distort our worldview. Through his *Dymaxion Map*, Buckminster Fuller (1895–1983) gave us an improved unfolded representation to make us aware of our interconnected world. The trip to the moon and Google Earth has now provided a new point of view, one of the wholeness of earth and of an ability to observe that boundaries are imaginary, because we all dwell together within the folds of a shared, delicate surface.

Topology is also a mathematical construct concerned with locations comprised of spatial relations through continuous surface transformations, mainly by pushing, bending, twisting, or folding. This notion extends to the way we use software to assist in the development of built surfaces in continuity with the natural surface as a dynamic structure. These deformations are more qualitative than they are vectorial measures. While geometry is concerned with shapes and sizes, topology investigates questions of connectivity and boundaries.

These topological variations compose place, location, and form relationships between surface and space interconnected with the material world. We are concerned with *placing* or *situating* forms that respond to their surroundings within a topological framework. Enfolded thinking of topology is an interrelationship of environment and building that is drawn from knowledge and information in our surrounding world.

Considerations on siting and making a building starts with an analysis of the spatial and morphological features of the site, by mapping forces and variables, form and material character, topography (both built and unbuilt), spatial dimensions, paths, and movement systems. Climate, degrees of light, wind, sound, and smells define the parameters. Next, the site's ecology describes interactions with living species and natural resources that affect living conditions. Finally, history (both in human and geological terms) and its inhabitants' economies, philosophies, beliefs, and inclusive values define culture and context.

We diagram these flows of information to demonstrate value and importance. Using this kind of comprehensive review of ecology, resulting social inequities emerge, and by cycling back through these varied considerations, we can make better decisions about building.

Design, structures, and ecology relate the built and natural environment to place. Philosophical and phenomenological questions present interrelationships between place and form, spaces and boundaries, elements and atmospheres, stasis and change, fact and feeling. Our discussions are not binary, but dialectic, a resolution of opposites, forming topological thinking.

This inquiry enables investigations into our world both *inside* and *outside* of our bodies, knowing that we are not only *in* space, but that we *inhabit* space. "The question of home, of living, and so of building is thus always and only a question that arises within a singular horizon, with respect to a concrete situatedness, in and through the unitary multiplicity of what is given *here*, within these *bounds*, in this *place*."[3]

## Situatedness

Buildings derive meaning from the *situatedness* of place, not by contextualization or by theoretical constructs. When observing context elementarily or atomistically, we often fail to understand the complexity required to interrelate our work with its location and surrounding place. To be substantial, the analysis of our surrounding world must be more than taxonomic. It must expose affordances between ecosystems, people, materials, animals, processes, and concerns.

The psychologist James J. Gibson (1904–79) informs us that perceiving

> an affordance, points two ways, to the environment and to the observer. So does the information to specify an affordance. But this does not in the least imply separate realms of consciousness and matter, a psychophysical dualism. It says only that the information to specify the utilities of the environment is accompanied by information to specify the observer himself, his body, legs, hands, and mouth. This is only to reemphasize that exteroception is accompanied by proprioception—that to perceive the world is to co-perceive oneself. This is wholly inconsistent with dualisms in any form, either mind-matter dualism or mind-body dualism. The awareness of the world and of one's complementary relations to the world are not separable.[4]

According to the mathematician Nikos Salingaros collaborator of architect Christopher Alexander, an organism that bases its behavior on direct sensor contact with the world is situated. He describes situatedness through an analogy of driving a car, which requires "continuous sensory input and interpretation of the immediate environment," with "decisions [that] are based on being situated in the physical road network, responding to every variation of the environment."[5] This description, however, does not account for the Global Positioning System (GPS) that digitally maps and locates us in space nor the mechanics now possible for self-driving. Together these technologies remove almost all bodily sensory actions required to operate the car. What is left is an affordance of comfort, safety, efficiency, and better experience for the passenger.

Situatedness gathers interrelated environmental, social, and cultural factors, in addition to psychological functions. It is topological as "it does not allow of any grounding of the structure as a whole by reference to any one element within that structure nor by reference to anything apart from that structure."[6] It is an affordance between the agent and the environment.

In architecture, situatedness applies epistemologies of location, grounding, and position, all while enfolding matters of atmosphere within a nested process enveloped by material and ecological concerns. This knowledge matters in the structure and character of what we do, what we say, and how we design.

Aalto describes a process of intuitively sketching to reconcile the complex and contradictory requirements of an architectural design:

> I forget the entire mass of problems for a while, after the atmosphere of the job and the innumerable difficult requirements have sunk into my subconscious. Then I move on to a method of working which is very much like abstract art. I just draw by instinct, not architectural synthesis, but what are sometimes childlike compositions, and in this way, on this abstract basis, the main idea gradually takes shape, a kind of *universal substance* which helps me to bring innumerable contradictory component problems into harmony.[7]

Aalto's *Universal Substance* unifies many phenomena into one all-encompassing concept. This concept informs a rational yet abstract design method synthesizing science and technology with art and intuition. Aalto's rationalism did not apply reason as its principal source for justification. Instead, it was rooted in nature and being-in-the-world; it was ontological. Yet, the work is empirical. Its concepts were arrived at through experiment and observation. It was rooted in modernism, but its haptic sensibility and corporal empathies did not dismiss innate thoughts or traditions. It was phenomenological in structuring experience and the embodiment of a place. And it was existential and metaphysical in its transposition of physical matter and psychophysical phenomena.

Rather than having opposed science with art, Aalto situated architecture between science and art. Aalto said that the architect's role "is to restore a correct order of values."[8] His thinking is topological, elastic boundaries of interconnected ideas, concepts, and transformations. Thus, drawing and ordering content layers that connect situational matters of place cannot be separated.

The *universal substance* signified by Aalto is manifest by the theoretical physicist Karen Barad (b. 1956), who writes:

> Primary ontological units are not "things", but phenomena-dynamic topological reconfigurings/entanglements/relationalities/(re)articulations of the world. And the primary semantic units are not "words" but material-discursive practices through which (ontic and semantic) boundaries are constituted. This dynamism is agency. Agency is not an attribute but the ongoing reconfigurings of the world. The universe is agential intra-activity in its becoming.[9]

Architecture is an agent of boundaries, both physical and implied by the agency of transforming a location into a more meaningful place. Through its reconfigurings of the world, architecture is a powerful change agent, positive or negative. Considering boundaries, we distinguish between *contextualization*, primarily concerned with representation or replicating the character of a given location, and *situatedness*, concerned with responsiveness to the surrounding environment, the physicality of form, and the material nature of a place.

Making the headquarters for Enso Gutzeit (1962), Aalto uses what is for him a unique form-system. According to Norberg-Shultz, "the task entailed an adaptation to the neoclassical milieu of the esplanade, and Aalto assumed its rhythms and proportions."[10] The building situates itself within a neoclassical context, not by replicating the same patterns, but by inlaying material structure and form that compliment, rather than imitate, its surroundings. The building is "a modern complement, simultaneously classical and anticlassical."[11] Adaptive thinking and morphogenesis situate building with a context. The building is organized with respect for the material and scale of the prevailing atmosphere of its site. Most prominent is the placement of the void in the U-shaped plan and its relationship to the Upenski Cathedral and its ascending pathway (Figure 1.1). The space apprehends urban structure in its recognition of the monument and placement of the nucleus of the building; it extends its boundary to become one with the situated environment, rather than a mere representational *fit* to its context.

In defining situation, we would be remiss in not mentioning Guy Debord (1931–94) and the *Situationists* who in *The Society of the Spectacle* wrote, "Everything that was directly lived has receded into a representation." The situation of times reflects one's time. For Debord and Aalto, *Modern Times* was framed by Charlie Chaplin and his representation of technology consuming the *little man*. The writings of Debord and Aalto have become positions that represent a vision of the world through panning out illusion to find actuality.

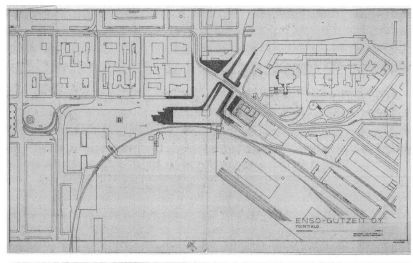

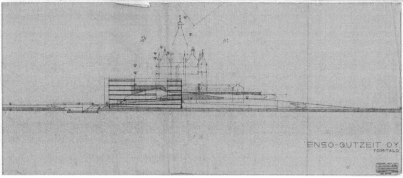

**FIGURE 1.1**   Enso Gutzeit—Situatedness Plan and Section

*(Credit:* Alvar Aalto Foundation drawing 60–4728 & 60–4716)

This thinking process allows us to embed working parameters or circumstances in a given location into our design methodology. Analysis of these parameters affords boundaries to test and develop *form-systems-material* topology by using elements that situate themselves around the needs of place, purpose, and people. Digital technologies are imbued with specific epistemic parameters that, when used correctly, are affordance tools that help us validate interactions and co-relate our work into the surrounding environment. In making this *form-systems-material* triad, the first act is knowing our location.

## Location

In 1956, the science fiction writer Arthur C. Clark (1917–2008) described the GPS concept almost 40 years before its use. GPS accurately predicts our location defined precisely by reference to a geo-coordinate system. We use maps in tandem with GPS coordinates to spot ourselves on the globe, but this does nothing to advance our location knowledge.

Location is the action or process of placing someone or something in a particular position, occupied or available for occupancy by people, plants, animals, and other distinctive elements. Features of a location define its situation. These features are both physical and perceptual.

The Finnish geographer Johannes Gabriel Granö (1882–1956) developed surveying of landscape geography where the perceived environment was as much a natural science as physical geography. For him, the view of the surrounding world is made by charting the situation of a landscape by observing not only geomorphology, topography, and location but bodies of water, living systems, culture, and human impact. Our view on the environment apprehends landscape "quantified by our sensual engagement."[12]

Aalto researcher Harry Charrington describes this engagement with our surrounding world: "First, a distant environment perceived by sight alone and dependent on a combination of topography and the spectator's vantage point 'that corresponding to landscape [constitutes] a locality,' and, second, a 'close, intimate world, which we always inhabit and in which context we perceive our geographical object with all our senses',"[13] a vicinity.

The basis of Granö's book *Pure Geography* (1929) includes human perception as an equal factor in defining a terrain. Considering that humans have impacted every terrain and territory on the planet, his work is quite prescient.

While living and working in Turku, Finland, between 1927–33, the Aaltos designed their most vital early works while making many influential contacts. The Turun Sanomat (1928–30), the Paimio Sanatorium and its eponymous chair (1929–33), and the Viipuri Library (1927–35) were all designed while in Turku. Alvar Aalto encountered Johannes Gabriel Granö at the University of Turku, and later built a house for Granö's successor August Tammekann in 1932 (now the Granö Center).

A report of the 2nd CIAM Conference of 1929 written by Le Corbusier (1887–1965) and Pierre Jeanneret (1896–1967) recorded an "Analysis of the Fundamental Elements of The Problem of *The Minimum House*." Le Corbusier remarks that "The dwelling place is a distinctly biological phenomenon" thus, the dwelling's function is revised, "this short, concise (and so very revolutionary) phrase as a slogan: *breath, hear, see* or again: *air, sound, light* or again: *ventilation and isothermics (even temperature), acoustics, radiation of light*, etc. . . . Everywhere, in everything, in our daily research, we lack scientific certainty . . . territories which we must prospect in search of sufficient truths."[14]

Aalto, present at the 1929 CIAM conference, met Walter Gropius (1883–1969) and Le Corbusier, as well as the architectural historian Sigfried Giedion and the artist and Bauhaus professor László Moholy-Nagy (1895–1946). At the Bauhaus, Moholy-Nagy structured a design exchange between nature, art, and technology, wherein the notion of "flexible" standardization and the structuring of light took shape. Aalto and Moholy-Nagy formed a lifelong friendship and shared the conviction that biology and technic are interrelated. The influence of Moholy-Nagy might be referenced in the Viipuri Library by way of its dynamic circulation and in the ceiling, where the grid of skylights recalls a screen of punched orifices in his work *Light Prop for an Electric Stage, 1930*.

In 1930, consistent with the aims of the 1929 CIAM congress, the Aaltos developed a 'Minimum Apartment.' The project was subsequently presented in a *Rationalization of the Minimum Dwelling* Exhibition, showcased that same year. The exhibition made concise statements on the necessity for housing to add psychological considerations and include cultural, emotional, aesthetic, economic, and social advancement in its design and production. "Biodynamic forms must serve as the basis for the internal divisions of a home, not obsolete symmetrical axis and standard rooms dictated by façade architecture." This Minimum Apartment was not a *machine for living*, but an *apparatus for living*, with standards that followed "the biological requirements of life includ[ing] air, light, and sun."[15]

In 1933, the Aalto's moved to Helsinki, Finland. After Paimio and Viipuri, the time between 1933 and the onset of WWII amplified ideas and production for the Aalto's. Soon they constructed a new house and studio, located just north of the city center. The house represented a new way of forming architecture and set the foundation for their next phase of work. They met Maire Gullichsen (daughter of industrialist Walter Ahlström), wife of industrialist Harry Gullichsen, and the art historian Nils-Gustav Hahl in 1935. Alvar and Aino, Maire Gullichsen, and Hahl started the Artek Company to produce and distribute Aalto furniture and glassware. Consequently, in 1936, the Aaltos designed the Sunila Pulp Mill and Housing in Kotka for Ahlström (Harry Gullichsen was the chairman), the famous Savoy Vase, and the Finnish Pavilion at the Paris International Exhibition.

In 1939, the Aaltos completed Villa Mairea, the acclaimed house for Maire and Harry Gullichsen in Noormarkku, and the Finnish Pavilion for the New York World's Fair, a project Frank Lloyd Wright (1867–1959) called "Genius." Soon after, he was appointed Research Professor at the Massachusetts Institute of Technology, but unfortunately, war broke out, and he returned to Finland to fight the Russian Soviet Union.

This chronology[16] marks the transformation, evolution, and situation of Alvar and Aino Aalto's design philosophies and their work. The first works are bound in historicism. The next are overt modernist. The latter are associated with an agenda that was mutually modern and grounded in the nature of Finland's surrounding location and traditions.

## The Surrounding World

In nature, an organism's interrelationship with its surroundings and one another defines an ecology. It is a reflexive relation that is simultaneously physical and perceptual. Evolutionary biologist Jakob von Uexküll (1864–1944) defines an organism's perception of its surrounding world as its *Umwelt*. "An Umwelt, according to Uexküll, comprises of two functionally distinct spheres or worlds: the world-as-sensed and the world of action." This function, according to Stanford Kwinter, provides an organism a "feedback circuit" where functions in an environment exist as "frameworks" that "impart and receive affects to and from its surroundings."[17]

Organisms situate themselves by using this sensory feedback framework, adjusting to environmental conditions. Likewise, buildings are situated, not by location, but by how they relate to surroundings and position respecting conditions and circumstances. Ecology may be defined as a topology of interrelated grounds that are adaptable, elastic, and evolve. Our view of the world influences what we do and make, thereby impacting bodies in their environment. It is an

> apprehended environment in which the organism relates to the world in a closed loop of interactions where the organism is acted upon, but in turn, acts upon the environment; so, Aalto envisages an empathetic environment in which spatial design is a unifying topology.[18]

Aalto used empathetic arrangements made for people and lived experiences of our environment in making architecture. The buildings are enveloped and grounded. Physical presence and composition do not overwhelm environment; they apprehend. The interrelationship of environment and elemental "living forms"[19] creates a unifying topology. The work methodically presents a sequential morphology of materially structured space in and around public life, where beneficial behavior patterns are stimulated, forming an interactive relationship to the surrounding world.

In addition, Aalto's "universal substance" and "conscious of the whole" closely follow Uexküll's Umwelt. This topological method extends into conditioning material form and tectonics, similar to Granö's concept of landscape, where values of location and proximity take precedence over formal constructs.

Paraphrasing J.J. Gibson, the *affordance* of a building or dwelling is what it *offers* the person, what it *provides* or *furnishes*, either for good or ill. Gibson's concept of affordances meant "something that refers to both the environment and the animal in a way that no existing term [had done]," implying that the person and the environment are "complementary." According to Aalto, building and setting are complementary and designed for human response.

Recognizing that conditions present in one location are not the same as those in another, Aalto adopted a *methodical accommodation of circumstance*, an adaptive, flexible design method that was employed in all of his work. Stanford Anderson (1934–2016) provided an astute description of the Baker House (1949) at MIT in Boston: "Aalto did not again create a building with serpentine curves or a dramatic hanging stairway. Forms were invented for a purpose, not as something to be visited upon other circumstances."[20] At the Baker House, the curvilinear shape delivers an arrangement that provides the inhabitants more light and views of the river and a constructive bi-product containing a continuous, flexible communal space developed between the rectilinear and curvilinear components. It is not the form itself, but what it affords, that makes the building's "irrational" shape become so accommodating to its use and thereby functionally rational.

Before settling upon the desired scheme, Aalto made many iterations to deliver this functional form. We can imagine Aalto using digital tools to manage the various parameters necessary to accommodate his intuitions and evaluate the practical necessities of the building program. The best solutions are not decided by the tool, but by the architect's record and analysis of the iterations.

He made clear in his writings a distinct attitude towards art, technology, and architectural problem-solving. In addition, he continually referenced nature and the impact of technology on environmental quality in his recorded statements and designs.

When making architecture, we all go through processes to develop successful outcomes. Sometimes, these processes involve experiments using analytical models and techniques to create or reinforce an idea; other times, the process intuitively relies on experience as a guide. Still, in all circumstances, the measure of architecture involves the review of information.

Information in architecture is multi-faceted. As we uncover the nature of a project, we ask questions answered by analyzing the pragmatic components. The architect's *language* is a form of discovery. Sometimes it underscores feeling versus thinking, offers vision versus language, or justifies difference versus similarity. Whatever the case, information is the basis for the discourse and formation of architecture.

Information cognition is a dual process—conscious and analytical, unconscious and intuitive. When using analytical cognition, our active mind involves conscious deliberation that draws on working memory resources. However, our unconscious mind uses situational pattern synthesis and recognition unconstrained by working memory limitations. This kind of cognition often exhibits a large capacity and fast responses independent of conscious, "executive" control. Intuition affords us the ability to understand something immediately, without the need for conscious reasoning. To be cognitive, as relating to cognition, is the mental action or process of acquiring knowledge and understanding through thought, experience, and the senses.[21]

Considerable quantifiable data about architecture and building needs to be unpacked and measured at a particular location. These include geology and topography, climate data, solar altitude and azimuth, wind speed and direction, heat and energy, utilities and systems, and other information obtained through historical data sets and recently as embedded information within digital design and engineering software. Other measures are more qualitative or empirical, such as the network of roads or building program types, demographics, local rules and regulations, or practical elements yet to be uncovered or rediscovered.

We can create intelligent buildings that apprehend their environment and adjust to the needs of their inhabitants. Consider digital design tools as *analytical cognition* machines that could support our intuition by iterating form to be more in tune with circumstance and situation by optimizing performance through specified input parameters. In addition, we can advance sensory feedback by embedding sensory devices and psychophysical augmentation systems. These new measures rely on growing our point of view towards understanding the interconnection between the building sensory system and human perception.

With all these measurable data sets, we still have the immeasurable, or the atmosphere of a place, the essential measure of architecture.

## Places and Boundaries (Being-in-the-World)

"For Aristotle, space was never disassociated from the notion of place (*topos*), which he defined as an envelope or boundary between an enclosed and an enclosing body."[22] Thus, with space enveloped by place, we understand the making of architecture, not as the space put between objects but as the envelopment of spaces defined by surroundings.

Place as compared to location is more ambiguous. We establish place by relying on human or social attributes rather than geography or geometry. Places are made distinct by overlapping morphological boundaries defined by geology, ecology, topography, climate, and other topological attentions. Enfolding these boundaries, perceptions of surroundings form a sense of belonging and respect.

Culture signifies place and thus contributes to our identity. Variations in social structure, ideologies, natural resources, and other situations found in a location signify one place or region from another. Language is also a significant identifier of place and culture, and it plays a vital role in developing the form and structure of a culture. For example, the Finnish language is "Topological" (relational), whereas the Swedish language (much like Indo-European language) is "Vectorial."[23] Alvar Aalto was bi-lingual with a Finnish father and a Swedish mother. During his childhood, he spoke both languages, and we might deduce that this dualism granted Aalto the inherent ability to reason synthetically.

Aalto was born in Kuortane, Finland, a small municipality 40 km east of Seinäjoki in 1898. As a young student, Aalto learned the role of seasons in nature by examining his native land and viewing and reading Nordic artists' landscape paintings and writings. In Finland, the landscape environment is considered the fundamental living space that changes with the seasons. For Aalto, nature soon became an extension of the inside world of the house. His "interconnecting" room concept will make house and landscape seamless.

These associations continually influenced Aaltos artful young mind. He drew and painted pictures of the forest, building shapes and masses, weather shelters, snow, ice, and contouring landscapes. His classical humanistic studies, natural imaginations, and building experience fused landscape with formal technical solutions that created a topological form-structure-material agency. Elements were used repeatedly through time, spaces, and scales. Within this crafting, the essential elemental forces of nature developed into new form-structures. Then, aided by the choice of materials, the architecture became determinate, involving sensory and memory experiences.

Aalto

> believed in the cross-inspirations of the various art forms; he sketched, painted, and sculpted all his life. The three art forms of architecture, painting, and sculpture are linked to one another in that they are all manifestations of the human spirit based on *materia*.[24]

These activities advanced an emergent *form-structure-material* topology that manifested simply in his travel sketches. In Italy, he drew landform buildings and protections against sun and wind. In Greece, he drew landscapes merging ruin with contour. Walls in Marrakesh. Windmills in Spain. Boats in Egypt. Storms in the United States.

Together with his childhood memories, view of nature, formal training, and building experience, these encounters all form a narrative. We know our world to be structured based on mental maps through neuroscience. For Aalto, the tracing and lived experience led to a transfiguration of historical, vernacular, and modern form into a new language of expression, memory, and experience (Figure 1.2). Material codification and signs expressed inside-out relationships with the landscape. Line, shadow, matter, color-matching the snow-covered, day–night landscape, and flowing space between cloud-form ceilings and free-form grounding portray the narrative.

Aalto's paintings made representations of the landscape and cultural *forest dreaming* later recalled in the Finland Pavilion at New York World's Fair (1939).[25] As Robert McCarter describes, Aaltos recall demonstrates an ability to metamorphose ceilings, furniture, glassware, and complete buildings using open-ended *flexible* contour, form, and figures. Similar remarks by Eeva-Liisa Pelkonen exemplify this idea more precisely:

> An aerial view of the Finnish lake landscape juxtaposed with the Savoy Vase, the plan of the Finnish Pavilion at the New York world's Fair, and an oblique bird's-eye view of Baker House visualizes the multitude of references and associations suggesting that the form has the power to metamorphose into anything at any scale.[26]

Philosophical realms in architecture also reside within a topological formation. The bending and twisting fields of influence around making and fabricating places delve into the ethical function of building and its responsibility outside its professional scope.

In his seminal text *Building, Dwelling, Thinking*, the philosopher Martin Heidegger (1889–1976) defined *dwelling* as enfolding the unity of earth, sky,

**FIGURE 1.2**   Northern Lights Image & Finish Pavilion Sketch

*(Credit:* Alvar Aalto Foundation drawing 68–371)

mortals, and divinities as the four-fold. For the architect, the divine resides in our imagination. We create worlds for corporeal use by living beings between the earth and the sky. Heidegger states,

> space is in essence that for which room has been made, that which is let into its bounds. That for which room is made is always granted and hence is joined, that is, gathered, by virtue of a location, that is, by such a thing as the bridge. Accordingly, spaces receive their being from locations and not from *space*.[27]

Christian Norberg-Shultz (1926–2000) describes *site* via its *genius loci*, or the pervading tone or mood of a place's environment—its *atmosphere*. When analyzing a place, we must understand topologies that represent the formative nature and development features (Figure 1.3). A place comprises overlapping spheres of influence demarcated by topographical, geological, political, and phenomenological boundaries. These boundaries intertwine climate, resources, culture, historical and ecological development of landscapes, buildings, streets, and cities in terms of architecture. An understanding of a place is more significant than visual observation; it is also what's felt.

In his book *Design with Climate*, the architect Victor Olgyay (1910–70) informs us that we must develop our work in harmony between a four-fold realm of ecology, technology, climate, and building. These overlapping realms provide a platform for us to consider the measure of our work. For example, his work on the *Bioclimatic Chart* develops boundaries of comfort, helping us observe contentment through a documented measurable instrument.

To design an architecture considering its place is to be responsive to all these boundaries. Considering these limits provides the freedom to make decisions. To be decisive is to believe in the wholeness of your measured actions. Only by empathizing with the nature of a location can you be sure that your efforts are responsible and respectful of the places in which we dwell.

William McDonough defines the place of dwelling in this way: "There are certain fundamental laws that are inherent to the natural world that we can use as models and mentors for human designs. Ecology comes from the Greek roots *Oikos* and *Logos*, 'household' and 'logical discourse.'"[28] Thus, it is appropriate, if not imperative, for architects to speak about ecology and our earth household through logic.

The dyad of location and place defines what we call *site*. A site is both a spatial location and a place or point for the start of an architectural exploration or building project. Siting our work involves positioning and situating oneself in a location, finding the characteristics that form the boundaries of a place.

Boundaries are a part of life. Our bodies are semipermeable boundaries, geological or climatological boundaries define ecosystems, and we dwell in structures that mediate inside and outside. Thus, all of where we live and what we make is a system of nesting and containment. Mark L. Johnson in *The Embodied Meaning of*

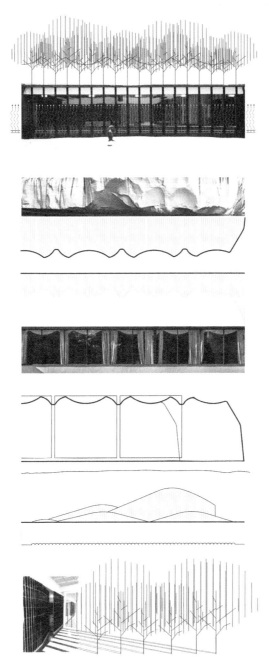

**FIGURE 1.3** Aalto's Topological Variations. Säynätsalo Town Hall Thermodynamic Landscape, Topological Situation, Tectonic and Technic in the Viipuri Ceiling, Rovaniemi Typological Ceramics and Metaphor, National Pensions Institute Topological Outside-Inside

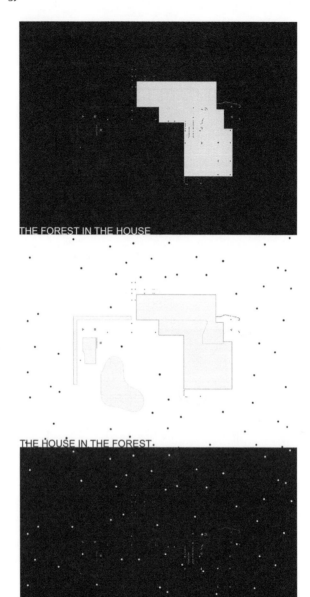

**FIGURE 1.4** Villa Mairea Forest Topology, House in the Forest | Forest in the House. The world of experience, according to the Villa Mairea, is a capturing of *forest dreaming* from mental imagery to bodily experience

*(Credit:* Steven Sculco)

*Architecture* tells us that "this kind of ecological logic lies at the heart of our experience of architecture, so that we learn the meaningful affordances of particular kinds of containment structures, in relation to our bodily makeup, needs, desires, and ideals."[29]

We can read these overlapping boundaries in the Villa Mairea. This villa can be understood as a flexible house *set* and as a *setting* of the landscape. It becomes a virtual topological condition as it *blurs* traditional site typology (Figure 1.4). The house was imagined and situated simultaneously as a metaphorical derivative of its forest setting, as a traditional and modern structure, and as an acclimatizing apparatus that functions between a *rural* villa and an *urban* gallery.

The rustic and modern villa accentuates its relation to time and place. So much has been written about its elements; its wood, steel columns, windows, stair, tile, and surfacing. What makes this villa so endearing is its ability to be read as modern and anti-modern, vernacular and universal, full of art and integrated with technology.

Juhani Pallasmaa compares the experience of this house to a walk in a forest in which we confront numerous stimuli and details integrated into the embodied perception of ourselves moving through the spaces. He states, "There is no given center point; the perceiver himself is the moving center of his experience, and the situations unfold as an unbroken flow of observations."[30] Detecting these hidden dimensions, Pallasmaa has speculated that for Finns, the myth of the forest has led to the organizing of space topologically, using "forest geometry" as opposed to the typological town planning of Indo-European cultures. We understand that what might be perceived by many as idiosyncratic, could very well be cultural correspondence.

Relating boundaries to the self, Pallasmaa writes,

> All art articulates the boundary surface between the self and the world both in the experience of the artist and the viewer. In this sense, architecture is not only a shelter for the body, but it is also the contour of consciousness, and an externalization of the mind.[31]

Furthering this notion of self-actualization invested in a work of art, Maurice Merleau-Ponty writes, "We come to see not the work, but the world according to the work."[32] (Also see Heidegger, "Origin of the Work of Art.")

## Grounding and Contouring our View

Christophe Girot, Director of Landscape Architecture at the ETH Zurich, defines topology as the interrelated cohesiveness of ground, things, and people, which requires a new set of disciplinary tools that are capable of responding to ground in any situation, through a form of physical continuity in the landscape.[33] This grounding is formed by the arrangement of features on and in the relief of a surface.

For many modern architects, grounding was made by building in juxtaposition to the earth, producing artificial horizon lines or figural autonomy. "In general, a building may stand 'in' the ground, 'on' the ground, or 'over' the ground.'"[34] Frank Lloyd Wright made extensions and multiple datum planes—what Leatherbarrow calls "topogenisis" or emerging from the earth. Mies van der Rohe builds platforms like the ancient Greeks or the "mediation element" resting upon the earth. Le Corbusier provides a pivoting axis elevated on pilotis, positioning his five points as a device to survey the world.

In 1925, discussing the landscape of Central Finland, Aalto stated, "Our buildings should not merely meet one or two aesthetic norms; they should be placed in the landscape in a natural way, in harmony with its general contours."[35] This attitude towards landscape corresponds with Girot's topological contouring and continuity of surface and ground.

For Aalto, the point of view is not about the horizontal like Wright nor the autonomous object like Le Corbusier, but a moving landscape. Like Wright, he creates mutual relationships between building and topography, architecture and nature. But in most cases, the outside is drawn in through the free-flowing section, which employs skylights and amorphic ceilings by interactions of light and air in the interior connected space, or by the arrangement of "mountain earth" developing synthetic contours between earth and sky.

In Le Corbusier's *Promenade Architecturale*, your gaze is transfixed by a contorted horizon line, eyes outstretched surveying the landscape and reaching towards the sun and sky. Aalto engages a similar gaze trope but is redefined as moving ground, a positioning system for active engagement, binding building to landscape. The new ground metaphor is a marriage of contours, taking place between *mountain earth* and *cloud sky*, where the resultant space is an expectant place for dwelling.

Santa Maria Assunta in Riola di Vergato (completed 1978), in the Bologna Apennines, was formed as a topological feature resulting from its situation. The topical dimension, or its study of place, has its origins in the site's scenic and geological material. The building is overtly grounded, taking shape from the background hillside and forming a structure that envelops a lived spatial experience (Figure 1.5). It emerges from the ground in a state of becoming. The modeled

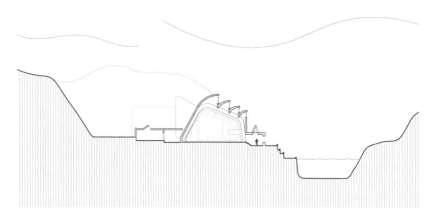

**FIGURE 1.5** Santa Maria Assunta Riola Church Grounding & Contouring

terrain is metaphorically "risen"[36] and a symbolic *Body of Christ*. This *form-system* affords function and provides a suggestive allegory of emergence from cave to water, developing deep significance to resurrection and purification.

The building is empathetic towards our need to associate the spiritual with lived reality. The material form-system contributes to this with a rational and figurative program interrelationship. The plan composition does so by engaging (not overwhelming) your awareness of place—the subtle moving terrain inside the complex and the relationships between space, site, structure, and event.

"The experience of depth, which is the point of departure for the Euclidean schema, stems from the topological relation that things are between each other."[37] The enhanced perspective made by the roof pitch, the section of the choir, the staircase leading to the organ, and, most notably, the descent to the baptistry with its view to the river with its crystal skylight, enable illusory grandeur and tangible anchoring to place.

The conspicuous structural system transforms the beam-column form-system previously used in the Auditorium in the Helsinki University of Technology campus at Otaniemi (1964). The precast concrete structure is modern yet derived from traditional Scandinavian technic used in wooden frames. These arches are like the bent lower chord of the wooden roof trusses in Stave churches, where the Norwegians accommodated the Gothic within circumstances of using wood. In works, such as the Storage Building in Toppila, Oulu, we see wooden arched roof beams, and in Aalto's drawings for the Institute of Physical Education of Vierumäki project (1930), we see development of a similar roof structure. In the Toppila Silo (1929–31), wood is transfigured into reinforced concrete.

In Riola, like windows of a Gothic cathedral, a high clerestory transmits light. Here the crest that rises above the rib-like precast concrete framing transposes a Gothic buttress deformed into a vault set perpendicular atop the beam–column arches.

Yet, we perceive the building not through parts, but by the *assemblage* of parts, positioned and fit together into the whole. The building is a part of its place, and it contours our view; "foreground, middle ground, and distant view, together with all the subjective qualities of material and light, form the basis of 'complete perception.'"[38]

Aalto teaches us that our work's artful, subjective nature is allowed through objective technological reconciliation. He wrote,

> In every case one must achieve a simultaneous solution of conflicting problems . . . Let us say that our purpose is to build a church. The nature of the foundation, the geographical and local siting, the building materials for walls and roof, heating system, ventilation, lighting, and surface treatment and innumerable other factors are basically independent of each other. Fundamentally these are independent problems, and as parts of the church structure they are often even in conflict with one another, and yet it is necessary to bring them into harmony. Only if and when this harmony is achieved does the building become a cultural factor of permanent value

to the society, and only in conflict-free unity do these factors create a temporal continuity.[39]

Anderson describes this comprehensive, integrated form-system logic in the church in Vouksenniska (1958):

> The circular arc moving walls require physical construction at the ceiling of much the same scale as the roof support beam, which continues in a straight line established by the beam and moveable wall extending from the entrance side of the church. Not by formal intention, but in addressing several problems of space and support, a fan of beams with intermediate webs is created at the ceiling along the far wall. Aalto then seizes upon these small, unique webs as the location for ventilation grills which might otherwise have occurred as minor disruptions in larger elements. A necessity of modern buildings is accommodated in the niche generated by larger complex organizations.[40]

In the case of Riola, the deliberate interrelationship of context, structure, and program brings the architecture into being. A condition where art and technology synthesize into a responsive form-system. The situatedness of building as landscape produces a metaphorical binding of the *four-fold*; a convergence of relationships; described by Heidegger as the existential purpose of architecture.

Aalto helps us see the world with our feet on the ground and our heads in the clouds. We daydream with the ascending vision of the work and remain rooted in the earth. This point of view from the ground was stated by Shigeru Ban: "In Aalto's architecture I found a space created to complement its context."[41]

For Aalto,

> architecture is, of course, tied to a locale in the sense that it is always fixed to the ground, and is not merely national but local in a special sense, though it can get an international response from what is happening in the world through its forms. In the end whatever the starting point or final goal, it is a combination of the two that attains the balanced result, which is essential in the modern world, which cannot really distinguish between the concepts national and international.[42]

Contemporary analysis of ground relies upon geotechnical data and surveys that determine adequate bearing capacity, excavation, and waterproofing strategies. Once in the hands of architects, these determinations now reside in the realm of specialists and consultants, which is better since we wish to reduce our burden to concentrate on the task at hand, building common ground for living between earth and sky.

Point cloud technologies offer opportunities to see the ground in new ways. These scanning systems provide astoundingly accurate representations of our surroundings. They are primarily skin information, not geological information; thus, they exist in the realm of architectural imagination. They provide topological evidence, logic, incredible accuracy, and intelligence about a place or terrain representing infrastructure and landscape all at once.

These clouds of data, providing multi-layered perspectives, are a conceptual revolution. They can help us see "landscape as a body"[43] and help us control our decisions. We can place our buildings in the cloud and simulate real situations—dealings with topography, water runoff, capture, flow control, and flooding. The point cloud is almost scaleless, allowing us to resolve design decisions at the measure of the hand to the infinite perceptions of the mind. This convergence of scales and realities is a new breadth of information, and it provides previously impossible investigations. This technology supports the future of our profession.

Aalto once said, "Realism usually provides the strongest stimulus to my imagination."[44] The point cloud provides more realism than could have been imagined by Aalto.

> Whatever our task, whether large or small, whether it arises from ugly banality or the most sensitive emotional element, be it a city or its part, a building or a transport network, a painting, a sculpture, or a piece of utility-ware, there is one absolute condition for its creation before it can attain a value that qualifies it as culture . . . in every case, opposites must be reconciled . . . Almost every formal assignment involves dozens, often hundreds, sometimes thousands of conflicting elements that can be forced into functional harmony only by an act of will. This harmony cannot be achieved by any other means than art.[45]

The point cloud puts these matters forward for reconciliation. Our task is to artfully, logically, and firmly position these matters into harmony.

## Position and Orientation

Topology is a positioning geometry without regard to the sizes or shapes of things themselves but their association to a particular place. Ordering space and its scalar measure are typological considerations; however, orientation and form are topological constructions. Furthermore, position and orientation affect building boundaries through topological variations adjusting to the sun, wind, water, and energy.

The morphology of a place, its ecology, its climate, and its social structure each provide specific parameters for measuring a building's performance and providing information about a situation. It is the job of the architect to advance and position these inputs together as they embody the program of building for our comfort and dwelling on the earth.

Buildings are positioned and placed in a particular way. This placement has to do with orientation, the way a structure is aligned or situated relative to the points of a compass or other specification. Our primary focus is two-fold: First, we aim to identify our position about what we feel the building should achieve experientially. Second, we seek to understand how the building should be oriented and shaped in relationship to the sun and other conditions of the site.

In making architecture, we take a position—an orientation or point of view in the forming of our propositions. This position is an essential attitude, belief, or feeling concerning a particular subject or issue. Our *disposition* is a prevailing tendency, mood, or inclination to act in a specific manner given the circumstances at play.

Orientation is also a change of position, responding to external stimuli, especially in regard to solar tracking or the changing seasons. For example, a sunflower is heliotropic, turning towards and growing with the sun. It has bodily growth and movement in response to light stimuli. Perhaps we can define optimal plan typology as heliotropic, developed so that the sun travels about the center of a plan or building mass.

In the *Athens Charter*, Le Corbusier told us, "To introduce the sun is the new and most imperative duty of the architect." The sun's transit provides light and energy, and buildings take shape to take in or repel these forces. Aalto understood this issue of orientation, daylighting, and natural ventilation. He used these parameters to enable a methodological arrangement of material, space, and positional and thermodynamic engagements of form.

Aalto buildings are situated to take advantage of natural phenomena. For example, he oriented the terraces at the Pamio Sanatorium not only to afford easy access and views, but for optimal exposure to sunlight.

"Light and Sun," Aalto said emphatically, before continuing,

> Under extreme conditions, one can no longer leave the dwelling's access to the sun to chance. Light and air are such important preconditions for living that haphazard conditions that prevail today must be changed. The norms should not only require that each dwelling get sun; the angle of incidence should always be decided, too, let us say, 1° leeway. The sun is a source of energy; but only if we use it in a scientific way and in exact qualities will become, under all circumstances, a positive factor for the biodynamic concept that involves the families and the single individual's life within the dwelling's walls. In a 50 m² dwelling we don't have, in this regard, the slightest margin to be left to chance, nor can we afford to allow the sun's and light's energy to remain unused.[46]

These standards set by Aalto can be readily quantified using contemporary digital design software. We can imagine making simple models that test these configurations, physical as had been done in the past, but now more accurate using computer simulations. Statements made by Aalto, "harmony cannot be achieved by any other means than art"[47] and "a harmonious result cannot be achieved via calculations, or with the help of statistical data or probability calculations,"[48] place imagination first and technical resolve second as harmonizing instruments. It is not software alone that will give us better buildings, but the architect's imagination in concert with our digital tools that will achieve greater harmony between our buildings and the living earth.

## Aalto's Form-System

Geometry was not an organizational measuring device for Aalto but an associative flexible proportioning system. Shigeru Ban describes,

> some of his early buildings were composed with golden-sectioned rectangles. Interestingly, the key elements of the structure-the corners of a room, the center of an undulating wall, or the slope of the roof are conspicuously positioned along the diagonal line of the rectangle, with a particular angle of 72 degrees.[49]

Distinct space and order is geometrical interiority, while the overall arrangement is variable exteriority, drawing outside-in and inside-out.

Where geometry is concerned with shapes and sizes, topology considers questions of connectivity and boundaries. Aalto's *environmental memory* helped him to develop an amorphous connection to the surrounding world, forming extended place boundaries. The topological method employed by Aalto is a philosophical common ground, a place of logic and intelligence about a place and its terrain. He uses elastic boundaries that interrelate architectural form with flexible systems that are solutions made according to the natural phenomena.

In his seminal essay, 'The Trout and the Stream' (1947), Aalto writes,

> Architecture and its details are in some way all part of biology. Perhaps they are, for instance, like some big salmon or trout. They are not born fully grown; they are not even born in the sea or water where they normally live. They are born hundreds of miles away from their home grounds, where the rivers narrow to tiny streams, in clear rivulets between the fells, in the first drops of water from the melting ice, as remote from their normal life as human emotion and instinct are from our everyday work. Just as it takes time for a speck of fish spawn to mature into a fully-grown fish, so we need time for everything that develops and crystallizes in our world of ideas. Architecture demands even more of this time than other creative work.[50]

This description invites us to understand architecture as both dialectical and paradoxical, inextricably bound to its present place, but also evolutionary as it belongs to different times and places.

Aalto's form-making is a systemic typology of varied indeterminacy, intersected with or overlapped by determinant systems. This system-oriented thinking interconnects forms and materials that are both local and universal.

Aalto's early work is a *form* strategy, a binary between itself and its image or representation, primarily made by altering classical typologies. The work originated in Turku represents a *form-system* dialectic because it was registered within the white functionalist agenda of early modernism but imbued with local characteristics (Figure 1.6). This form-system dialectic was then elaborated with material evidenced most strikingly in the Villa Mairea and later with more austerity in his brick buildings of the 1940s and 1950s, which became more critical towards the local situation. Aalto's later work became what we describe as a *Form-System-Material* triad that interrelates notions of meaning and material, function, and human nature.

In the proposed project for the Vallila Church (1929), Aalto began altering classical forms. The curved ceiling developed an acoustic model like Gustave Lyon's Salle Pleyel (1927) in Paris.[51] The transfer from *form* to *form-system* was conceived in the arch window transept demarking the sanctuary and, more interestingly in the roof windows, a system that Aalto would recall in later church designs.

The Helsinki University of Technology campus planning at Otaniemi provides an elaborate form-system strategy. "As a serious student of nature and the organic models its system provides for building forms, Aalto was acutely aware of this embodiment and its extensions."[52] The auditorium roof is like a Greek theater. The administrative center rests upon a synthetic mountain recalling the acropolis, and the library emerges from the ground as if resting on ruins. These associative memories form a social landscape.

In early writing from 1925, Aalto defines "architecture as refined landscape."[53] At Otaniemi, the stairs, terracing spaces, and the grounded amphitheater are all situated towards this refinement. The forms may elude a scenographic aesthetic or mnemonic formalism, reminiscing bygone orders or patronizing a bucolic landscape. However, the architecture is also ontologically grounded in utility and technological reality. It is equally abstract and real, art and non-art, and concurrently past, present, and future. The scenography is representational, but the tectonic is ontological.

This ontological grounding is manifest in the form and systems of the auditorium theater. Its shape is born from functional necessity artfully deformed into a precise figure about a specific place. The form affords function of inside/outside theaters and the purposeful integration of form and technology, or its *form-system*, which shapes the metaphysical grounding of thought and human experience.

The auditorium form-system is a complete fulfillment of Aalto's assertion that "building is not in the least a technological problem; it is an archi-technological problem." Here, a fully formed synthesis of space and structure is composed to heighten the senses. The form-system strategy delivers functional sensitivity

| Classical | | Modern | | Regional | | Future | | |
|---|---|---|---|---|---|---|---|---|
| Vernacular | Order | Type | Standard | Situated | Variation | Organic | Metaphysical | Existential |
| Body | **FORM** | Rational | Functional | Production | Flexible | Biology | Sensory | Mind |
| Proportion | Harmony | Evolution | FORM | **SYSTEM** | Vital | Ecology | Nature | Synthesis |
| Art | *Materia* | Representation | Universal | Adaptable | FORM | SYSTEM | **MATERIAL** | Customized |
| Humanism | Ontological | Metaphorical | Technology | Perception | Experience | Simulation | Energy | Optimization |

**FIGURE 1.6**  Form–System–Material Lotus Diagram

towards acoustics and light and a harmonious and artful interrelationship of form, structure, and mechanical operation. The expression of form and building systems is archi-technologically composed multidimensionally. Automated systems, seamlessly integrated around and between the arched beams, are not a typological system but a systemic topology.

The Cultural Center in Wolfsburg, Germany (1958–62) adds material into the form-system, exhibited by material positioning within a variable column geometry in the loggia. The regular column spacing along the western facade, facing the piazza, turns unequal when rotating the corner towards the north. The irregularity transposes regularity above as these columns support the ordered, fan shape plan of the lecture halls (Figure 1.7). Clad with copper and shaped like inversions of a Greek column, these columns are simultaneously historically representative, functionally rational, and referential to nature. The resultant *forest geometry* visually draws in the stand of trees from the surrounding piazza, uniting the building *form-structure-material* to place.

Designed and constructed during the same period, the Seinäjoki Civic Center (1958–65, 1987) extended Aalto's earlier planning concepts in Säynätsalo and Otaniemi and introduced another form-system-material strategy. The Town Hall, like at Säynätsalo, is a *landform structure*, an emerging synthetic landscape. The building's contouring of earth impacts associations with its surroundings, affecting its physical presence and its psychophysical and thermodynamic sensitivity, both inside and out.

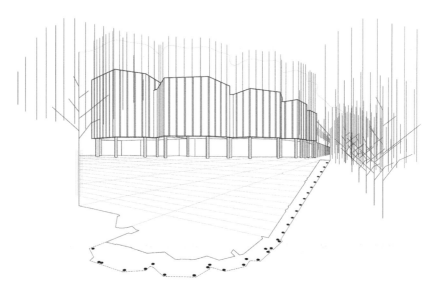

**FIGURE 1.7** Wolfsburg Cultural Center Situated Form-System

Aalto's two type-forms, the *interconnecting room* and the *city crown* helped fix building to *place*, especially in developing *place-form* strategies. In both Säynätsalo and Seinäjoki, the mound is a respite, a binding between building and ground. It is a composition of the soil, flora, and a welcome memory of nature in the city's center. In both cases, the mound ascends from the piazza to the crown of the landscape, corresponding to Aalto's observations and sketches of Italian hill towns.

Recalling Gottfried Semper (1803–79) *bekleidung*, dressing is an expressive adornment, not a protective covering or cloak. However, Frederick Kiesler, an acquaintance of Aalto, reminds us, "The house is neither a machine nor a work of art. The house is a living organism . . . the skin of the human body."[54] When considering the envelope as clothing, we begin to perceive the principle of building as a body. Depending on its location, the body's skin needs varying degrees of protection and expression—dressing the Town Hall in glazed blue tile cladding and copper roofing complete Aalto's *form-system-material* triad.

Reading *Theory of Colors* (1810) by Johann Wolfgang von Goethe (1749–1832), we can imagine Aalto drawing the glistering pageantry of the iridescent glazed tiles and the copper roof surfacing.[55]

> As the sun at last was about to set, and its rays, greatly mitigated by the thicker vapors, began to diffuse a most beautiful red color over the whole scene around me, the shadow color changed to a green, in lightness to be compared to a sea-green, in beauty to the green of the emerald. The appearance became more and more vivid: one might have imagined oneself in a fairy world, for every object had clothed itself in the two vivid and so beautifully harmonizing colors, till at last, as the sun went down, the magnificent spectacle was lost in a grey twilight, and by degrees in a clear moon-and-starlight night.[56]

The cladding tiles Aalto developed are both expressive and functional. In Finland, the way light grazes a surface in the winter is starkly different from summer because of the latitude. In both Säynätsalo and Seinäjoki, Aalto's choice of material, texture, and color, together with the form of the building, celebrate this solar dialectic. The rounded shape of tiles affords acute angle refraction of sunlight varied throughout the day and the year.

Across from the Town Hall is the library building. The plan of the library is made of a linear bar intersected by a fan-shaped reading room. Its high windows face south, tracing the transit of the sun. The horizontal light shelves refract light inward and afford glare protection from the low sun. Wall apertures are made only for diffused light provided via light refraction. They are not for viewing, and thereby maintain a sense of focus for people reading inside. A union of function and form, this example demonstrates how a synthetic form–system can alter exterior forces to create harmonious internal accord with nature; no external energy source required.

In *Aalto and Methodical Accommodation of Circumstance*, Anderson writes, "The architect as viewed by Aalto must attend to circumstances: climate, landscape, site, culture, materials, tectonics, and more."[57] Aalto uses location, position, and grounding circumstances in response to natural landscape and site-specific daylight conditions in Finland. The work is also *transpositional*, made *more* by enfolding elements bound to its place and those brought from other places in time, resulting in a transfigurative architecture.

The fan shape seems born in the *topos* of Pergamon in ancient Greece or the Etruscan ruins in Fiesole, Italy, then transposed by Aalto as a new three-dimensional spatial form (Figure 1.8). These forms were then bound to the landscape and deformed using the daylight characteristics of the region. The shape in the building's section is reminiscent of a flower opening towards the sun. From within, it appears like a cloud-form ceiling. This organic form to function system, most helpful in admitting light into the main reading space, was first *informed* by its location, and then molded by function through variable place-form expression systems.

The unification of space and place was vital to Aalto. For Aalto, the interior was often treated like an exterior subject, and spaces conjoined with the natural landscape. Peter Buchanan points out, no matter how "quirky, arbitrary and irrational" they appear, Aalto's plans are

> surprisingly pragmatic, compact and efficient, the distorted spaces tailored to function as well as fluidly flowing into each other, either minimizing or making the most of major circulation routes, with long diagonals increasing the apparent size of spaces, and the whole enveloped in a compact exterior volume.[58]

The variable geometry system of the plan is methodically ordered, yet the section is a free-form daylight system. Topology is geometry, but it is non-Euclidean; rather its properties are understood by continuous deformations. With this in mind, we can imagine the daylight forms of Aalto as stretched deformations in patterns of "becoming," a space of potentialities that illuminates further architectural possibilities.

The regular geometrical structure joins a more flexible topological system—a continuous and stretchable, irregular, or foldable geometry. In Aalto's forms, it does not matter if dimensions change; the deformation or flexibility of the system is a natural operation. For Aalto, architecture was both an *enfolding* and *unfolding* of situations; it was a substance of locality that also approached universality.

In *Space, Time, and Architecture* (1941), Sigfried Giedion (1888–1968) juxtaposes images of the Finnish Pavilion with a Finnish lake landscape. We could also view the Pavilion's curvilinear form related to the Baroque buildings that Aalto had visited and metamorphosed into the locality of his work. Giedion defined Aaltos double nature as being between "Irrationality and Standardization" and

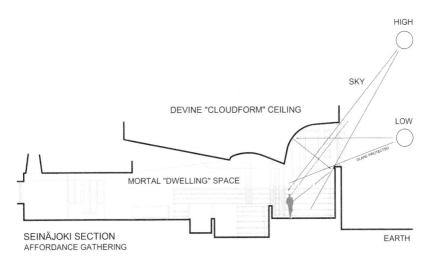

SEINÄJOKI SECTION
AFFORDANCE GATHERING

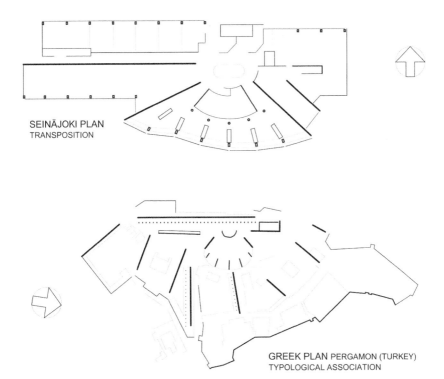

SEINÄJOKI PLAN
TRANSPOSITION

GREEK PLAN PERGAMON (TURKEY)
TYPOLOGICAL ASSOCIATION

**FIGURE 1.8**　Seinäjoki Library Daylight Form–System and Transposition

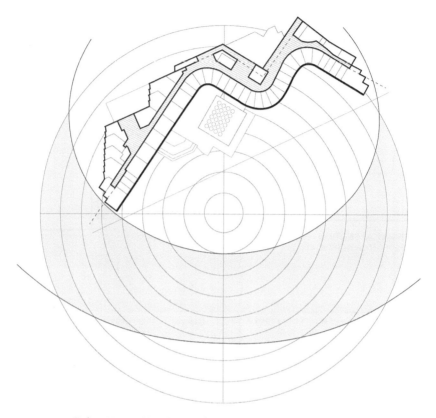

**FIGURE 1.9**  Baker House Site Oriented Form-System

"Elemental and Contemporary." Giedion described Aalto's Baker House MIT Dormitory as part of a continuing "tradition," starting with Borromini's facade of the Chiesa di San Carlino alle Quattro Fontane (1646) and the Royal Crescent in Bath by John Wood (1774).[59] *Irrationality*, which we distinguish as *accommodation*, takes the place of transparency and other terms of space/time synthesis as the new epitome of the program of humanizing architecture.

"For Giedion, Baker House revealed a link between the plasticity of the Baroque, the formal invention of eighteenth-century English town planning, and the sculptural shapes of modern architecture."[60] The curvilinear form is opposite that of the rectilinear brick. However, as previously discussed, the form-system of the Baker House emerges from situatedness, building between river and street, campus and open space. This double-sidedness is far from a simple formalist approach (Figure 1.9).

Contrary to Gideon's characterization, the Baker House is in no way irrational; however, Aalto's form-system does have relationships to Baroque form and planning. Like the Baroque light of Bernini's Sant'Andrea al Quirinale (1670) in Rome, the light in the work of Aalto is both a form generating device and an enigmatic substance.

As within the Baroque, the experience of daylighting in Aalto's work is harnessed and distributed in innumerable ways. He uses a multitude of apertures developed to manage daylight: window walls, skylights, cloud-like ceiling forms, clerestory lines of high or low light, downward glow, cleft surface light, double layer light walls with ghost-like shadow, light scoops, and baffles to complete the sculpted nature of the space. In addition, this lighting affects the physiological atmosphere of the architecture.

Aalto used the conditions of place to shape meaningful form strategies. These are beyond style; they enfold situations of place and time to endure history and meet human needs. Aalto created, as Anderson writes,

> a world in which there is more of the complexity and conflation of the natural and the man-made, of the new and the old . . . he had concern to find reciprocity between "his world" and the world. "His world" was held back from utopian idealism and was informed by the conditions of the world around him.[61]

## Enfolding our Surroundings

In nature, each part of our surroundings is interrelated to the nature of its place. So, too, buildings should be made as integral parts of the surrounding world. Architecture and urban design are not defined by whole to parts but by parts that make up a whole. For Aalto, "each element—in this case, space, light, walls, steps, rails and their supports—its independent role while defining its complementarity within the whole."[62] A world of ideas, places, and corresponding elements provides an enfolded whole.

We can view the work of Aalto as *Classical*, following the Vitruvian point of view that the parts relate to the whole. Aalto's work could also be viewed through the lenses of various other architectural periods and styles: *Medieval*, in its accommodation to its surroundings and human scale; *Gothic*, in that the details are vital rather than purely formal; *Renaissance*, in its humanist ideal; *Baroque*, in its equilibrium of naturalism and allegory. It also fits with the *Enlightenment* through its logical discourse, rationalization, and synthesis of art and technology. Finally, it is *Modern* in its form and function and *Postmodern* in that technology is suspect unless developed co-dependently with nature and human life.

The physicist David Bohn compares the universe's structure to a hologram wherein each part is distributed throughout the whole. Conversely, each part of the whole is internally related to one another. Consequently, the hologram of the universe (or point cloud) cannot have separations into pieces; it can only exist in wholeness. Information is enfolded and decoded. The whole is unfolded, and each part is enfolded into the whole. This idea can confer our proposition that the virtual model made for simulations is a whole structure, much like Aalto's *form-system-material* triad or *universal substance*, a completeness wherein each part constitutes a whole—biologically, metaphysically, and materially.

Gottfried Wilhelm Leibniz (1646–1716), in *Monadology* (1714), describes the Baroque "universal substance" as the "monad," the soul of sufficient reason. In *An Enfolded Membrane*, Georges Teyssot explains aspects of Leibniz's thought: "A monad is 'a simple substance . . . that has no parts,' for monads constitute 'the true atoms of nature.' Natural changes and transformations in a monad occur as a result of 'an internal force, which one might call an active force.'"[63] A monad is the site of changes in what we call perception. Each monad unfolds to become the whole and vice versa.

*The Fold: Leibniz and the Baroque* (1993) by Gilles Deleuze (1925–95) begins by explaining, "The Baroque refers not to an essence but rather to an operative function, to a trait. It endlessly produces folds." These traits, first described by the historian Heinrich Wölfflin (1864–1945), classified the Baroque as "Open Form" and Renaissance as "Closed-Form." In the Baroque, we can read the early stages of topological space that is non-metric and has the capacity to be twisted and deformed without losing its characteristic properties.

In his essay 'Electronic Baroque' (2001) Stephen Perrella (1956–2008) tells us:

> Architectural topology is the mutation of form, structure, context, and program into interwoven patterns and complex dynamics . . . Topological "space" differs from Cartesian space in that it imbricates temporal events-within form. Space then, is no longer a vacuum within which subjects and objects are contained, space is instead transformed into an interconnected, dense web of particularities and singularities better understood as substance or filled space.[64]

In *Parametric Semiology: The Design of Information-Rich Environments* (2013), Patrik Schumacher wrote,

> Morphological features, as well as colors and textures that, together with ambient parameters (lighting conditions), constitute and characterize a certain territory can now influence the behavioral mode of the agent. Since the "meaning" of an architectural space is the (nuanced) type of event or social interaction to be expected within its territory, these new tools allow for the re-foundation of architectural semiology as parametric semiology.[65]

Aaltos curvilinear forms and deforming transformations of bending and stretching are a substantive function of the *form-system* employed within many of his works. Within this form-system is a discreet and purposeful, figural logic that folds together the pragmatic and the poetic, the ambient and the material. Each figure is deformed and meshed into a single continuum. The result is morphogenetic, where the changing states of space, form, and matter are actively composed into a topological formation. These formations reside within a territory where meaning is a semi-semiotic to place and form. The form–system–material triad is self-referential but symbolically extracted from its context.

Here we can speculate that this review of Aalto's architecture can help us move into the future with a new ability to work through meaningful, simulative environments in the making of architecture that is actively responsive to physical environments and the poetic situatedness of place.

## Topological Parameters

Ecology is the science of ecosystems, consisting of sets of interrelationships between species constrained by the physical environment. Locally, the situation makes the diversity of a place. Topology, as an ecology, represents the shape and structure of networks as an interaction. It is not a taxonomy of living things, but a set of nodes developed as surfaces. We have learned that our ecosystem is intertwined; a fluttering bee on one side of the globe could affect the weather in the Himalayas.

According to Salingaros,

> All organisms are situated, because they are embedded in the natural environment. They possess sensory mechanisms that dictate and adjust the organism's behavior through feedback. Organisms are constantly sensing their surroundings. Buildings normally don't do that, yet with recent advances in technology, we now have the capacity to create intelligent buildings.[66]

A surface of interactions forms the basic structure of our thoughts and is the basis for the parametric network used to develop architecture ecologically.

A lesson of Aalto that remains most resonant today is his synthetic combination of ideas with material construction as it relates empathetically to its environment. For example, today we can simulate the effects of climate and daylighting of a place. Using these tools to evaluate and uncover the natural logic surrounding buildings and places can lead us to new, more responsive environments.

Unlike Aalto's buildings, which in their time could be designed and detailed by a single architectural office, significant works today require teams of specialists to execute the design and construction. Moreover, due to the complex nature of building codes and legal responsibilities, we need engineers and consultants to have diverse expertise to provide us with degrees of certainty that a design will perform as planned. Therefore, the new tool of the architect is no longer a static pencil on paper or printouts from a Computer Aided Design (CAD) program, but the integrative active computer model that assists in evaluating design solutions, providing simultaneous structural analysis and environmental performance.

According to Göran Schildt, Aalto often repeated the mantra, "you cannot change the world, but you can set an example to it."[67] Today, this mantra requires us to develop our work by forming relationships between form, place, shape, structure, and thermodynamics. Information technology, computer-assisted design, and animation software can not only present our work but facilitate dynamic form variations. Topological formation leads architectural design towards new and often spectacular plasticity and forms a more responsive design.

## The Zollverein School

Kazuyo Sejima + Ryue Nishizawa integrate the situatedness of location in the Zollverein School in Essen, Germany (Figure 1.10). The building is an informed design concept that uses latent energy from a defunct coal mine coupled with a Thermally Active Surface (T.A.S.).

The building does not adhere to a teacher-centered, classroom-corridor model. It is flexible, open, and composed of vertically organized floors that accommodate many uses. A raised floor addresses ventilation for air distribution interconnects with courtyards at the roof. At the roof garden, the unique penetrating courtyards continue the topology of the facades. The quality of light and air and flexible planning make this whole building system a bodily experience.

The imagination of the project evolved from these formal ambitions and its location. The initial vision was based on finding a solution that allowed concrete—a heavy bearing material—to appear light and translucent. The discovery of the latent energy at the site made the schematic vision possible. The material performance of the concrete is both a design idea and a technical functionality, displaying how a simultaneous resolution of opposites could produce significant architecture through an understanding of ecological tectonics.

The external walls are structured using a more conventional concrete structure. However, within the walls is an active insulation system consisting of a network of embedded pipes, where hot and cold water is pumped and recycled between layers of concrete and insulation (Figure 1.11). The idea of a building as a heat exchanger is compelling, enacting material that integrates tectonics and thermodynamic systems.

Heat energy from the mine is extracted from the mineral-saturated water by pumping and recycling between the adjacent river and the mine shaft (Figure 1.12). The result is a resourceful use of heat energy. This energy is dispersed in the building using a structured T.A.S. of the reinforced concrete floor and façade systems.

The structure is high performance and minimal in embodied, operational, organizational, energy systems. The concrete slabs use an innovative approach, lightened with plastic balls to reduce depth, weight, and material. Two slender

**FIGURE 1.10**   Photo, Zollverein School, Germany, SANAA Architects, 2005

*(Credit:* Michael Hoefner)

steel columns used to reduce deflection enhance the image of gravity defiance. The network of pipes runs vertically through three circulation cores.

T.A.S. systems are more sensitive and perceptive to the human body's physi-ological processes and thus connect us to architecture more powerfully. Dense material surfaces are made active by storing, radiating, and circulating energy. The mostly free energy from the mine provides synergy between location and building.

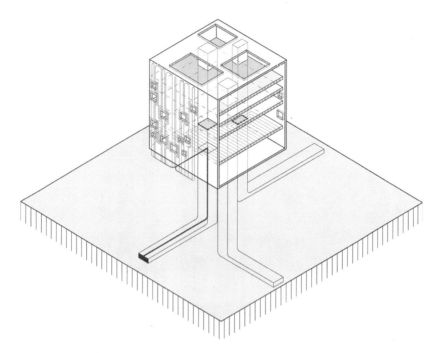

**FIGURE 1.11**   Zollverein School Thermally Active Concrete S. Axon

## The Helsinki Central Library Oodi

The Helsinki Central Library Oodi (Figure 1.13) is situated topologically considering location, culture, and climate (Figure 1.14). The competition required an accommodation of future urban infrastructure in the form of a tunnel to be constructed under the building. With their winning entry, ALA Architects enfolded the public square inside the building, employing a structure that would bridge the tunnel and create a light-filled public space.

A library is significant in Finnish culture. It is the place of community interaction, especially in winter when daylight hours decrease. Enacting a place of light for knowledge and vital social interaction is possible through correlating topology and Aalto's concept of archi-technical resolution.

The building engages the public square with its warm wooden facade and its warped arching cantilever structure. Here, material choices embrace the surroundings and cultural history. Locally sourced wooden claddings of various tones along with frit patterns in the glass help the exterior facades function in connection with the interior wooden finishes, for a calming, well-lit experience.

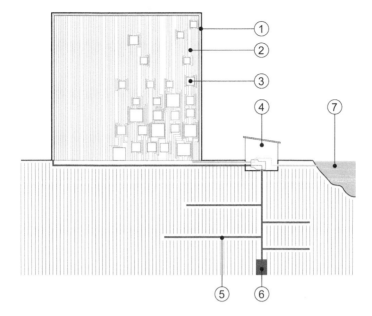

1. Thermally Active Concrete (T.A.S.) Façade System
2. Embedded Hot and Cold Piping with Insulation in TAS
3. Window Openings
4. Pump System for Heat Exchange
5. Geothermal (Mine) Piping System
6. Defunct Mine Heat Energy
7. Lake Water Heat Exchange

**FIGURE 1.12**   Zollverein School Site Section

At the highest level, the white cloud-like ceiling contains a variable grid of circular skylights that enhance daylighting (Figure 1.15). Artificial light illuminates the fritted glass walls, extending the interior atmosphere to the exterior and simulating daylight during darkness (Figure 1.16).

Technical considerations influenced the position of the main reading room at the top of the building. This room is column-free, enabling a free flow of space. Perhaps more significant is the ceiling, the source of light and imagination. Here, a contour between the ground and the sky is created, situating a simulated sunlit room to illuminate the plaza. This room is accompanied by an open-air terrace that is created by the overhang protecting the forecourt to the square.

The structure spanning over the future tunnel behaves like a bridge comprised of two arches. Cantilevered trusses are structured perpendicular to these arches, affording the entry cantilever's topological deformation and upper terrace to take shape.

**FIGURE 1.13** Photo, The Oodi Helsinki Central Library, ALA Architects, 2018

(*Credit:* Author)

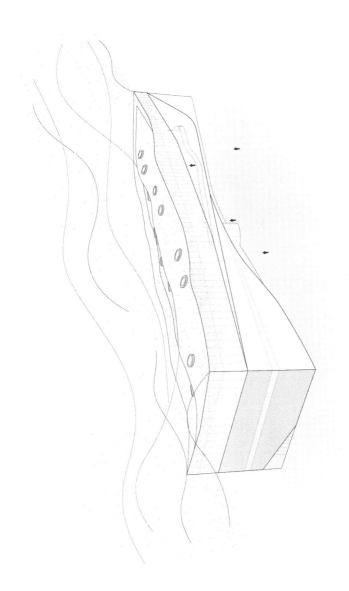

**FIGURE 1.14**  Oodi Topological Isometric

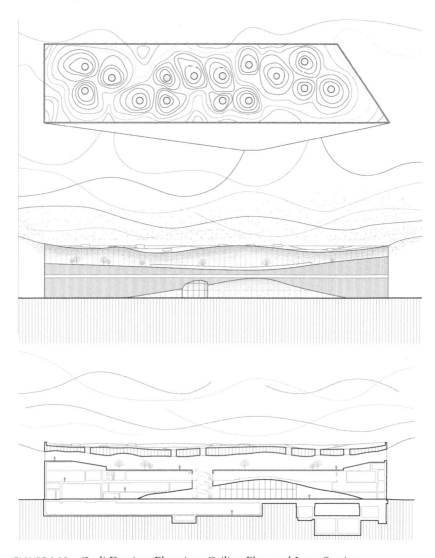

**FIGURE 1.15**   Oodi Daytime Elevation, Ceiling Plan, and Long Section

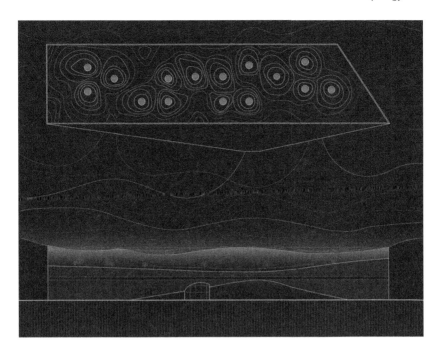

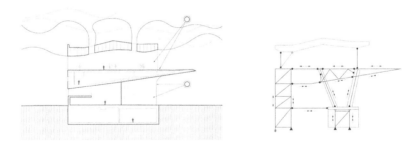

**FIGURE 1.16** Oodi Nighttime Elevation and Ceiling Plan, Short Section & Bridge Structure Diagram

From a structural design point of view, the deformation and deflection of the arches and cantilever to the building size are high. Design and Building Information Modeling (BIM) and algorithm-aided parametric design helped to anticipate and resolve the complex curved geometry of the connections (none of which are the same). Pre-cambered steel members optimized this situation.

Passive solar design, highly efficient building systems, and the BIM model helped to keep the library's energy demands to a minimum. As a result, the energy target is equivalent to $120kWh/m^2$ per year, a new benchmark for energy consumption in a high-technology library facility.[68]

## Notes

1  Bulletin of the American Geographical Society. *Topology, Topography and Topometry*. Bulletin of the American Geographical Society, 1912.
2  See discussion on Norberg-Shultz, Christian. *Schematization and Topology in Intentions in Architecture*. MIT Press, 1965, pp.43–48.
3  Malpas, Jeff. *Heidegger, Aalto, and the Limits of Design*, p.29. https://jeffmalpas.com/wp-content/uploads/Heidegger-Aalto-and-the-Limits-of-Design-Man.pdf (Accessed 05 March 2022).
4  Gibson, James J. *The Ecological Approach to Visual Perception*. Taylor and Francis, 1986, p.141.
5  Salingaros, Nikos. 'Architecture: Biological Form and Artificial Intelligence,' *The Structuralist*, Volume 45–46, 2006, pp.54–61.
6  Malpas, Jeff. *Heidegger's Topology: Being, Place, World*. MIT Press, 2008, p.42.
7  Quantrill, Malcolm. *Alvar Aalto: A Critical Study*. Shocken Books, 1983, p.5.
8  Aalto, Alvar. 'Between Humanism and Materialism,' in *Sketches*. MIT Press, 1978, p.131 (Aalto—Sketches).
9  Barad, Karen. *Meeting the Universe Halfway: Quantum Physics and the Entanglement of Matter and Meaning*. Duke University Press, 2007, p.141.
10  Norberg-Schulz, Christian. *Nightlands*, MIT Press, 1996, p.179.
11  ibid.
12  Charrington, Harry. 'A Persuasive Topology, Alvar Aalto and the Ambience of History,' in *The Cultural Role of Architecture*. Taylor & Francis, 2012, p.105.
13  ibid.
14  Congrès Internationaux d'Architecture Moderne (CIAM, 1929, 2nd., Frankfurt-am Main) 'The Minimum House' as reproduced in Le Corbusier, *The Radiant City: Elements of a Doctrine of Urbanism to be Used as the Basis of Our Machine Age Civilization*. Orion Press, 1933.
15  Aalto, Alvar. 'The Housing Problem,' *Alvar Aalto in His Own Words*. Ed. Schildt, Göran. Otava, 1997, p.80 (Aalto).
16  Timeline of events and meetings are from the MoMA Alvar Aalto Timeline. www.moma.org/interactives/exhibitions/1998/aalto/timeline/ (Accessed 05 March 2022).
17  Kwinter, Sanford. *Architectures of Time: Toward a Theory of the Event in Modernist Culture*. MIT Press, 2002, p.136.
18  Charrington, 'A Persuasive Topology,' p.106.
19  See Aalto discussion 'Motifs from Times Past,' Aalto—Sketches, p.2.
20  Anderson, Stanford. 'Thinking in Architecture,' in *Ptah 08 Yearbook*. Ed. Laaksonen, Esa. Alvar Aalto Academy, 2009, pp.72–86.
21  Patterson, Robert Earl, and Eggleston, Robert G. 'Intuitive Cognition,' *Journal of Cognitive Engineering and Decision Making 2017*, Volume 11, Number 1, March 2017, pp.5–22.

22  Kwinter, *Architectures of Time*, p.94.

23  See Strømnes, Frode. 'A Semiotic Theory of Imagery Processes with Experiments on an Indo-European and a Ural-Altaic Language: Do Speakers of Different Languages Experience Different Cognitive Worlds?' *Scandinavian Journal of Psychology*, Volume 15, Number 1, 1974.

24  Pallasmaa, Juhani. Alvar Aalto, Synopsis for more detailed review of Aalto's artistic endeavors in Ban, Shigeru. *Alvar Aalto: Through the Eyes of Shigeru Ban*. Black Dog Publishing, 2007, p.26.

25  See Pelkonen, Eeva-Liisa, *Forest Dreaming with Aalto*. www.serpentinegalleries.org/art-and-ideas/forest-dreaming-with-aalto/ (Accessed 05 March 2022).

26  Pelkonen, Eeva-Liisa. 'Reading Alvar Aalto Through the Baroque,' in *The Baroque in Architectural Culture, 1880–1980*. Eds. Leach, Andrew, and Macarthur, John. Taylor & Francis, 2016, p.143.

27  Heidegger, Martin. 'Building, Dwelling, Thinking,' in *Poetry, Language, Thought*. Harper & Row, 1975.

28  McDonough, William. 'Design, Ecology, Ethics and the Making of Things,' in *The Sustainable Urban Development Reader*, Ed. Wheeler, Stephen M., Routledge, 2014, p.183.

29  Johnson, Mark L. 'The Embodied Meaning of Architecture,' in *Mind in Architecture: Neuroscience, Embodiment, and the Future of Design*. MIT Press, 2017, p.42.

30  Pallasmaa, Juhani. 'Image and Meaning,' in *Alvar Aalto, Villa Mairea*. Alvar Aalto Foundation, 1998, pp.70–125.

31  Pallasmaa, Juhani. *Lived Space. Embodied Experience and Sensory Thought*. OASE, 2002, p.14.

32  Maurice Merleau-Ponty, as quoted in Iain McGilchrist, *The Master and His Emissary: The Divided Brain and the Making of the Western World*. Yale University Press, 2010, p.409.

33  For more information see, Prof. Girot, Christophe, *Topology: Thinking About Ground in Landscape Architecture*. https://girot.arch.ethz.ch/research/topology (Accessed 05 March 2022).

34  Norberg-Schulz, Christian. *Genius Loci: Towards a Phenomenology of Architecture*. Rizzoli, 1980, p.177.

35  Aalto, Alvar. Architecture in the Landscape of Central Finland, 1925, p.21.

36  See Aalto's conversation about his obsession with the "rising town" and its unpredictable line and contrast between brutal mechanicalness and religious beauty in life, in 'The Hilltop Town,' In his own Words, p.49.

37  Norberg Schulz, Christian. *Intentions in Architecture*. University Press, 1966, p.47.

38  Holl, Steven. *Questions of Perception: Phenomenology of Architecture*. William Stout, 2006, p.45.

39  Aalto—Sketches, 'Art and Technology,' pp.127–128.

40  Anderson, Stanford. 'Aalto and Methodical Accommodation to Circumstance,' in *Alvar Aalto in Seven Buildings*. Ed. Tuomi, Timo et al. *Museum of Finnish Architecture*, 1998, p.148.

41  Ban, Shigeru, *Alvar Aalto: Through the Eyes of Shigeru Ban*, p.66.

42  Aalto, Alvar. 'National-International,' *Finnish Architectural Review*, Arkkitehti Number 7–8, 1967.

43  For more information on Point Clouds see, Prof. Girot, Christophe, *Topology: On Sensing and Conceiving Landscape*. Lecture at Harvard GSD, 17 November 2014 and https://girot.arch.ethz.ch/tag/point-cloud. According to Girot, with Point Clouds it's a "conceptual revolution that's happening with this with this tool it's to me it's of the same order as a Albertian revolution it's really a way to grasp the world to work with the world in a very different way than just the old you know orthographic projection and perspectival mode that we've been trained in."

44 Aalto, 'Interview for Finnish Television, July 1972,' p.174.
45 Aalto, 'Art and Technology,' p.174.
46 Aalto—Sketches, 'The Dwelling as a Problem,' p.32.
47 Aalto, 'Art and Technology,' p.174.
48 Aalto—Sketches, 'Art and Technology,' p.128.
49 *Encounters with Aalto*, in Alvar Aalto through the eyes of Shigeru Ban, p.94 note 17, The examples include the Paimio Tuberculosis Sanatorium (the proportions of the patients' room); the Viipuri City Library (the plan/elevation/section), the Experimental House (the relation between the main building and the annex, and the angle of the logs laid as foundations); Villa Mairea (the L-shaped wall standing on the site boundary), the National Pensions Institute (the angle of the glazed window of the top light); La Maison Carré (the pitched roof), AA-System Houses (the proportions of rooms).
50 Aalto, 'The Trout and the Stream,' pp.108–109. https://www.alvaraalto.fi/content/uploads/2017/12/AAM_RN_Passinmaki.pdf.
51 Schildt, Göran. *Alvar Aalto: The Complete Catalogue of Architecture, Design, and Art*. Random House, 1994, p.46.
52 Quantrill, Malcolm. 'Lateral-Mindedness Versus Literal-Mindedness,' in *Alvar Aalto's Uses of History*. U+U 8903, p.12.
53 Aalto, Alvar. Sisä-Suomi newspaper, 26 June 1925, p.21.
54 Kiesler, Frederick, 'Manifeste du Corréalisme,' *L'Architecture d'Aujourd'hui*, Volume 2, June 1949, pp.79–105.
55 Aalto, p.37. According to Schildt, Aalto shared Goethe's view that man is an integral part of nature's cycle, and therefore cannot stand on the outside as an ostensibly objective observer of isolated phenomena.
56 Goethe's Theory of Colors; translated from the German: With notes by Charles Lock Eastlake, R.A., F.R.S. https://www.Gutenberg.Org/Files/50572/50572-H/50572-H.Htm#Page_29.
57 Anderson, 'Aalto and Methodical Accommodation of Circumstance,' p.143.
58 Buchanan, Peter. 'The Big Rethink Part 6: Learning from Four Modern Masters,' in *Architectural Review*. EMAP Publishing Ltd, June 2012, pp.83–95.
59 Giedion, Sigfried. 'Alvar Aalto: Elemental and Contemporary,' in *Space, Time and Architecture*. Harvard University Press, 1962, p.586.
60 Bentel, Paul. 'The Significance of the Baker House,' in *Aalto and America*. Yale University Press, 2012, p.236.
61 Anderson, Stanford. 'Fiction of Function,' *Assemblage*, Volume 2, February 1987, pp.18–31, 29.
62 Anderson, 'Aalto and Methodical Accommodation of Circumstance,' p.192.
63 Teyssot, Georges. 'An Enfolded Membrane,' in *Architecture in Formation: On the Nature of Information in Digital Architecture*. Ed. Eiroa, Pablo Lorenzo. Taylor & Francis, 2013.
64 Perrella, Stephen. 'Electronic Baroque,' in *AD: Architecture and Science*. Ed. Di Cristina, Giuseppa. Wiley-Academy, 2001, pp.149–150.
65 Schumacher, Patrik. *Parametric Semiology: The Design of Information-Rich Environments*. Architecture in Formation, 2013.
66 Salingaros, Nikos Angelos. 'Lecture Notes for the Thirteenth Week: Architecture Itself as a Biological System,' in *Unified Architectural Theory: Form, Language, Complexity—a Companion to Christopher Alexander's "The Phenomenon of Life: The Nature of Order, Book 1."* Sustasis Foundation and Vajra Books, 2020, UAT, Chapter 29.
67 Aalto, . . . but you can set it an example. p.201.
68 https://www.arup.com/projects/helsinki-library (Accessed 05 March 2022).

# 2

# TYPOLOGY—ENVELOPMENT(S) OF SPACE

---

**Typology** = a classification or structuring according to the general type.
(*Túpos*: "sort," "example," and "model")

---

From Plato, we understand that pure *a priori* form is the intrinsic fundamental characteristic of an object. In architecture, objects and elements associate, and elements define formal or standard features when arranged or shaped in specific ways. Produced by reassembled forms in time, the architectural object develops. The act of naming these objects, elements, and forms defines verifiable *types*. Types establish characteristics, and forms evolve from a recognized *túpos* or prototype. The comparative study of these transformed types is *typology*. A formal repeating model appears by structuring elements through typology, called *Architecture*.

According to Douglas Kelbaugh, *type* "is like a three-dimensional template that is copied over and over in endless variations. It is a norm, an abstraction, not an actual building."[1] There are different views on types that have been established and altered throughout history. In *Precis* (1802–05), J.N.L. Durand (1760–1834) provided techniques for assembling *type-forms*. However, he did not call them types, but *genres*.[2] The characterization of formal genres provided techniques for composition without specific regard to use. Later, as defined by Quatrèmere de Quincy (1755–1849) in the *Dictionnaire Historique de l'Architecture* (1832), "*type* present[ed] less the image of a thing to copy or imitate completely than the idea of an element which ought itself to serve as the rule for a *model*."[3]

DOI: 10.4324/9781003160571-3

In *The Architecture of the City* (1982), Aldo Rossi (1931–97) told us that "type developed according to both needs and aspirations to beauty,"[4] which derive from different locations and social systems. By this definition, it seems clear that typological questions are important. Rossi began this argument with Quatrèmere's definition of type:

> The model, understood in terms of the practical execution of art, is an object that must be repeated such as it is; type, on the contrary, is an object according to which one can conceive of works that do not resemble one another at all. Everything is precise and given in the model; everything is more or less vague in the type.[5]

Rossi then defined typology as "the study of elements that cannot be further reduced, elements of a city as well as of an architecture."[6]

Studying types matters; it forms architecture's very idea and essence. It provides information for a model, and without it, there would be no architecture. *Type* distinguishes itself from a *model* by utilizing its replicability or sublimation of characteristics. History embeds type; models transcend and help instigate change into the future. New models often originate from novel typologies and are not recognized until we distinguish differentiation from the original. Models can become a *standard*, replicated or used as a baseline for advancement. Therefore, understanding typology in architecture remains useful as a measure of obsolescence and discovery of change.

To analyze *type-form* and morphology in typology, we must engage with conceptual and formal reasoning, not copying but decoding. As Giulio Carlo Argan wrote, typology is a "function both of the historical process of architecture and the thinking and working processes of individual architects."[7] Through Argan, we learn that form as type is not formed *a priori* but deduced from a series. Typology, the formative process, consists of two salient facts: First, typological series do not arise only concerning physical functions but through configurations; and second, formal architectural typologies have three categories—complete arrangements, structural elements, and aesthetic motif or the process of planning, structuring, and surfacing.

During the Modern Movement, architects looked to technology instead of historical typology (though the idea of type would endure in retrospect). In the early 20th century, Le Corbusier broke with traditional housing typologies and invented a new model for the future: Maison Domino (1914). Rafael Moneo describes, "Mass production in architecture, focused chiefly on mass housing, permitted architecture to be seen in a new light . . . type had become prototype."[8]

The modern attitude rejected historical types and concerned itself with methodology and solutions. This idea led to the imposition of universal structures within any given context. Concurrently, the 1914 Muthesius/van de Velde,

"Werkbund 'theses' and 'antithesis'" debate on typology discussed whether type was a fixed arrangement or the generative idea of form. In this discourse between standard *type* and flexible *typology*, Hermann Muthesius (1861–1927) advanced standardization and the universal type in his practice, while Henry van de Velde (1863–1957) pronounced: "protest against every suggestion for the establishment of a cannon and for standardization."[9]

While the Modern Movement rejected the imitation of the past, Aalto, a friend of van de Velde, saw typology and flexibility as critical tools for discovery. In 'The Reconstruction of Europe', Aalto wrote, "The purpose of architectural standardization is that not to produce types, but instead create variety and richness which could, in the ideal case, be compared with nature's unlimited capacity to produce variation."[10] Types are standard, but typology, a study of standards, is flexible. Though often seen as a form of convention, type should not be followed as a mere set of rules. Establishing the role of nature and precedent in design, the methodology outlined in this book is a search for *new* models, which cannot be discovered through mimicry, but through translational, transpositional, and transformational analyses. Through the work of Aalto, we see the development of a new type-form through typological discovery: an associative plan type and flexible typology accommodating surrounding conditions into a project.

For Moneo, Typology meant to "raise a question of the nature of the architectural work itself." To answer this question, he explained, "means, for each generation, a redefinition of the essence of architecture and an explanation of all its attendant problems."[11] Redefining the essence of architecture has to do with the needs and nature of society. Accordingly, one's choice of a model implies a judgment intended towards formulating a new value. Today, typology requires a thorough examination of new model *types*, wherein the baseline includes environmental concern, social and economic variables, and human comfort as necessary, functional measures of performative responsibility.

Buildings cannot exist solely as type objects, nor should they be conceived as pure image production. In other words, the study of types cannot result in mere composition or representation but must help define an *inner form structure*. To apply metrics for form verification, we must be aware of typology and its varied structure. For example, the ordering system of a Renaissance Palazzo no longer applies to contemporary typology. One type of space requires more lighting than another, specific heating and cooling or humidity limits or air changes per hour, and other degrees of privacy or access. All of these have an impact on the comprehensive formation of our work. Types are not immutable standards, but references are altered and administered through typological decoding and referencing.

## Vernacular Typologies

In 1977, Anthony Vidler defined three typologies: the abstraction of nature (the primitive hut), the technological utopia (prototype housing), and the city.[12] He argued that the city, like the first two, is based on reason and classification and that it is ontological, not metaphorical. By the latter part of the 20th century, as many architects sought to discover a richer vocabulary than the one introduced by modern architecture, this third typology, a pretext to postmodernism, drew from the vernacular.

The traditional city first established itself around resources, transportation, and distance. Historically, cities were unique places with distinct morphologies and cultural identities. Today, with resources depleting, transportation has made local universal and distances nil by technology.

But we can still learn from the vernacular type, where morphologies of material, structure, and form are shaped by utility, climate, and legacy systems, not by theories. Patrimony expressed by a common type becomes engrained in social consciousness. Types, by their very nature, are ontological structures. They belong to objective memory and reason. They are reproductive and purposeful.

A Gothic cathedral, its prearranged shape, is a type, whereas starting with Leon Battista Alberti (1404–72), architecture that grows by an ordered definition and an intentioned argument is typology. In many ways, the Gothic type cathedral is more natural, more human in rooting emotive sensation than the Renaissance typology of abstract geometry. The Gothic is objective and unintentional; it grows from trial and error. The Renaissance is fully intentioned and more subjectively designed. Yet, the Gothic type is intentioned in its structure, whereas the obsolescence of the Renaissance inflexible order is an unintended consequence of its standard design.

According to Moneo, for Rossi, "the logic of architectural form lies in a definition of type based on the juxtaposition of memory and reason."[13] Can we reposition these words not based on formal typology but on experience? On our memory of how a building type makes us feel and why this has happened, ascribing validation for form-making that is less subjective?

Aalto searched for objective evidence by looking to the vernacular Finnish farmhouse:

> It is forest architecture pure and simple, with wood dominating almost one hundred percent both as a building material and in jointing . . . Another distinctive feature about the Karelian house is its origin in terms of historical development and architectural function . . . its internal structural scheme is the outcome of a methodical development of flexibility.[14]

From this typological discovery, Aalto goes on to say,

> This architectural freedom holds a special interest for our day and age. The architectural reform movement of our time, the Renaissance that we see

throughout the world, has consistently sought to liberate architectural form and to achieve a flexible unity in town planning and architecture.

This study validates Aaltos intentional typological thinking, that of *flexibility*.

## Extended Typologies

Beyond formal type, typology is the measure of order and organization. We can use typology to position spaces expressly linked to each other by association to their environment. Extended parameters classify these arrangements to respond to both the building performance and the body. Function is attached to form by ordering and corporeal experience. Moving from one space to the next involves thresholds and boundaries. These boundary zones are sometimes open, sometimes closed, but they always demarcate experience, the sequence, and plan event.

Our earliest lessons on the interrelationship between physiology and the thermal milieu of buildings come from Vitruvius. In describing the *Education of the Architect* (1st century BC), Vitruvius stated that

> the architect should also have a knowledge of the study of medicine on account of the questions of climates (κλίματα), the healthiness and unhealthiness of sites, and the use of different waters. For without these considerations, the healthiness of a dwelling cannot be assured.[15]

There is history and tradition in architecture to advance the concepts and methods of building to be in harmony with its environment:

- Alberti urged architects to *imitate the modesty* of nature.
- Palladio created varying microclimates, an oblique solar positioning, an elevated floor for passive heating control, and natural breezes at the Villa Rotunda.
- Labrouste's daylighting strategy and underfloor heating and energy control at the Bibliothèque Sainte-Geneviève in Paris.
- Frank Lloyd Wright and the Organic.
- Le Corbusier and his infatuation with the sun.
- In his lectures in London from the mid-1930s, Gropius aimed to reinforce a design method for human life in harmony with nature's biological forces.
- Aalto and his belief that architecture and its details are all part of biology.
- Murcutt touching the earth lightly.

If we tie these thoughts together, new typological standards emerge. Planning for natural somatic pleasure, mental visual desire, and intentional earthly discourse bring forth a new ecological typology, not as formal rules but as a body of measured understanding.

## Envelopment(s) of Space and Material

The experiential conditions of architecture are directly associated with its material and immaterial boundaries. In architecture, the boundary between inside and outside must not be considered a sealed envelope but rather like a breathing skin that envelops the body's organs. Architecture surrounds and enhances our somatic sensation. Physical forces can be conditioned by how we use elements in design for movement, people, air, and energy to activate programs by relationships and understand the circumstances that form in interaction with our surroundings. For example, enacting thermal thresholds and developing contrast between inside and outside make expanding or contracting boundaries for human experiences.

The word *somatic* is from the Greek word *soma*, which means body. Describing *Nested Bodies*, Sarah Robinson writes,

> We are bodies who start inside other bodies. Most of us think we know what our body is: it is the fleshy whole we inhabit; but the dictionary defines the word "body" much more broadly. A body is the entire material or physical structure of an individual organism; it is also an entity composed of numerous members—of people, things, concepts, or processes—a student body, a body of work, a body of evidence, the body politic. Body is used to describe the main or central part of something—the body of a temple, for instance. It can also describe a mass as distinct from other masses—a body of water or a celestial body. Body can also be used to describe a qualitative measure of physical consistency; wine and sauces have a certain body. Shakespeare used body as a verb, "To body forth the forms of things unknown."[16]

What does a defined "body" mean to architecture? In some of these meanings (though not all) the body is a material entity. These meanings share that a body is a boundary that delimits qualities, persons, ideas, substances, objects, or processes. Therefore, we can infer that since a building is a material entity, it is a body, and that when our body is within it, we are part of the body of the building. If the body of a building supports our body, we need to define the physical attributes that have a passive and active envelopment of, and connection with, our body.

Thermodynamic buildings, like bodies, are embodied and situated to take advantage of natural flows and forces that provide heat, cooling, or dynamic comfort. Much of the comfort people experience is sensorial, and we respond negatively to unfamiliar heat patterns. Some of this has to do with cultural perception and innate associative memory. Still, more has to do with our exteroceptors that convey sensations of heat, cold, touch, and pain to our central nervous system.

This information, combined with proprioceptors—the nerves that evaluate position and space perception—help us to observe the world and convey to our mind if a space, or organization of spaces, is sensibly satisfactory or not. Knowing this, making places that impact our mind and memory, architects must order space not to be visual or *formal*, but to have empathic arrangements that are sensorial and psychophysical. In thinking about architecture, we must apprehend the body and mind together.

Organisms move from hot to cold. They bask in the sunlight, look for shade, hibernate, and migrate. Buildings cannot move, but its inhabitants can. How might we consider the use of architecture linked to bodily experience, and how does our choice of orientation, organization, material, and threshold impact the making of architecture?

As Rayner Banham (1922–88) wrote, "Architecture, indeed, began with the first furs worn by our earliest ancestors, or with the discovery of fire—it shows a narrowly professional frame of mind to refer its beginnings solely to the cave or primitive hut."[17] We can assess this remark by confessing that the first advance in creating an adapted somatic experience was made by adding a second skin, one that was fully operational; it could be put on or taken off, left opened, or closed. The second moment was when we first took shelter.

## The Cave and Envelopment

The cave was the first dwelling place. Understanding that the cave was the first space for storytelling and artistic production connecting our bodies and minds, Paul Valéry (1871–1945) wrote, "An artist is worth a thousand centuries."[18] Juhani Pallasmaa elaborates,

> The hypnotic power of the cave paintings testifies to this longevity of artistic images. The interaction of newness and the primordial in the human mind is yet another aspect of the artistic and architectural image that can be understood through neuroscience research, I believe. Our neural system seems to be activated by newness, and we seek novel stimuli, whereas the deepest emotive impact arises from the primal layers of our neural system and memory. We, humans, are essentially creatures suspended between the past and the future more poignantly than other forms of life—it is the task of art to mediate between polarities.[19]

According to Inaki Abalos, "the grotto [or cave] is the ultimate architectural interior." It makes an envelope for the interior. Its mass can create a sensory experience within its boundaries, a threshold between interior and exterior.

> Since its revival in the imagination of the English picturesque empiricists of the eighteenth century, the grotto has continued to exert a fascination

that has secretly run through modernity, always vying with the supremacy of the idea of exteriority which here and there delights in taking flight and dominating from a panoptic viewpoint. The grotto represents the very core of architecture, the need for inner force, an obscure, atavistic center that refuses, opposes and counters transparency, visibility, and lightness. This fascination exerts a generalized attraction that transcends professional debate.[20]

Abalos associates the typology of the Office for Metropolitan Architecture (OMA) project for the Bibliothèque de France (1989) to the cave. He regards the library's section as the seminal outline for contemporary architecture and a new prototype of planned atmospheres. The encasement with a clearly defined set of bodies represents contemporary architecture's spatial paradigm. It also hints at the possibility of dynamic inter-configurations of thermodynamic bodies within an elastic envelopment of space.

Looking to Le Corbusier in his project Basilique (1948), La Sainte-Baume, France, the scheme "comprises the Basilique, cut in the rock, the two ring-shaped hotels, and the Permanent City on the other side of the plateau."[21] He envisioned a section of the basilica carved through the mountain, two spaces connected by a gallery memorializing a pilgrimage to the La Basilique de St-Maximin. Le Corbusier writes,

> The Basilique was a remarkable architectural enterprise, invisible, enormous effort expended on the interior destined to move only those souls capable of understanding. The building was entirely within the rock; partly artificially and partly naturally lit, it ran from one side of the rock at the entrance of the cave of Mary Magdalen to the other, opening suddenly on the blinding light and the distant sea.[22]

We can imagine the experience of this journey; it is primordial and encapsulates our senses. Le Corbusier later consecrates this enigmatic space in Ronchamp (1955) and in the Saint-Pierre Church at Firminy Vert (1963, completed 2006).

Frank Lloyd Wright's Unity Temple (1908) central space captures the hollowness and sensory experience of a primitive cave, referencing the traditional nave or court and creating a new type-form. Wright abstracted Lao-tzu's concept of the void from *The Book of Tea* (1906) by Okakura Kakuzo, stating, "In it [*The Book of Tea*] I read this—the reality of the building does not consist of the four walls and the roof but in the space to be lived in!"[23] This thinking considers the envelopment of space, not a non-existent void. The space forms a sensory experience of its enclosure, materiality, mass, environmental differences, and a touch of the body expressed with nature.

Turning to Finland, Elias Lönnrot captured earthly notions in 19th-century Karelian-Finnish mythology and poetry in the Kalevala, as did Aalto in his architecture. In his study on Aalto, Robert McCarter writes,

> The Finnish landscape endless weave of forest and lakes with its ever-receding horizon and the straight vertical tree trunks that slice below the light and deny the sky any unifying effect for those on the ground below, have led the inhabitants since early times construct caves of wood, as Norberg-Shultz names them. In Finnish vernacular buildings of all types, the walls and roofs were almost invariably merged to form a continuous, shell-like skin, enclosing and protecting the interior volumes.[24]

According to McCarter, the undulating wood ceiling of the Viipuri Library lecture hall (1935), with its curving vaults reminiscent of village parish church vaults and typical finish farmhouse, "may also relate to the sky above."[25] Aalto's work exemplifies cultural form and its repositioning as a thematic and technical acoustic device. Much later, in the Rovaniemi Library (1965), Aalto creates a ceiling of light, shaped from inside as a cave of melted ice formed by light. This forming demonstrates skillful technical ability to manipulate structure and material, arranged as a functional form for developing specific light zones, enhanced spatial perception, and practical use.

In *Sources of Modern Eclecticism*, Demetri Porphyrios writes on Aalto's influence on type and typology: "The locus which now legitimizes architecture is no longer the laboratory where science practices its technological strides, but culture conceived as an everyday consciousness, diffused in time and alert to the multivalent myths of form."[26]

## Finding Type Form *(the court, the hall, and the interior)*

Gottfried Semper, in a footnote in *The Four Elements of Architecture* (1852), proposed that large indoor spaces (theaters, auditoria, cathedrals) were, historically, external spaces, roofed atria, or courtyards with ceilings: "There is actually no significant architectural form that did not arise from the original concept of the court."[27]

Aalto translated a court concept in 'From Doorstep to Living Room' in the 1926 Finnish journal *Aitta*. He described the house he designed for his brother, which was modeled after a traditional vernacular ancient Roman house with its open-roofed hall. Aalto deemed that the interior must have dealings with open-air from the exterior. He explained that the Nordic climate and tradition should not make Finnish architects stumble for solutions. Accordingly, he deemed the atrium equal to the hall and that the hall was the essential room of the house.

Aalto's poetic reading of history and his idea of the court, its threshold, and boundary, begins with his interpretation of Fra Angelico's painting L'Annunciazione (1440–45). Fra Angelico, a highly devoted man, was famous for his religious themes. In *Lives of the Artists* (1550), Giorgio Vasari called him "a rare and perfect talent." Aalto did not point to the artist's religious or technical proficiency. Instead, he alerted us to the image of unity and its representation of the ideal hall—offering what he called a *"demarcation line"* between the function of the house, the exterior wall (garden wall), and the garden. This line signifies the place between man and nature, the divine threshold where one enters the home. Aalto wrote, "The picture provides an ideal example of 'entering a room.' The trinity of human beings, room, and garden."

Aalto questions how the "elegant ceremonial form" of the atrium hall can exist in a cold climate. An intimate perspective drawing of Casa Aalto depicts a central hall, evoking the atrium of a patrician's house in Pompeii. The atrium becomes a double-height hall, the central gallery, and in concept, the open-air space of the home. Not literally outdoor space, but an open hall or boundary interconnecting two sides: entry and garden.

Aalto goes on in reverence describing the Pavilion de L 'Esprit Nouveau (The New Spirit) constructed at the Paris Exposition des Arts Décoratifs of 1925 by Le Corbusier:

> "Latter-day classicism." A brilliant example of the affinity of the home interior and garden. Is it a hall, beautifully open to the exterior, and taking its dominating character from the trees, or is it a garden built into the house, a garden room?

Le Corbusier would later write,

> it represents the entire "furnishing" of a home, leaving a maximum of unencumbered space in every room, and only chairs and tables to fill it. The scientific study of chairs and tables has, in turn, led to entirely new conceptions of what their form should be: a form which is no longer decorative but purely functional.[28]

Aalto would soon adopt functionalism as a pretext to his early buildings, especially the Paimio Sanatorium. But later he would assume the image of interior and garden and Fra Angelico's trinity as a humanist model in all his projects, especially the houses.

In many cases, the central hall or court is part of an archetypal house plan, from the Roman and Chinese Atrium House, to Palladio's Houses, to the American plantation house and other vernacular examples. The idea of a central place of exchange for the passage of people and goods and socializing is significant. Yet, more importantly, this space is for the exchange of air. The stair and the fire were active participants that affected the form of the hall. The focus of this center was passive air dynamics, ideal convection in a vertical hall that offered potential for spatial, sensory experiences that worked in tandem with the envelope, the site, and material.

In these Classical or traditional house types, the center was the focal point for the axially developed plan—a centripetal space, where the action moved back to the center. In contrast, in modern architecture, particularly in the De Stijl echoing Frank Lloyd Wright's *Destruction of the Box*, the spatial force was centrifugal, directing motion away from the center.

In reading the work of Aalto, we understand a proclivity to use arrangements that are of a regional historical tradition. Yet, the whole markedly fit within the zeitgeist of the Modern Movement. This synthesis of local and universal is a theme that emerged in Aalto's work soon after his writing 'From Doorstep to Living Room' (1926), the construction of the Viipuri Library (1927), and his travels to France, the Netherlands, and Denmark (including his visit to Johannes Duiker's Zonnestraal Sanatorium at Hilversum) in 1928.

Between 1935 and 1936, Alvar and Aino Aalto began work on their new home in Helsinki—an experiment in regional form, materials, climate, light, and function. The Aalto House is a variant of the Nordic vernacular L-shaped type-plan (Figure 2.1). In *The Environmental Imagination* (2008), Dean Hawkes writes,

> Pallasmaa has commented on the utility of the L-shaped plan when adopted in the Nordic countries, "deriving as it does from an attempt to respond to such conditions as basic orientation and sun, the direction of arrival, views and the opposition of public and private realms."[29]

The principal wing contains living spaces, while the secondary wing, slightly raised, contains the studio. The secondary wing is enveloped by a solid wall that faces south. It is covered with vines for shade in summer while affording solar heat gain in winter. The bedrooms are sunlit by the southeast orientation and through the second-floor garden to the west. Aalto said of the house,

> We wanted to make the best use of natural lighting inside the house, the orientation of the terraces and the different rooms, shelter from the wind and so on, so because of our climate, we were forced to take a complex solution in the walls. This required a thorough investigation of the insulating properties of the walls.[30]

Aalto declared that the Finnish home should have two faces:

> One is aesthetically direct contact with the world outside; the other, its winter face, turns inward, and this is seen in the interior design, which

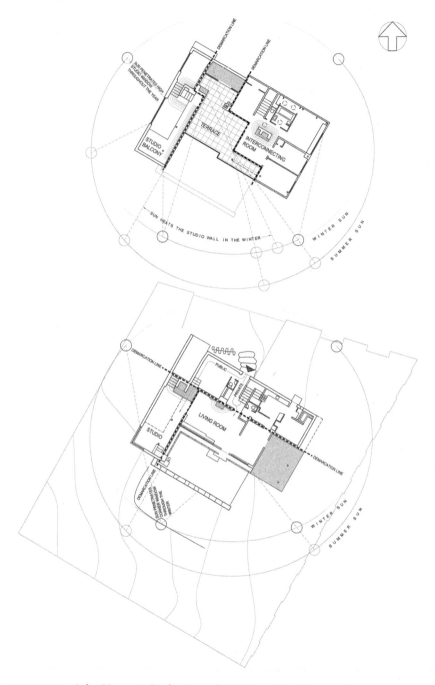

**FIGURE 2.1** Aalto House & Studio 1st and 2nd Floor Plan Demarcations

emphasizes the warmth of our inner rooms . . . I see the garden and the interior decoration as a closely-knit organism.[31]

The faces are layered with various lines of demarcation from street to garden. First, a fortified wall protects inside and outside and separates public and private, beginning at the entry. Second, is the thickened wall between the service and the domestic. This wall is also an energy boundary in winter with fireplaces. The third layer is transparent. This transparent layer thermodynamically separates the living room from the garden while connecting inside and outside, all within one interconnected space. The final layer is the landscape wall, which marks the boundary of the house and the geometric room  Here, interior and exterior living are commonly linked.

These lines continue to the upper floor, where they help separate spatial and programmatic components. In the middle of this level, a roof garden faces south. The roof garden is the intermediary between the private bedrooms and the upper level of the studio. The bedrooms are *compartitioned*, meaning that, rather than each room being enclosed, spaces are joined around an interconnecting hall, which also connects to the exterior garden. The fireplace in the center of the hall completes the ensemble of thermodynamic elements. The details of the entry thresholds offer framed views and controlled flows of air, light, and occupancy; these are inextricably linked to the whole, and they affect the trinity of the *body-room-garden*.

In contrast to pure formal modernism, centripetal and centrifugal forces for Aalto were about path and sensation, movements with the sun and season. Often situated around landscape, elements became an assemblage of interconnecting volumes, articulated by walls and apertures and typically organized obliquely. The travel of space, light, and material delivered an architectural experience that was not static. The envelopment of space and material were an antithesis to the reductive modernist paradigm.

## The Courtyard

For Semper, the historiography of architecture and the court pointed to the mound, hearth, enclosure, and roof. We can say that these elements are derivative primordial mass (earth), fire, air, and water. Aalto understood this idea and the court's potential as an interconnecting space. According to Aalto, the archetype to these ideas is the Pompeian Atrium house, with its core of fire, air, and water in which the central hall is an open-air space with roof apertures, where *the ceiling is the sky*.

A courtyard gathers at any scale. Place and patterns—natural, social, cultural, and aesthetic—relate hierarchically across boundaries, from small to large assemblies or shifting details in time. For example, the courtyard, originating as a space in front of an early Christian church, was typically flanked or surrounded by porticoes. Later enfolded as a cloister, it was perfected as the central space of the Renaissance Palazzo.

The courtyard is a prime vernacular and indigenous typological spatial device for passive cooling and natural ventilation. Aalto often spoke from his experience as a traveler, practitioner, teacher, and student. His stories interwove vernacular examples, technical descriptions, poetics of history, and economic considerations of both 'the modern gentlemen' and 'the little man.' His priority was 'archi-technical,' with formations often starting from vernacular considerations to prior-itize climatic questions, while calling for no sacrifice to expressive form or human comfort. For Aalto, the court or the courtyard also acted as a 'forum of reform.' It was a place for dynamic interconnectivity and *tempering* between the inside and the outside.

Concerning Aalto's open-plan architecture, functionally an environmental technology device, Ulrike Passe wrote,

> The courtyard atrium or inner landscape, Aalto's major spatial devices act as an interface to create an intermediate microclimate. This microclimate mediates between the severe outside climate and a more moderate, com-fortable, or even delightful interior. The courtyard has to be inside, (i.e., protected to protect); the surrounding building thus acts as its interface. The house acts as a climatic membrane. The main material needed to cre-ate this interface is air and its ventilation patterns, which are shaped through the spatial composition.[32]

Throughout modernism, the dominant plan emphasized analytical spatial hierarchy to address functional associations and meaning, usually strictly rational and perhaps with new materials and structural innovations. Plans were not always made attentive to thermodynamic boundaries of interior and exterior, hot and cold. Recently, the operative envelopment strategy has changed from a modernist visual image towards energy efficiency, responsibility, and affect. Subsequently, a new type-form can emerge that contemplates thermodynamic boundaries through typological discovery, with technological and scientific advancement.

Aalto knew thermodynamic type-form. He configured pragmatic transitions as physical boundaries and somatic experiences of light and energy. These were not precisely calculated but intuitively apprehended. Today, we must consider a calculated thermodynamic model.

## Compartition

In the Joseph Rykwert translation of *On the Art of Building* (1452), Alberti stated, "The elements of which the whole matter of buildings is composed are clearly six: locality, area, compartition, wall, roof, and opening." As we focus on one of these elements, *compartition*, we recall Alberti's definition as, "the process of dividing up the site into yet smaller units so that the buildings maybe considered as being made up of close-fitting smaller buildings, joined together like members of the whole body."[33] In a plan, compartition is not mere partitioning but the distribution of spaces that make up the whole.

The planning type of Aalto consists of volumes interacting with a clearing, the interconnecting room. This type-form enacts a natural compartition of space that can adapt to many circumstances. As seen in his varied works, this strategy works well in any building type. The Aalto plan type is a transcendent typology when considering differences in solar orientation, occupancy requirements, conditioning systems, and flexibility.

Architectural form is a derivative of climate, use, culture, context, and meaning. It is responsible for developing comfort and health, vested with adequate thermal sensations and airflow. We may consider the thermodynamic use of space by a compartition of cyclic rooms—uses that follow a circadian rhythm and encourage movements from one part of the house to another, daily and seasonally.

Today, compartition also relates to the way we interact as a society. For example, private spaces require connectivity, specific lighting, and digital connections, yet they also need demarcation for health and energy control conditions. Ideally, buildings should be interconnected volumes that are bound by active, static, and buffer zones—spatial continuities and boundary events made for thermodynamic sensation. These matters relate directly to the work of Aalto and to the necessary typological investigations required in the design of a building.

Architecture is an instrument to dwell. To embrace our human bodies and accept the rhythm of life, we must contemplate nature and the function of the organs in the body of architecture. Compartition is contingent upon good companionship with the surrounding world. Spaces oriented east arise filled with light, while south-oriented spaces capture and condition light and energy. Moreover, west-oriented spaces shield and north-oriented spaces protect. These spaces may be internally integrated within an envelopment made by material formations, derived by adaptable considerations related to place-specific nature and gradients of exchange between inside and outside.

## Aalto's Typologies

Demetri Porphyrios referenced Aalto's design memory and typological concepts with two quotes: first from Quatrèmere de Quincy in *Dictionnaire Historique d'Architecture* (1832), "the art of building is born out of a pre-existing germ; nothing whatsoever comes from nothing . . . the type is a sort of kernel around and in accordance to which the variations that the object is susceptible of are ordered," and second from Alvar Aalto in *Painters and Masons* (1921), "Nothing old is ever reborn. But it never completely disappears either. And anything that has ever been always re-emerges in a new form."[34] Though these references help clarify Aalto's idea of the type, his typological considerations are far more complex and enigmatic.

Aalto is often affixed with romantic metaphors and an intuitive, interpretive practice concerning nature, climate, and materials. However, as Alan Colquhoun wrote, "intuition must be based on a knowledge of past solutions applied to related problems, and that creation is a process of adapting forms derived either from past needs or from past aesthetic ideologies to the needs of the present."[35] Aalto translated the past through cultural signification into functional form beyond his intuition.

Porphyrios writes that Aalto's conception of representation was concerned with *propriety*, though more in tune with conveyance than fit. Social cognition required that architectural form be typologically *codified*, that is, grounded more on a taxonomy of form as it related to the structure of human behavior and recognition, and less on building program and style. Propriety, as defined by Vitruvius, is the perfection that comes when a work is authoritatively constructed on approved principles and natural causes.[36] One example of Aalto's concern with propriety was his articulation of semiotic elements surrounding his churches; the campanile, roof profile, repetitive massing, and vertical fenestrations are each recognizable within an ecclesiastical typology. Here, the familiar develops an embrace that enriches our encounters with the world. It grounds our experience.

Aalto developed a new type that interrelated considerations of two existing types. The first consideration, a plan type, was an interconnecting hall with demarcations that enable associative expansions and contractions. It is an elastic form-system that permits the development of a free-flowing section while "blurring" the inside and outside. This interconnecting plan, and its corresponding section, composes a cohesive natural typology. The second consideration was a type of questioning: What is type? What is its expression of mood (atmosphere)? Who is it for ('the little man')? How does it respond to its place (material)?

Aalto's typological thinking is manifest in his plans. The court evolves into two primary plan type-forms: the interconnecting room and the fan shape. Another type-form, the iconographic "city crown,"[37] a Classical/medieval element, becomes an *extended phenotype*,[38] an outward and visible manifestation of the themes within Aalto's mind. This *sectional* type-form connects Aaltos *architechnical form-system* strategy. Other tropes and elements also reoccur, but none more quintessentially *Aalto* than these types.

The interconnecting room type-plan "has perhaps never been more fortuitously applied in a typological sense than in Aaltos Hansaviertel apartments,"[39] wrote Kenneth Frampton. The Hansaviertel apartments, a stacking of single-story courtyard houses, embody Aalto's flexible production concept (Figure 2.2). Moreover, the repeated interconnecting plans represent a transfigured city morphology.

**FIGURE 2.2** Hansavertel Apartments Interconnecting Plan Typology

## Orientation and Boundary Typology

The idea that our physical and mental health varies with the sun and seasons goes back a long way. In the 1st century BC, Vitruvius wrote,

> from astronomy, we find the east, west, south, and north, as well as the theory of the heavens, the equinox, solstice, and courses of the stars. If one has no knowledge of these matters, he will not be able to have any comprehension of the theory of sundials.[40]

Around 300 BC, *The Yellow Emperor's Classic of Medicine*, a treatise on health and disease, described how the seasons affect all living things. For example, in winter—a time of conservation and storage—one should "retire early and get up with the sunrise . . . Desires and mental activity should be kept quiet and subdued, as if keeping a happy secret."[41] In line with this way of thinking, architectural planning requires comprehending orientation and empathy towards circadian cycles.

Making an architectural form that is orientated and enveloped by context, climate, and occupancy cycles is not easy. Moreover, considering ambient conditions of solar gain, personal energy, light, air, and the functionality of space makes this task ever more complex. Nevertheless, we can see that by ascribing to auspices of proper solar orientation, many canonical freestanding buildings—with defined attributes, orifice, or compartments—position themselves to establish site relationships through arrangements that take advantage of solar orientation and the sun's arc.

To elaborate on orientation and effective passive performance, we will discuss four houses: the Villa Tugendhat (1930) in Brno, the Czech Republic by Mies van der Rohe (1886–1969); the Schminke House (1930) in Löbau, Germany by Hans Scharoun (1893–1972); the Loomis House (1937) in Tuxedo Park, New York by William Lescaze (1896–1969); the Villa Mairea (1939) in Noormarkku, Finland by Aalto. Each house has an intended solar orientation, exterior wall invention, compartition of space, and interior winter garden (Figures 2.3A and 2.3B).

The Villa Tugendhat is orientated approximately 45 degrees north, with the southwest part of the building left glazed or open. This configuration maximizes solar gains. In addition, the lower floor embeds into the sloping terrain.

The plan organized north-south with the living rooms around a central stair containing various partitions that delineate zones of space for different uses at different times. Each of these zones is responsive. The western corner, for example, is made with an overhang to protect the interior from the intensity of the afternoon sun while simultaneously creating daytime shade for summer comfort. The southern corner has a protecting trellis, terrace, and winter garden. The living space takes in solar gain as its internal partition demarcates hot and cool zones.

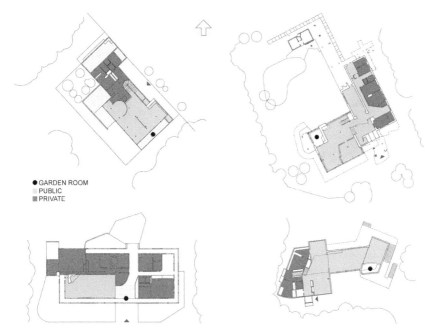

**FIGURE 2.3A** Orientation & Boundary Typologies, Villa Tugendhat— Garden Room Buffer (top), and Loomis House—Garden Room Envelopment (bottom)

**FIGURE 2.3B** Orientation & Boundary Typologies House, Villa Mairea—Garden Room Interconnection (top), and Schminke House—Garden Room (bottom)

The western space contains the dining room. It is immediately adjacent to the kitchen, internally bound by the west terrace and the interior rooms of the servant quarters.

The winter garden, which extends along the entirety of the southeast facade, provides a stratified thermodynamic boundary. At the same time, the interior partitions demarcate thermodynamic zones within, which aid in forming a responsive form-system.

The southwest wall made with retractable glass further substantiates the effect of the different zones in the plan. At the southeast, retractable canvas awnings along with deciduous trees provide shading. The trees also protect the winter garden, and their placement brings in nature.

The floors, along with the travertine walls, work well as a heat sink, accumulating sun in winter to re-radiate heat at night. With awnings fully extended and the window wall retracted in summer, heat naturally transfers from the southern to the northern zone.

The Schminke House, aside from the 35-degree twist of the second-floor dining room and terrace, is oriented primarily on an east–west axis. It has a winter garden with a canted glass wall facing south. The envelopment of the dining space is made by the glass wall of the garden room, as it continues below the curvilinear terrace of the second floor and folds to meet an interior wall.

The interior rooms take advantage of solar gain, while the overarching form makes for a diversity of use for different times of the day and year. On the exterior, the terrace's twisted form and stairs are pragmatic, and functional elements formed to take advantage of orientation and provide shading.

At the main entrance, the double-high welcoming space functions in two ways: First, it expresses the formal twist at the rear of the house, creating a visual unity with the angle of the forward-facing dining room. Second, it develops a flow of air siphoned from the lower floor to the north side of the upper story. It is a simple and effective passive form-system.

The Loomis house was the most technically inventive of all Lescaze's houses. The unique element is its double exterior walls, constructed two feet apart and connected with a similar space between the ceiling and the roof. This 'house-within-a-house' establishes a complete envelopment membrane. Outfitted with a fully controlled heating and cooling system, it functions accurately and economically, without moisture accumulating in the double wall. In winter, a separate heating system between the membrane tempers the space.

As written by Lorraine Lanmon,

> The double construction also insulates against outdoor noises. Noise control within the house was further facilitated by mineral wool insulation, vibration dampers on mechanical equipment, a cork-insulated air conditioning room, insulated air ducts, and acoustical materials throughout the house. An awning (which extends the full length of the house), the doors, and the screens all operate electrically.[42]

Lanmon emphasized that

> the house expresses the prevailing ideology of the thirties-the scientific attitude as a way of life and the belief in technology for a better society. In this regard, Loomis invented a "sun machine" to record the angle of the sun's rays at different times of the year in relation to the topography. In order to site his house most favorably in relation to the sun, models of the house were placed on the machine and the amount of sun that came through the windows at any time of the day during the entire year was recorded. Loomis's "scientific" attitude was further manifested in his effort to create a highly controlled, artificial environment.[43]

To Aalto, nature was a complex organic system in which all the subsystems of biology, soil, plants, man, and sunlight interact.[44] Consequently, many of his buildings are situated and oriented to capture reflections of light off the snowy ground, directing the horizontal rays of the Scandinavian latitude inward and developing a perception of more light than is actually present. In the south, people seek shade and shadow, but in the north, they seek light.

At the Villa Mairea, Aalto formed a situated understanding of place. The house is oriented approximately 35 degrees north. The southwest corner is glazed, and the wall facing the courtyard, also glazed, is fully operable. This configuration maximizes solar gain from the clearing in the forest to the north while protecting from the southwest winter wind. In addition, the outside trees and interior plantings provide both shade and glare reduction in the summer.

The plan, an L-shaped typology, surrounds a courtyard with a west-facing dining room as the central figure; living spaces make up the west half, and service spaces are on the east. The ground floor is for entertaining, while the upper level is private. The sauna and irregular-shaped swimming pool are seen across the courtyard's clearing.

The northwest wall is glazed, providing a view to the courtyard and affording ample late afternoon sun penetrating deep into the living room. Adjacent to this wall is the fireplace, a companion in winter. Behind the mass of the fireplace, the winter garden faces the clearing on the west/northwest corner. The overhang of the studio above shelters it.

The living room is thermodynamically apportioned, with floor material changes corresponding with temperature gradients. While this room is oriented to the southwest, the garden room faces the northwest corner, and the sitting room faces north. Central to this entire composition is the fireplace. The ceiling, made of wood slats, provides visual continuity and hides the interconnecting ventilation system.

The upper level contains a painting studio, bedrooms, children's bedrooms, a playroom, and several guest rooms, all configured around a large hall facing the garden and outfitted with various windows. In particular, the children's rooms' windows were designed to face south and east simultaneously with glare controlled by the stepped solid volumes of the parent's rooms with solid walls facing west.

In describing the Villa Mairea, Aalto understood the house as a typological experiment for solving the relation between architecture and the fine arts. He studied solutions later applied in larger buildings under different conditions. Aalto stated, "this means that you are not only a poor architect with a single temporary client, but you are working as a responsible designer who is responsible for an entire nation and for the social life of the entire world."[45]

## Aalto's Typological Elasticity

In his essay 'Temple Baths on Jyväskylä Ridge' (1925), Aalto discussed a monumental stair in Jyväskylä, Finland. He critiqued the stair and its origin from the grid of the old town plan, stating that its function and form stood against the Jyväskylä Ridge. "The stair leads to nowhere," he wrote, just before recommending a program: the sauna, for him a most logical end-use for this enormous stair.

For most, the idea of placing a sauna in such a prominent location made no sense, but in Finnish culture, as Aalto put it, "the land of the sauna," this program made perfect sense. Within the essay, his assertions about form, context, function, and cultural significance—all concepts that he would model in his future architecture—began. The sauna, atop the mount, amplified Aalto's aspiration for northern Finnish culture to be equal to that of the Classical world down south.

In 'Hilltop Town' (1924), Aalto discussed a fresco in Padua by Andrea Mantegna (1431–1506). The painting combines forms and lines that blend earth and walls, illustrating a *synthetic landscape*. This reading of Mantegna depicting "the rising town" predicated Aalto's story of the Temple Baths on Jyväskylä Ridge.

Aalto's notion of the synthesis between landscape and building was first expressed in his metaphorical sketches of "fantastic mountain landscapes with cliffs lit up by many suns in different positions," as he dreamed of the spatial configuration in the Viipuri City Library in 1929. Aalto realized the potential for planning a contiguous moving space—a space of flows and interactions that became choreographed in a dynamic operational environment. This plan was later combined with landform, monumentality, symbolic reference, local material, and thermodynamic performance in the Säynätsalo Town Hall (1949) (Figure 2.4).

The Town Hall is composed of two brick buildings that make a courtyard. The northern building, made of three stories, is U-shaped and contains offices, apartments, shops, and the council chamber, which rises monumentally from the eastern corner to crown the composition. The southern building closes the "U" with shops at the lower level and the library at the courtyard level (now a two-story library). The ground level is accessed from the perimeter, whereas the second level is met by the courtyard.

At each level, the building has been articulated in multiple functions. Its primary brick material does not create a dominance of any kind. The windows and their lack of repetition are a mix of wood and metal, creating various readings towards the interior functions. The stair and variation between solid bricks and facade openings invite a visit to the court on the second level—an intimate yet publicly accessible space for the town. The court emerges at a modest and embracing scale, unexpected from the impression of monumentality seen in many of the published photographs. The idea that a town can gather with such a feeling of intimacy is a welcome surprise when considering the political nature that a town hall represents—all part of the magic of this multi-use program. The overall scale and articulation of the interior circulation around the court enable the reading of layers and transparency, interconnecting inside and outside across a thermodynamic material boundary.

Reminiscent not only of the Karelian vernacular farmhouse, the courtyard type-form is composed of multiple formal readings. The courtyard is a mound, the consecration between man and earth. It is a grand piazza reached by ascension and comparable with the program and arrangement of both the center of Bergamo and the landscape of Fiesole in Italy. And it is a synthesis with surroundings ceremonially and monumentally risen from a plateau.

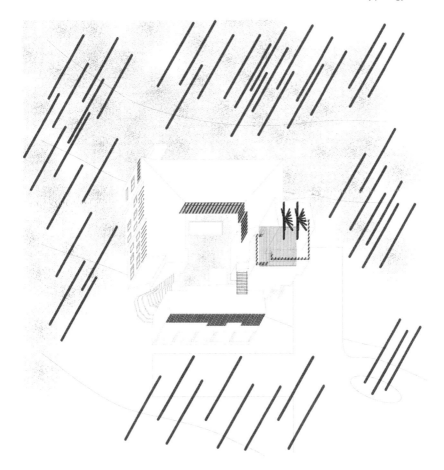

**FIGURE 2.4**   Säynätsalo Town Hall Courtyard Typological Elasticity

Stairs flank each side of the court—one formal and the other informal. For Aalto, the perception of moving up a hill, an image of landscape, and external nature transmitted to the inside were essential features.

Like a Japanese garden, the court makes an intimate space, complete with vegetation, water, and well-proportioned window screens. Aalto's connection to Japan came from an interpretation of spiritual space related to varied internal and external positions. Aalto wrote about Japan in 'Rationalism and Man' (1935):

> There is a civilization that, even in its traditional phase, its handicraft era, showed enormous sensitivity and tact toward the individual in this regard. I mean parts of the Japanese culture, which, with its limited range of materials and forms, inculcated a virtuoso skill in creating variations and almost daily recombination. Its great predilection for flowers, plants, and natural objects is a unique example. The contact with nature and its constantly

observable change is a way of life that has difficulty getting along with concepts that are too formalistic.[46]

According to Göran Schildt (1917–2009), "When designing buildings, Aalto liked to start out with one or several kernels, letting other motifs grow around them to produce a complex, crystallized entity."[47] Multiple readings are apparent; a formal composition interpreted with many languages harmoniously spoken together.

The courtyard is not only symbolic but functional. This raised volume captures the sun, protects from the wind, and has a low height-to-area ratio that allows the low sun to penetrate and warm the whole inner space. Courtyards are often said to employ "ingenious natural cooling strategies."[48] Here, we can see how the courtyard can become a microclimate, aided by the position of a building mass, the biomass of the plantings, and water for evaporative cooling.

As noted by Francine Battaglia and Ulrike Passe,

> A courtyard in northern climates can also protect from detrimental winds and create a sheltered space. Studies of the relationship between wind velocity, pattern, and direction concerning the proportions of the courtyard itself (height and width) support this approach. A courtyard creates a microclimate and protects from the excessive wind while still enabling natural ventilation from the warm inner courtyard through the circulation space into the surrounding rooms.[49]

The window wall is a transparent demarcation and a mediator between visual and thermodynamic perception. The glass provides a clear visual connection towards the courtyard and a boundary for sensation when paired with the brick.

The brick is a phenomenological presence in the building. It is not just a material but a substance that is simultaneously the walls, the stairs, the floor, the benches; a scalar sensation of details that mark the worker's hand.

Dean Hawkes describes this material arrangement of brick and its heating system as a thermodynamic bodily experience:

> Throughout the building, Aalto took great care to integrate radiators into the fabric in ways that meet the particular needs of each space and its function. In the light-filled cloister, the radiators sit beneath a massive brick sill that runs continuously beneath the windows . . . Warm air passes through a gap between the sill and window frame, and the brick itself becomes warm to act as a secondary heat source. Brick pavers extend partway across the floor and absorb heat from the radiators to extend the sense of the warm perimeter. The rear wall is exposed brick, and this absorbs direct sunlight to retain its heat. The whole is a sophisticated environmental micro-system that combines the natural and mechanical with ease.[50]

The bricks function as a material technic, the glass as an immaterial boundary, and the wood as a tectonic and mnemonic device. This synergistic understanding

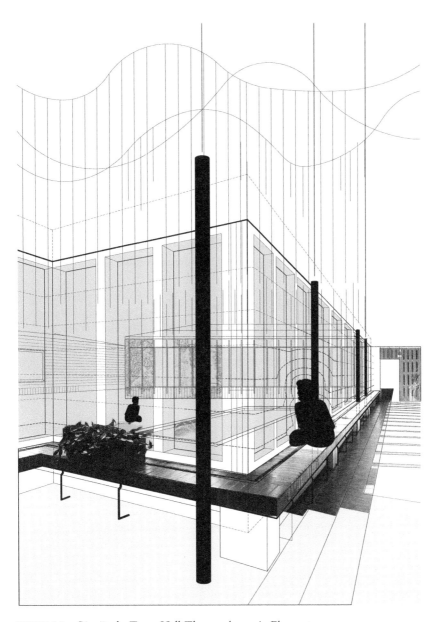

**FIGURE 2.5**   Säynätsalo Town Hall Thermodynamic Element

of structure and material becomes a semiotic, functional form (Figure 2.5). Hawkes tells us that

> the image of the roof trusses in the Council Chamber at Säynätsalo is one of the most familiar in the whole of twentieth-century architecture. These have been interpreted variously as 'upturned hands'—Porphyrios—or as an evocation of a 'great barn'—Quantrill—but they have a significant environmental function in allowing, by supporting the secondary roof framing, unrestricted ventilation between the interior and exterior surfaces of the double roof construction that is necessary for Finland's winter climate. This may be 'prosaic,' as Richard Weston suggests, but a crucial part of Aalto's genius was his ability to transform necessity into poetry.[51]

In this way, Aalto was a *transcendental* architect, straddling the traditional and modern concepts of building. Like an alchemist transforming forms of tradition and the standard technics of material construction, he created a transmutable substance of sensation, light, and energy. Still today, the work of Aalto delivers a potent imagination that we can journey with into the future.

## Aalto's Thermodynamic Building Typology

A study of two unbuilt Aalto houses in Italy—the Villa Sambonet (1954) on Lake Como, and the Villa Erica (1967) near Turin—reveals how Aalto shifted his planning when designing outside of Finland. The houses accommodate his typological model considering the material culture and climate of Italy.

Aalto's description of The Villa Sambonet is as follows:

> The part of the house where studio, living-room, dining-room, and kitchen were intended to receive the most light and is open to the garden and the surrounding landscape, whereas the bedrooms were conceived of as appended, pavilion-like volumes discernible as separate units from the outside. From the inside, there is no direct contact between the bedrooms and the garden. This arrangement was intended to emphasize their function as a zone of rest and privacy, in contrast to the open public part of the house.[52]

The compartition of the plan also has thermodynamic rationality. The bedrooms have a conical roof reminiscent of the southern Italian Trulli to emulate natural stack ventilation, "the skylight over the bedrooms serves simultaneously for ventilation, especially during the hot summer months (Figure 2.6). The windows can thus remain closed, and the interior can be shielded from direct sunlight."

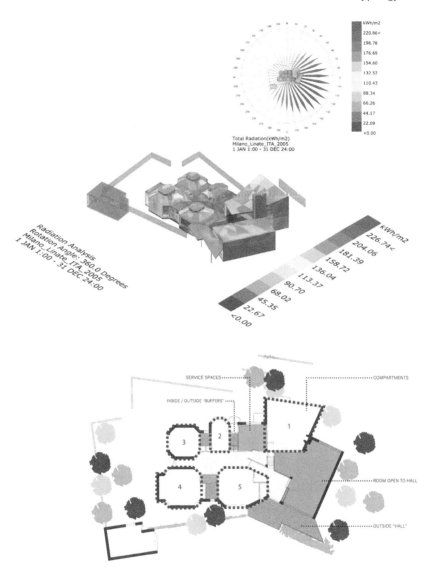

**FIGURE 2.6** Villa Sambonet and Radiation Analysis

We can see that the rooms are separate chambers connected to the open-air hall, and can imagine, on a hot day in Como, opening the living room window adjacent to the garden and shaded overhang. The ventilation cupolas of each trullo chamber would temper and moisten the air by a passive thermal chimney and evaporative cooling. Here, the cleverness of form fits the climate and the client's request.

The Villa Erica was organized to accommodate privacy and flexibility. The design, according to Aalto, "was intended for the entertainment of house guests and as a stimulating milieu for the owner; it was planned as the locus of an active social and cultural life."[53] The house was also a place where large social gatherings would take place during different seasons (Figure 2.7). Its arrangement of form and space would have delivered a noteworthy passive heating and cooling strategy, employing demarcated boundaries of hot and cool areas, each oriented in a particular way to the sun and direct natural airflows.

The pool, on the southwest corner, was envisioned as a winter garden that would include a shaded space or *grotto* enveloped by the ground. The interior living space, an open room, would be connected to the outside and to the hall, configured like a heat exchanger. An open-air hall and stairs interconnect the upper floor. This spatial arrangement would create a thermodynamic situation similar to the *Venturi effect* made by the entry and the free flow of the interior void in the Viipuri Library. This intuitive and experimental understanding of the technical function of form is why continued investigations of Aalto is fitting to 21st-century discourse, as it can contribute to the advancement of technological strategies elaborated by new methods of analysis.

## The 21st-Century Building Type

In his treatise titled *Building* (1928), Hannes Meyer (1889–1954) made several design rights discussing physiological heat transfer. In unambiguous terms, he observed that "Building is a biological process. Building is not an aesthetic process. In its design, the new dwelling becomes not only a *machine for living*, but also a biological apparatus serving the needs of body and mind." He continued to explain how

> we calculate the angle of the sun's incidence in the course of the year and in relation to the latitude of the site, and with this knowledge, we determine the size of the shadow cast by the house in the garden and the amount of sun admitted by the window into the bedroom. We work out the amount of daylight falling on the working area of the interior, and we compare the heat conductivity of the outside walls with the humidity content of the outside air . . . we consider the body of the house to be a storage cell for the heat of the sun.[54]

Meyer's proclamation, formed in the 1920s, is already 100 years old. We have since seen many buildings and volumes of literature expound on similar notions. However, this process has yet to become standard. To design and practice sustainably, we need to evaluate types differently; a typology that looks not to review historical types for only form and shape, but to help us consider our future.

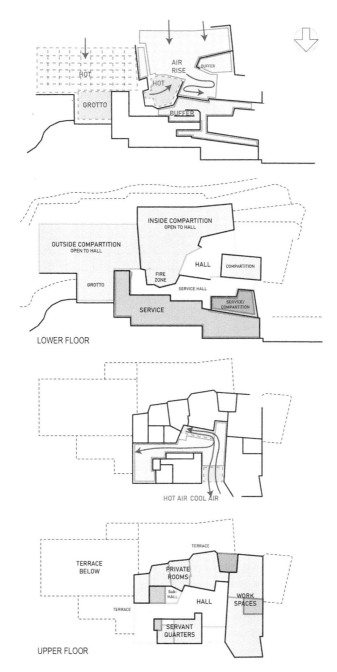

**FIGURE 2.7** Villa Erica Compartition of Thermodynamic Zones

The widespread loss of local technical traditions has resulted in expression and construction as contradictory to context, culture, and climate. Technology alone is not at fault, but it is also far from the solution to our problems. As Martin Heidegger reminds us,

> We can use technical devices, and yet with proper use also keep ourselves so free of them, that we may let go of them any time. We can use technical devices as they ought to be used, and also let them alone as something which does not affect our inner and real core. We can affirm the unavoidable use of technical devices, and also deny them the right to dominate us, and so to warp, confuse, and lay waste our nature.[55]

Perhaps quantifying local types and contemporary design through qualified software could develop a new type-form. As discussed, the hall was a place of exchange for passage and socializing; more importantly, it was also for air exchange. Early modernism gave clues for adapting these exchanges by spatial organizations and assemblies of materials. But unfortunately, the simple passive systems in these traditionally informed houses of early modernism went lost as modernism soon proliferated as a universal style. Instead of integrating the *passive* strategies learned from tradition with new *active* systems, air-conditioning technology supplanted the operable and adaptable boundary with the hermetically sealed box—also not the best plan concerning our post-pandemic world.

Passe reminds us why we need natural ventilation:

> The amount of air needed to transport heat is much larger . . . In our contemporary mechanized world, most of this heat is removed using forced-air cooled by refrigeration technology that relies on compression refrigeration machinery consuming large amounts of electrical energy. In fact, delivering plentiful fresh air into a space with as little energy as possible is a complex endeavor and can be tricky. But natural ventilation is truly underrepresented and could pick up much more of the load than in current practices.[56]

Though we cannot yet process fluid dynamic systems all at once with our computational devices, we can look back at the past to reestablish the future.

Instead of searching for energy efficiency in a building, we should focus on the convergence of material form and energy. Matter is "captured energy," Kiel Moe describes, and this convergence is "the thermodynamic premise that architecture should maximize its ecological and architectural power."[57] A new methodology must not begin with pure aesthetic concerns but with the conception of architecture as a thermodynamic bio-network *and* as an adaptive system informed by its local environment. Considerations of new measures and operative envelopments of form, space, and material can help us fulfill this vision.

Perhaps simply planning for those autumn and spring days, the natural breeze and warmth of the sun must again be prominent parameters informing our design philosophy as architects.

The accelerating movement away from oil and gas towards solar and wind has already begun to open a new economy. Once better integrated into our homes and buildings, life-cycle costs will be reduced as healthy living environments become the new standard. As urban power grids stress to their maximums, and as the prices of solar and super-efficient HVAC systems drop, an approach that incorporates passive and active strategies will soon become a political, cultural, and economic reality. This convergence will require us to adapt and employ an integrated design-thinking process.

In *The Task of Architecture* (2012), Patrik Schumacher tells us,

> Traditional schemes of classification are thus augmented by the possibility of hybridization, and the ordering of a spectrum of smooth transitions between types via ordinate or quantitative (parametricized) concepts. Function-types are thus placed within a continuous order and redefined as variable, parametricized constructs. The result is more complex than a traditional typology. This increased complexity does not only result from the addition of the in-between variants, but is also due to the much stronger sense of integration achieved within such a topo-typological system.[58]

Thus, typology evolves to form variety and customizations within a topo-typological framework. Finally, we should "get into the habit of analysis—analysis will, in time, enable synthesis to become your habit of mind."[59] Since digital tools and computation platforms have built-in standards, augmented by custom parameters and iterative variability, analysis using models should become our design habit.

## The W.I.N.D House

The name W.I.N.D. House (Figure 2.8), an acronym from the family's initials, is fitting to the cross breezes created by the building configuration. As Ben van Berkel of UNStudio states,

> a challenge for the architect in the design of today's single-family home is a response that accurately reflects the degrees of flexibility, sustainability, and automation required by the residents and the incorporation of these into the overall concept of the design.

Through its immersion in the landscape in North Holland, Netherlands, the house responds to context and the seasonal conditions of its surroundings. The

**FIGURE 2.8**   Photo, W.I.N.D. House, Netherlands, UN Studio, 2008–2014

*(Credit:* Fedde de Weert)

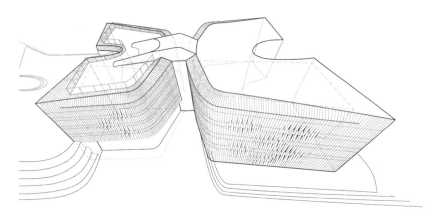

**FIGURE 2.9**   W.I.N.D. Situated Plan Boundary

more public living and dining areas look south to polders, the Dutch reclaimed landscape, while the private sleeping and working spaces look north into the woods. The east and west are predominantly closed, affording privacy against the neighboring houses.

The house loosely follows a centrifugal split-level arrangement derived from the changes in grade at the site. The pinched court-form at the open staircase

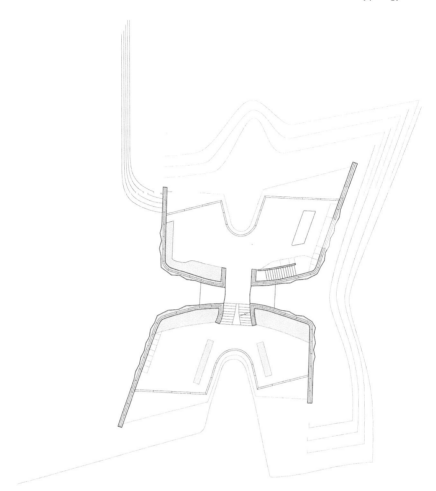

**FIGURE 2.10**  W.I.N.D. Type-Form Volume Envelopment

connects the front and back wings, creating an effective type of compartition. Configured like a flower, the flexible floor plans open to the landscape, enabling an interplay of sunlight, prevailing breezes, and functionality (Figure 2.9).

The front and rear are fully glazed with overhangs made by the wood-slat siding that envelope the exterior. The glass is tinted to protect the interior from glare. With the glass inset within the envelope, canopies, terraces, and blinders are created. On the sides of the house, the wood slats bulge outward, creating ventricles for airflow into the house (Figure 2.10).

Standard clay terracotta bricks infill the concrete walls with a straightforward construction system. The clay also provides thermal regulation and humidity control. In addition, the walls and ceilings are coated with natural clay stucco,

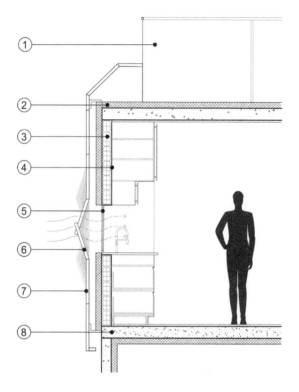

1. Glass Railing around Roof Terrace
2. Continuous Insulation on Concrete Floor Structure
3. Clay Terracotta Brick Infill Walls
4. Natural Clay Stucco on Interior Surfaces
5. Operable Windows with Insulating Glass
6. "Ventricles" Openings in Façade Envelopment System
7. Wood Panel Façade Envelopment System
8. Concrete Structure on Grade

**FIGURE 2.11**    W.I.N.D. Ventilated Wall Section

which aids in providing a healthy indoor climate due to the evaporating effect of the clay (Figure 2.11).

An integrated automation and energy management system manages the distribution of air. The heating and cooling operation uses a central air/water heat pump system with waste heat recovery and solar panels. Vents are placed near the floor to maintain cool air while the warm air flows up, allowing for faster cooling with less energy. In addition, heat gain is reduced through the glass, the overhangs, the outer wooden envelope, and the thermal mass.

**FIGURE 2.12** Photo, Perez Art Museum Miami, Herzog & de Meuron, 2013

(*Credit:* Paolo Gambo, CC by 2.0)

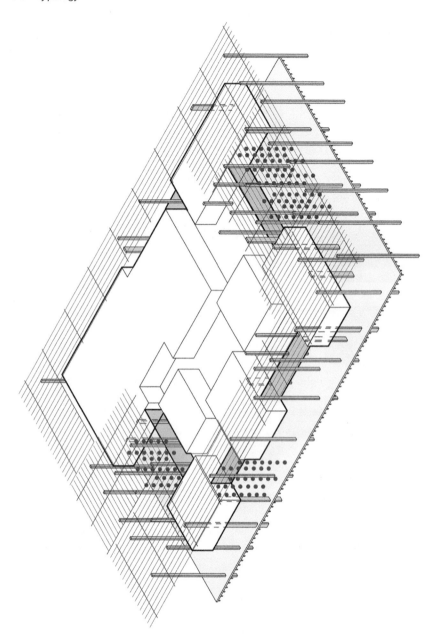

**FIGURE 2.13** PAMM Temperature Gradient Conditioning Typology

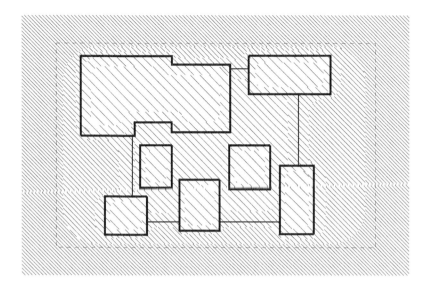

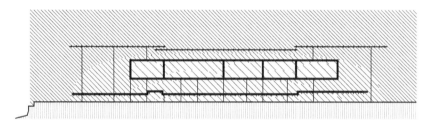

**FIGURE 2.14**    PAMM T. G. Compartition Plan & Section

## The Perez Museum

The Perez Museum in Miami, Florida exemplifies a building that subtly alters type towards a typology attending to its environment (Figure 2.12). This plan is more than a typical museum with rooms connected by a hall. It presents a different type-form configured to harmonize its situation. Herzog & de Meuron have flipped the conventional type and extended the design to unite its surroundings.

In Miami, the tropical climate with a hot, wet season (high sun summer) and warm, dry season (low sun winter) sets up typological parameters (Figure 2.13).

The building is elevated upon a platform that raises the main floor above the floodplain while affording significant natural airflow to cool the surroundings. The roof, covered with a shade canopy, forms a veranda, a vernacular device in a tropical climate.

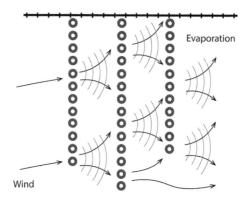

**FIGURE 2.15**  PAMM Platform, Veranda, & Air Flow Typology

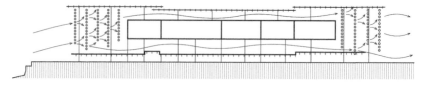

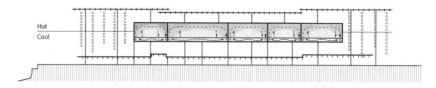

**FIGURE 2.16**  PAMM Air Distribution System Type

Plants in the veranda, hung vertically from the canopy, envelop the building with a microclimate between the gallery volumes and their surroundings. This intermediary boundary between inside and outside offers gradual transitions from hot to cool and humid to dry.

The adaptation of the veranda and its microclimate create a pool of shade. Evaporative cooling through natural airflow advances the diversity and flexibility of the garden room and temper the building by reducing energy loads as it provides added environmental comfort (Figure 2.14).

The lower floor forms the entry and the interconnected public room. The upper floors contain compartitioned galleries accessed from within the two-story, glass-enclosed mixing chamber. The solid galleries extend outward from this chamber, furthering effective shading and defining the varied outdoor spaces within the veranda (Figure 2.15).

An underfloor, low-velocity air distribution system provides radiant cooling that helps to decrease the energy usage of fans. As a result, only the lower strata of the rooms are conditioned, which provides occupants access to high-quality air and requires significantly less ductwork than an overhead alternative. This concept continues through the glass-enclosed mixing chamber, where the air is co-mingled and pre-tempered (Figure 2.16).

While the solid, rough textured concrete is reminiscent of Miami's Art-Deco buildings, a custom concrete mullion system, holding the largest hurricane-proof glass in Florida, is incorporated to enhance the transparency.

The galleries have wooden floors and concrete ceilings with recessed lights organized in repetitive linear rows. Outside, the platform uses greenheart wood that was left unfinished in order to weather into a silvery tone. The wood canopy battens, laid in opposing directions and at varying heights, govern the sun by creating various lighting and shading patterns throughout the day and changing seasons.

## Notes

1　Kelbaugh, Douglas. 'Typology: An Architecture of Limits,' in *Urban Design Reader*. Taylor & Francis, 2007, Chapter 9, p.87.

2　Forty, Adrian. *Words and Buildings: A Vocabulary of Modern Architecture*. Thames & Hudson, 2004, "Type," p.304.

3　Vidler, Anthony, translation and introduction to Quatremère de Quincy, 'Type,' *Oppositions*, Volume 8, Spring 1977, pp.146–150.

4　Rossi, Aldo. *The Architecture of the City*. MIT Press, 1982, p.40.

5　Quatremère de Quincy, 'Type,' as referenced by Rossi, *The Architecture of the City*.

6　ibid.

7　Argan, Giulio Carlo. *On the Typology of Architecture*. n.p., 1963.

8　Moneo, Rafael. 'On Typology,' *Oppositions*, Volume 13, Summer 1978, pp.22–45.

9　Conrads, Ulrich. Ed. 'Werkbund Theses and Antitheses,' in *Programs and Manifestoes on 20th-Century Architecture*. The MIT Press, 1970.

10　Aalto, Alvar. 'The Reconstruction of Europe,' in *Alvar Aalto in His Own Words*. Ed. Schildt, Göran. Otava, 1997, p.154 (Aalto).

11　Moneo, 'On Typology.'

12　Vidler, Anthony. 'The Third Typology,' in *Oppositions Reader: Selected Essays 1973–1984*. Princeton Architectural Press, 1998, pp.13–17.

13　Moneo, 'On Typology.'

14　Aalto, Karelian Architecture,' pp.118–119.

15　Pollio, Vitruvius. *Vitruvius, the Ten Books on Architecture*. Harvard University Press, 1914.

16　Robinson, Sarah. 'Nested Bodies,' in *Mind in Architecture: Neuroscience, Embodiment, and the Future of Design*. MIT Press, 2017, p.137.

17　Banham, Reyner. 'Stocktaking,' *Architectural Review*, Volume 127, Number 756, February 1960.

18　Valéry, Paul. 'Eupalinos, or the Architect,' in *Dialogues*. Princeton University Press, 1989, p.69.

19  Pallasmaa, Juhani. 'Body, Mind, and Imagination,' in *Mind in Architecture: Neuroscience, Embodiment, and the Future of Design.* MIT Press, 2017, p.66.
20  Abalos, Iñaki, and Renata Snetkiewicz. *Essays on Thermodynamics: Architecture and Beauty.* Actar D. Inc., 2015, p.33.
21  Le Corbusier. *Œuvre Complète: Volume 5: 1946–1952.* Birkhäuser, 2015.
22  ibid.
23  Nute, Kevin. *Frank Lloyd Wright and Japan.* Routledge, 2000, p.123.
24  ibid.
25  ibid.
26  Porphyrios, Demetri. *Sources of Modern Eclecticism: Studies on Alvar Aalto.* Academy Editions, St. Martin's Press, 1982, p.38.
27  Roberts, John. *Clouds and Sky Ceilings*, Imagining . . . 27th Annual Sahanz Conference I Newcastle, 2010.
28  Le Corbusier, *Oeuvre Complète, Volume 1: 1910–1929.* Birkhäuser, 2015.
29  Hawkes, Dean. 'Rationality and Domesticity,' in *The Environmental Imagination.* Ed. Pallasmaa, Juhani. Alvar Aalto Foundation, 2008, Volume 6, p.71.
30  Lahti, Louna. *Alvar Aalto, 1898–1976: Paradise for the Man in the Street.* Taschen, 2009.
31  Aalto, 'From Doorstep to Living Room,' pp.51–52.
32  Passe, Ulrike. *Alvar Aalto's Open Plan Architecture as an Environmental Technology Device.* Working papers—Alvar Aalto Researchers' Network, 12–14 March 2012, Seinäjoki and Jyväskylä.
33  Rykwert footnote 84. "compartmentalization" provides the closest translation of Alberti's partitio. However, Leoni's "compartition," though obscure, is perhaps more convenient, but see glossary, s.v. Compartition.
34  Porphyrios, *Sources of Modern Eclecticism*, p.25.
35  Colquhoun, Alan. 'Typology and Design Method,' in *Theorizing a New Agenda for Architecture: An Anthology of Architectural Theory 1965–1995.* Ed. Nesbitt, Kate. Princeton Architectural Press, 1996, p.254.
36  Vitruvius, Book One, Ch. 2, The Five Fundamental Principles of Architecture, "Propriety."
37  Porphyrios, *Sources of Modern Eclecticism*, p.28.
38  Extended Phenotype in this context. Dawkins, Richard. *The Extended Phenotype.* Oxford University Press, 1999, p.109.
39  Frampton, Kenneth. *Aalto in Retrospect Six Foci for the Next Millennium.* Domus, 1998, pp.45–56.
40  Vitruvius, the Ten Books on Architecture.
41  Geddes, Linda. 'Will Norway Ever Beat the Winter Blues?' *The Atlantic*, 14 March 2017.
42  Lanmon, Lorraine Welling. *William Lescaze, Architect.* Art Alliance Press, 1987, p.116.
43  ibid, p.117.
44  Schildt, Göran. *Alvar Aalto, The Mature Years.* Rizzoli, 1991, as cited in Shifting contours, Experiencing the landscape in Aalto's architecture. An exhibition in the Gallery at the Alvar Aalto Museum 20 May to 27 September 2009.
45  Aalto, 'The Villa Mairea,' p.226.
46  Aalto, 'Rationalism and Man,' p.93.
47  Aalto, 'Plan Descriptions,' p.225.
48  Passe, Ulrike, and Battaglia, Francine. *Designing Spaces for Natural Ventilation: An Architect's Guide.* Taylor & Francis, 2015, p.36.
49  ibid, p.39.
50  Hawkes, Dean. *The Environmental Imagination: Technics and Poetics of the Architectural Environment.* Routledge, 2008, p.78.
51  ibid, p.79.
52  Alvar, Aalto. *Alvar Aalto—The Complete Works.* Birkhäuser Verlag GmbH, 2014. Volume III, p.18.

53 ibid, p.34.
54 Schnaidt, Claude. *Hannes Meyer: Buildings, Projects and Writings.* Niggli, 1965.
55 Heidegger: Discourse on Thinking as quoted in Passinmäki, Pekka. *The Trout, the Stream, and the Letting-Be. Alvar Aalto's Contribution to the Poetic Tradition of Architecture.* Working papers—Alvar Aalto Researchers' Network, 12–14 March 2012, Seinäjoki and Jyväskylä.
56 Passe and Battaglia, *Designing Spaces for Natural Ventilation,* p.2.
57 Moe, Kiel. *Convergence: An Architectural Agenda for Energy.* Routledge, 2013.
58 Schumacher, Patrik. *The Autopoiesis of Architecture, Volume II: A New Agenda for Architecture.* Wiley, 2012, p.29.
59 Attributed to Frank Lloyd Wright.

# 3

# TECTONICS—ELEMENTS AND ATMOSPHERES

> **Tectonics** = processes affecting the structure and choice of the material system.
> (*Tektōn*: "carpenter, joiner, maker")

Until recently, the study of material has remained bound inside the limited performance metrics of gravity and durability. While still critical to making buildings, what has evolved is a more profound knowledge of materials, their costs, uses, and impacts. What we build with must be carefully considered against this expanded definition of material.

In *Architecture of the Well-Tempered Environment* (1969), Reyner Banham frames our conversation about the essence of material in architecture. Paraphrasing, he notes that the emergence of architecture is marked by the decision to use a pile of wood to make shelter rather than to make fire.

Thus, the first act of architecture was a future decision, choosing between immediacy, burning the wood for passing comfort, or constructing a place to dwell, for now, and into the future: to shelter or structure is a choice between the provisional and the permanent. Today, our option of using one material over another profoundly impacts our future. An architecture that embodies the elemental forces that shelter us; gives meaning to material matters through its capacity to turn construction elements into atmospheres of sensation, projected into the future.

Matter defines elements of architecture, mechanical and physical properties that embody energy, and its *Materia*, the imaginative artful ingredient that activates its sociological, psychological, and psychophysical properties.

DOI: 10.4324/9781003160571-4

The Periodic Table arranges the most fundamental building blocks of matter. These elements, in combination, make up all matter in the universe. While *matter* is associated with the physical characteristics of material—compounded elements extracted from the earth—*material* can be understood as the composition of matter used for construction. The material of architecture is also a container of energy past and future.

We can describe elements in architecture in many different ways:

> Plato described the elements—Earth, Fire, Air, Water—that form the universe. Vitruvius explained a triad of principal elements: *firmitas, utilitas,* and *venustas*; or *stability* (solid), *utility* (useful), and *delight* (beauty). These together defined architecture and building. Alberti's treatise *On Architecture* (1485) outlined parameters, measures, and techniques that derived beauty through arrangements of parts so that all things were composed together in harmonious accord.

Le Corbusier provided *Five Points* that ultimately defined the elements of modern architecture. One of those points had to do with building displacement: elevated buildings with a new ground on the roof enabling freedoms for buildings and landscapes to unite.

Rem Koolhaas describes architectural elements as a primordial toolkit used to understand how seemingly stable elements are in constant evolution.[1] Investigations of window, facade, balcony, corridor, fireplace, stair, escalator, elevator are the primary characters in architecture, and their evolving histories provide insight into each of their futures. Curiously, Koolhaas omitted the column from his elements; accordingly, we may interpret that, according to Koolhaas, columns are structural components, not architectural elements.

We can understand elements through their material qualities and cultural associations. Our long history helps to inform our material choices in the making process. Traditionally, material usage had a relationship with time and place. Gothic history is of stone. With columns stratified, merged, and re-articulated in relation to the wall, this period reconsidered structural possibilities with materials properties, producing a new form with the innovative use of matter. Today, the architectural elements need reassessment beyond structural analysis and towards ecological knowledge.

In an interview in 1969, Aalto defined how materials can become embodied understandings:

> The three art forms, architecture, painting, sculpture, are connected or interrelated because they are an expression of human intellectuality based on '*materia*'. . . I primarily mean matter as a substance, and yet the word *materia* means more to me, for it translates purely material activity into the relate mental process. The principles of human civilization are largely

based on materia. I even think that this wonderful word, materia, is ultimately that which connects the three art forms architecture, painting, and sculpture.[2]

He continued to say,

material is a link. It has the effect of making unity. All art forms are based on matter; they must confront materiality. The links in materia leave open every opportunity for harmonious synthesis for ultimately the three categories of art are one and the same they are identical in their working theory and even in their results as long as we are prepared to examine things in a deeper context. Art is a continuous process of refining and reworking matter—not for its own sake, but in order to satisfy human demands.[3]

Aalto was expressly interested in the harmonious agreement between art and technology, where "in every case, one must achieve a simultaneous solution of opposites."[4] In Aalto's work, the tectonic arrangement of *Matter, Material*, and *Materia* represents a *Form-System-Material* triad, where form and material are bound together in systemic artful harmony—what Aalto called "technical functionalism."[5]

*Materia* is the embedded matter that informs the atmosphere of architecture. It embodies sensorial properties and the interrelationship of elements in our imagination. We often limit our conversations and critical judgment to the visual sensation of our constructions; however, the whole sensory experience provides comfort and pleasure in architecture.

Material information can help provide better judgment, while software and fabrication hardware help develop better metrics and greater sustainability. Still, we must maintain that "art as an element controls or guides technology."[6] With all this in mind, an understanding of *materia* provides new light.

## Architectural Tectonics

Tectonics in architecture is a framework of understanding. The concepts and processes affecting the structure and choice of material vary. Most options begin with economy and resource, then historical and cultural analyses, leading towards structural or material expressions that eventually inform new fabrication strategies.

The igloo is a vernacular structure situated in its environment. Its material construction relies on local resources and customs that have developed over time. Its material, blocks of frozen matter harvested from its location, are shaped to make a shelter with extraordinary thermal comfort. Made by little more than ice, saw, skin, and fire, the elementary nature of this structure is an ecological embodiment; form, matter, and thermodynamics bound in a systemic triad of location, material, and custom. Architecture, however, is defined less from tradition but more by designed intentionality.

In 1851, Gottfried Semper described building in terms of its elemental components of construction: 1) hearth, 2) earthwork, 3) framework/roof, and 4) enclosing membrane. Each of these components has a connection with a specific production characteristic: 1) ceramics, 2) stereotomy, 3) carpentry, and 4) textiles. Semper regarded joinery as "the primordial tectonic element" with which building is defined.

The joining or weaving of a *tectonic frame* versus using a *stereotomic block* of elements is influenced by culture and location. Semper referred to architecture that maintains its cultural expression as hand-crafted. Although applicable in his time, adopting this view today would marginalize possibilities for using contemporary technologies to form new modes of tectonic expression. However, combining Semper's four-assembly system into one comprehensive building technic could produce more appropriate outputs. As handcraft and machine-craft give way to digital craft, we see a synthesis of mechanized fabrication informed by human assembly and management processes.

According to Kenneth Frampton,

> tectonic cannot be divorced from the technological, and it is this that gives it a certain ambivalence. In this regard, it is possible to identify three distinct conditions: 1) the technological object, which arises directly out of meeting an instrumental need; 2) the scenographic object, which may be used equally to allude to an absent or hidden element; and 3) the tectonic object, which appears in two modes. We may refer to these modes as the ontological and representational tectonic.[7]

Karl Bötticher (1806–89), a contemporary of Semper and an associate of Karl Friedrich Schinkel (1781–1841), discussed reciprocity between *ontology* and *representation* of form. These modes can be resolved by understanding the two opposing conditions: 1) the "Kernform" form of *structure* (elemental form), the functional, physical, and cultural vernacular; and 2) the "Kunstform" form of *expression* (atmospheric form), the aesthetic, expressive, and cultural imagination. These two bodies form a synergy between the element and the atmosphere, making a whole architectural concept. This discourse was an extension of a question posed by Schinkel,[8] later adapted by Aalto, about how architecture is elevated to a fine art despite its primary associations between function and utility.

Max von Pettenkofer (1818–1901), known as the "father of experimental hygiene," investigated concepts of clothing and dwelling skins as "breathable walls" in a performative tectonic that was largely overlooked until recently. We now see an effort, in some instances, towards the bifurcation of the building envelope, becoming an inhabitable interface between inside and out.

In his seminal text *Structure, Construction, Tectonics* (1965), Eduard Sekler (1920–2017) writes,

> When a structural concept has found its implementation through construction, the visual result will affect us through certain expressive qualities which clearly have something to do with the play of forces and corresponding arrangement of parts in the building, yet cannot be described in terms of structure and construction alone. For these qualities which are expressive a relation of form to force, the terms tectonic should be reserved.[9]

Here, tectonics is characterized as an expressive cohesion of the nature of material and its visual effect.

In *Studies in Tectonic Culture* (1995), Kenneth Frampton described the tectonic as "poetics of construction" and stated that the elements of architecture do not exist independently. Elements are both interrelated and interdependent—not singular constructs, but genealogy and cultural manifestation derived from the characteristics of place and the intentionality of the architect. This conversation recalls the tectonic matters of construction and material versus the architectonics of space and form. From Frampton, we understand architecture as a culture of making. This concept combines physical elements with an atmospheric imagination informed by underlying artistic and social ethics.

More recently, Neil Leach describes a tectonic where the old opposition between a digital culture of seductive images and a tectonic culture of the poetic and pragmatic building has led to a collaboration between the two domains. Leach's concept of *digital tectonics*[10] provides an approach to architectural tectonics where data is an embedded part of the form-making process.

The architect's material choice wraps an understanding of form-making traditions and the technology involved in the form-making process. These tracings on tectonics provide a point of overlay for new subsets to incorporate the latest digital-craft technologies. Without removing the hand or mind from the equation, this leads us to a new model of tectonic thinking.

As described by Rivka Oxman, *informed tectonics*[11] is "the explication and transparency of information that provides the holistic integration of design . . . [and] is mediated, by being computationally '*in-formed*' by explicit knowledge of its design, making, and fabrication." This information processing starts with material knowledge expected to be implanted responsibly within our design tools. Embedded information provides an "intelligent integration between material, structure, and form within the logic of advanced design and fabrication technologies." The *what-if* questions of this integration include research into material-based design and conceptual models, along with principles or theories which maintain a balance between structure and construction, space and form tectonic frameworks.

*Ecological tectonics*, the next tectonic turn, considering material, structure, and form systems, responds to the effect of buildings upon living beings, natural resources, and energy—including social, psychological, and psychophysical forces. In *Towards an Ecology of Tectonics* (2014), Claus Bech-Danielsen describes this new tectonic:

> The concept of buildings as parts tied together as a whole in a broader con-text of natural and cultural systems. This understanding feeds a new ethical dimension into tectonic practice that recognizes the correlation between the materials used, the ecosystems they form a part and the resources we share as common members of the global community.[12]

The ecological use of materials is more ontological than representational; its effects are interrelated and far surpass our visual preoccupations in the construc-tion of images (Figure 3.1). With today's vast data sources, we must be more motivated to acutely depict and measure the environmental impacts of our deci-sions in the making of buildings.[13]

The joining of energy, matter, and life is the contemporary poiesis of tectonic form. Ecological tectonics begins not with *material expression* but with *fabrication necessity*. Material, thermodynamic, and biotechnical knowledge form a complete pedagogy and praxis. Familiarity with these matters is vital to practicing architec-ture. As Nader Tehrani reminds us, "In the absence of tectonic considerations, architecture severs its capacity to generate effects specific to the discipline and risks diluting its social and political agency by ignoring the instrumentality of its medium."[14]

## Aalto's Tectonic Imaginations and Form Systems

Aalto's departure from functionalist modernism allowed him to develop a rationalist naturalism that fused modern ideals with regionalist romanticism. He considered construction and material, space and form, not only as pri-mary elements but as atmospheres and ecology. His method was enigmatic—a tectonic aggregation of Semper's four components, Bötticher's ontology and representation, Pettenkofer's hygienic performance, Sekler's form to force, and Frampton's material joinery and visual poetics. Contrasting these past and present tectonic frameworks, we can imagine how Aalto's design process and philosophy can help to inform a new synthesis of material performance and biological matters.

Aalto did not emphasize one single element or type. Instead, he established an accretion of component-sets that synthesized composite forms. When deployed, the frame *and* the block system achieved a co-existent harmony. Opposing forces—elements and atmospheres, structure and plan, architecture and nature, rationality and irrationality—were formed together in an evolving, circumstantial decision-making process that looked both inward and outward to develop rela-tionships that blurred conventional boundaries.

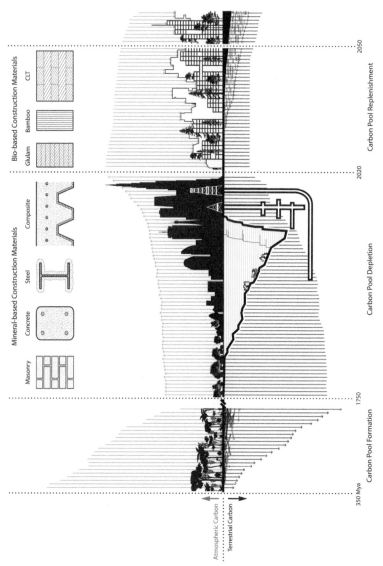

**FIGURE 3.1** Processes responsible for formation, depletion and potential replenishment of land carbon pool and changes in atmospheric CO2 concentrations over time

(*Credit:* Churkina, G., Organschi, A., Reyer, C.P.O. et al.)

This process activated a metamorphic typology rooted in architecture's fundamental form-making discourse: *Place-form, Earth-form, Frame-form, Surface-form,* and *Somatic-form.* The synthesis and interrelationship between these basic understandings have given much to what we see in Aalto's work. Considering how the relationships between elements developed form-systems, material structuring, and associative plans, Aalto's work can be reassessed as a *precursor* to ecological tectonics.

In a lecture in 1938 titled, 'Influence of Structure and Material on Contemporary Architecture,' Aalto described the relationship between man, nature, and architecture:

> Through the ages, we can observe in man's struggle with nature a conscious striving to deal with any problem he encounters in such a way that the importance and life-inhibiting effect of the problem diminishes as the ideal solution is approached. Looking at architecture from this perspective, as part of the struggle between man and nature, we find its most distinctive inner character—constant, systematic change. The number of problems and, with them, the number of basic elements in the inner process of architecture is increasing continually, reducing the importance of previously predominant issues. This natural thematic turnover is, therefore, one of the intrinsic qualities of architecture, and it is just as vital as ever to make provision for it in our work today.[15]

Aalto considered architecture a symbiotic relationship between nature, humans, and dwelling. To understand his ecological way of thinking, we can imagine an inseparable differential equation that the separation of variables cannot solve. The whole function of form, material, and delight contribute equally to sustainable thinking, necessary for any practice.

In the same 1938 lecture, Aalto also stated, "The very essence of architecture consists of variety and development reminiscent of natural organic life," following László Moholy-Nagy's definition of the word *biological*, which "stands generally for laws of life which guarantee an organic development."[16]

In 1955, Aalto gave a speech titled 'Art and Technology,' in which he stated,

> In every case, one must achieve a simultaneous solution of opposites . . . Nearly every design task involves tens, often hundreds, sometimes thousands of different contradictory elements, which are forced into a functional harmony only by man's will. This harmony cannot be achieved by any other means than those of art.[17]

Technology's marginalization of the *little man* was a concern for Aalto and is a continuing concern today. "We should work for simple, good, undecorated things," he explained in his 1957 RIBA speech, "things which are in harmony with the human being and organically suited to the little man in the street." Aalto's concern for social reform, combined with his choice to use local materials and apprehension towards mass-production, maintains relevance today.

For Aalto, material also afforded intimacy. *The door handle and the distant view* at the Villa Mairea provide one example. While the door handle is high resolution, the distant view is low resolution. Your moving perception apprehends the different images and textures, and you assemble them to form a *human-scale* resolution. This resolve is further manifest in his material explorations. For example, his research with wood incorporated tradition (*craft*), bodily comfort (*ergonomics and acoustics*), mass-production (*economy*), and, most importantly, flexibility (*digital craft*). Aalto tells us that "there are only two things in art: humanity or not." These experiments also extended to furniture design: the Paimio Chair, for example, displayed an intimate bond of art and technology with comfort.

## The Agency of Material—Elements

Materials have agency. Agency is the ability of something or someone to produce an effect. As we have seen since the industrial revolution, the materials we use have had the ability to affect the *equilibrium* of our environment.

Material matters in architecture have concerned themselves with construction or performance and imagination or representation but too often without concern for energy resources. Today, energy matters are of equal importance, and we must concern ourselves with using less and reducing embodied carbon when considering building materials.

Material properties classify into technical properties (structure and skin), economic properties (cost per manufactured unit and efficiency), properties influencing health (adverse toxicity and favorable thermodynamics), psychological properties (affective nature), and ecological properties (energy and resources).[18]

Structural materials have characteristics related to their use and form that matter when thinking about ecology. Fundamentally, masonry is stacked, concrete is fluid, steel is frame, and wood is joined. Today's production and fabrication methods have altered these precepts, at times allowing these characteristics to morph together. Looking forward, one can imagine masonry being robotically fastened and positioned, concrete losing its formwork when shaped through tubes, steel molded into any shape, and wood plaited and contorted into any form imaginable.

Construction methodologies other than those impacting production costs have been slow to progress, which has hindered the adoption of new material technologies. Concrete has seen significant improvements in structural performance. Yet, this material still requires a considerable amount of formwork to develop shape, and often the formwork is used only once, significantly adding to waste during construction. Steel has progressed slightly in categories of optimization and direct fabrication, but unless made of recycled content, this material also has a diminishing ecological impact.

Brick and wood, measured by their embodied carbon, remain the most ecologically preferred materials. Although we have seen some robotic masonry assembly, very little has changed. Wood, however, has seen the most advancement in categories of material properties and fabrication technologies. Of these materials, only wood can significantly mitigate the damaging impacts of climate change. After all that has progressed, timber, the most primitive supporting element, is the new performance agent.

Evidenced by his proclivity for designing buildings in brick or wood, Aalto intuitively understood the ecological properties of materials. As written by Kenneth Frampton, "among the pioneers of the Modern Movement, Alvar Aalto remains the one figure whose seminal contribution to the field seems just as valid now as it was at the end of his life." This claim may be justified on many levels, not least of which is the inherent sustainability of Aalto's architecture. For Aalto, wood was either equal or superior to any other material—not only for its firmness or association with nature but also its effect on the body and mind.

Elemental forces in architecture are formed in equilibrium. Le Corbusier tells us,

> It is natural that, in seeking happiness, we should strive towards a sense of equilibrium. Equilibrium means calm, a mastery of the means at our disposal, clear vision, order, the satisfaction of the mind, scale, and proportion—in fact, it means creation. Disequilibrium witnesses to a state of conflict, to disquietude, to difficulties not resolved, to a state of bondage and of questioning. It is an inferior and earlier stage of preparation. Lack of balance is the equivalent of a state of fatigue and balance the equivalent of a state of well-being.[19]

Equilibrium is a natural force for recognizing how the built environment is interconnected with the earth's surface.

A new architecture equilibrium model could be "a supersession of measuring but as the interplay between intensive and extensive differences." According to Reiser and Umemoto, these differences are not extensive reciprocities between form and matter, but "intensive differences . . . conceived as gradients, properties of matter that are indivisible [inseparable], such as weight, elasticity, pressure, heat, density, color and duration."[20]

Ecological properties of manufactured materials represent the dynamic interplay between extraction, production, delivery, environmental disturbance, and social equity. These properties concerned with embodied energy, are the combined consumption of material resources. When working with any material, we must consider the degradation of an ecosystem—pollution, waste, loss of habitat—and its impact on society. The most significant contributing factor to climate change is the release of carbon into the atmosphere.

Carbon emissions are the energy lost and released into the atmosphere during the production and deployment of materials. The environmental costs of these emissions are a factor in developing ecological tectonics. For example, suppose we design for carbon sequester and build our work following the principle of "doing more with less." If so, we could make a profound difference and set an example with our work.

This question balances concepts of *informed tectonics* and *ecological tectonics* towards an active engagement with *material agency*, or the underlying equilibrium inherent within an element that is understood as a part of a larger ecology. Knowledge can be gained through novel explorations of material ecologies and differential parameters.

Buckminster Fuller defined design science as "the effective application of the principles of science to the conscious design of our total environment in order to help make the earth's finite resources meet the needs of all of humanity without disrupting the ecological processes of the planet."[21] This process guided Fuller in the development of his lightweight structures, such as the Geodesic dome and Tensegrity structures. However, there is a difference between weight and lightness. Weight is a measure, whereas lightness is a way of seeing the world through science and philosophy. We need not fixate on weight, as this should not be the architect's sole preoccupation; rather, our focus should be on *elemental performance*, or in the words of Glenn Murcutt, "touching the earth lightly." Accordingly, we must ask the following questions: How much carbon will my building release because of my choice of material? How much carbon can I sequester in the mass of my building? Has my choice of material affected me, made me feel lighter, without carrying the world's weight?

## The Agency of Material—Atmospheres

The fundamentals of architecture are not only materials of construction or diagrams of a *parti*, but elements of an atmosphere. As stated by Pallasmaa, "Buildings are not abstract, meaningless constructions or aesthetic compositions; they are extensions and shelters of our bodies, memories, identities, and minds. Consequently, architecture arises from existentially true confrontations, experiences, reflections and aspirations."[22]

The word *atmosphere* has two definitions in the Oxford Dictionary: 1) The envelope of gases surrounding the earth or another planet or air around us and 2) The pervading tone or mood of a place, situation, or work of art. Architecture involves both.

The sense of an atmosphere unites material effects within an environment. These include thermodynamic phenomena, which have inherent relationships with climate, its forces, and the ecological matter of place, space, and imagination.

Architecture is then an enveloping spatial condition caused by material effects of place and surrounding influences.

In *Atmospheres* (2006), Peter Zumthor constitutes architectural atmospheres as a "singular density and mood, this feeling of presence, well-being, harmony, beauty . . . under whose spell I experience what I otherwise would not experience in precisely this way."[23]

Architecture must be made *delightful* (pleasing), not just *beautiful* (attractive). Delight is a bodily term excited by all the senses, unlike beauty which is beholden to the eye. We are no longer subject to a world of orders and preconditions, those aesthetic concerns outside of corporality. Buildings are now subject to performance measures, and in the beauty of this, we can take pleasure in making things full of delight.

Buildings provide multi-sensory experiences, and materials impact our collective memory, imagination, and sensory perception. The architect's agency comes in making atmospheres, balancing performance, and affect. When arranging the function of performance, it is best to consider its impacts on human bodies *and* on the body of nature.

Zumthor encourages us to experience the envelopment of architecture "as a bodily mass, a membrane, a fabric, a kind of covering, cloth, velvet, silk, all around me. The body! Not the idea of the body—the body itself! A body that can touch me."[24]

In great works of architecture, there is a unity between visual stimuli and structural logic, impacting our mental perceptions and our bodies. At Ronchamp, Le Corbusier captures an atmosphere of light(ness) or weight(lessness). Gaps of light, color, and apparent mass give us the feeling of weight, when, in fact, it is a lightweight construction. The ambiguity between visual intention and structural necessity contributes to this reading as opposing points of light help achieve the architect's desired effect.

As David Leatherbarrow tells us,

> neither stone nor glass possesses any essence or 'truth,' nor is one or the other singularly apposite to our time. The whole matter rests on the ways the materials are shaped and transformed, the ways they become what they had not been before, the ways they exceed themselves.[25]

Light and material are mutually dependent. Surface finishes (honed, milled, glossy, polished, reflective) or topological conditions (bent, curved, twisted, bowed) interact with light differently. The properties of light in space—color and intensity, transmittance, and refraction—are directly impacted by our choice of materials.

Although not a tectonic element but a transparent membrane, glass plays an essential role in creating an atmosphere, emitting and refracting light, air, energy, and imagination. At the Barcelona Pavilion, Mies van der Rohe displayed an atmosphere of immateriality. The glass, the highly polished stone walls, the chrome cross columns, and the reflecting pools all contribute to a vanishing effect. In *Eyes of the Skin* (2005), Pallasmaa wrote, "Mies van der Rohe's architecture a frontal perspectival perception predominates, but his unique sense of order, structure, weight, detail, and craft decisively enriches the visual paradigm."[26]

In discussing *firmitas*, Jacques Herzog provided an observation of his own:

> It is not the fact of the stable materiality but the immaterial, spiritual quality that is communicated to our senses through the material solidification. It is the indissoluble bond between material and immaterial characteristics of architecture that attracts us and refuses to let go; it is that to which we submit ourselves like to a beloved body that takes us away for a moment into a magical world.[27]

At the Villa Mairea, Aalto captured an atmosphere of place as *old world* notions of the forest combined with conditions of the present enhanced his architectural vision for the future. Early in his life, Aalto wrote,

> I am led to believe that most people, but especially artists, principally grasp the atmosphere in a work of art. This is especially manifest in the case of old architecture. We encounter there a mood so intense and downright intoxicating that in most cases we don't pay a great deal of attention to individual parts and details, if we notice them at all.[28]

The material nature of architecture is both a situation of structure and its mood. As written by Pallasmaa,

> Materials and surfaces have a language of their own. Stone speaks of its distant geological origins, its durability, and inherent symbolism of permanence; brick makes one think of earth and fire, gravity and the ageless traditions of construction; bronze evokes the extreme heat of its manufacture, the ancient processes of casting, and the passage of time as measured in its patina. Wood speaks of its two existences and time scales; its first life as a growing tree and the second as a human artifact made by the caring hand of a carpenter or cabinetmaker.[29]

## The Agency of Material—Ecology

In philosophy, *poiesis* (from ancient Greek: ποίησις) is "the activity in which a person brings something into being that did not exist before." It is an act of thinking, making, and revealing.

Throughout history, people made dwellings that existed in harmonious accord with their environments. Primitive structures used local materials and construction methods, evolving and representing a social vernacular. Building with nature concerned the ecological circumstances present in place and the social network of location. Over time, Architecture came to into being as a poetic manifestation in the joining of life and place.

In the early 20th century, modern architecture promised a new model: the performance-enhanced *machine*. This model was forward-looking, made to improve life for the greater population. This moment in history was one of a well-intentioned revolution, bringing significant changes in the idea of architecture as a *social condenser*. Modern architects' quest to enhance the quality of life in their models persisted until the end of WWII. After the war, however, many architects looked to resolve concerns of economy and performance in a process of reduction.

Provisional thinking can no longer persist in architecture. Consider the matter required to burn fire hot enough to smelt iron. It is difficult to justify the persistent use of high-energy, carbon-insensitive materials like concrete and steel when low-energy, carbon-sequestering alternatives are available to perform the same service.

In the 21st century, earlier tectonic frameworks in architecture must adapt to become *ecological tectonics*. To form ecological tectonics, we bear in mind this suggestion by Kenneth Frampton:

> Rather than join in a recapitulation of avant-gardist tropes or enter into historical pastiche or into the superfluous proliferation of sculptural gestures—all of which have an arbitrary dimension to the degree that they are based in neither structure nor in construction—we may return instead to the structural unit as the irreducible essence of architectural form.[30]

In ecological tectonics, this unit is an element of equilibrium merged with an atmosphere of imagination in services of our environment.

This service is two-fold; first, unlike material elements and atmospheres imbued with a form to force tectonics, ecological tectonics are revealed through considerations of responsibility, understood as functions, ethics, and information. Second, resource scarcity and carbon footprint require us to reconsider energy usage in our designs, not only by increased efficiency but by enhancing comfort through material choices and recruiting the structure as an agent of change.

We participate in material agency when we step outside of the architect's persona as *Master builder* and consider our role as listeners and orchestrators. Information is our instrument of control. Our mastery is no longer solely bound to our personal experiences but to how we manage data and allow new possibilities to emerge.

Aalto expounded this understanding through an analogy of the architect as the *conductor*: "Aalto, who had a strong interest in cinema, film, photography, and theater, quoted Fernand Léger by calling himself a '*chef d'orchestre,*' conducting all the arts to synthesize a harmonious, symphonic whole."[31] Aalto had an uncanny ability to form details without losing sight of material performance. In art, we perceive a combination of technical, physical, and psychological phenomena that resolve to give an overall impression of a work. By composing elements and embedding technology to make space, we partake in the art of building.

Today, the conductor metaphor still fits the method of making buildings. Quite often in the field of architecture, an endless array of considerations, committees, consultants, materials, specifications, fabricators, and critics have influences in the process. According to Aalto, the architect "must attend to circumstances: climate, landscape, site, culture, materials, tectonics, and more."[32] As a facilitator in addressing these circumstances, we can imagine software as our *assistant conductor*, keeping all our material decisions in tune so that we can spend more time orchestrating design.

With information as our instrument, we can better track the life cycle of materials—how and where they are extracted, delivered, fabricated, used, and maintained. We can also think about how materials return to the earth or how they can be repurposed. In *Cradle to Cradle* (2002), William McDonough described a circular strategy for expanding guidelines and standards for building materials and consumer products.

As we continue to set goals for the future, data can help us make better material decisions as we coordinate our designs through construction, into the life of the building, and thereafter. As written by Kieran and Timberlake,

> '*Life Cycle Assessment*' (LCA) is a method for rigorously tracking the embodied carbon associated with materials and construction processes across a building's full life cycle, from material extraction and manufacturing through construction, use, and eventually demolition . . . These tools give us the ability to rapidly evaluate and compare the embodied carbon contained in different building materials during design. They also help us find opportunities for strategic carbon reduction at no additional cost.[33]

LCA involves decisions about building and includes concerns about social justice and socio-economic impacts. It helps us measure environmental and human health impacts and guide decisions to reduce harm. Material data analysis must not only include technical properties and economic concerns, but also decisions about human life, health, psychology, and ecological futures.

The "only way to humanize architecture," Aalto believed, was to interrelate aesthetic, technical, physical, and psychological phenomena. Aalto also believed that "technical functionalism is correct only if enlarged to cover even the psychophysical field." It is the responsibility of the architect to balance these effects.

In line with thinking about equilibrium, we should go back to questions: How much carbon would my building emit during construction? How much of my building's weight sequesters carbon? Asking, why is this important?

The construction industry is responsible for approximately 39 percent of total greenhouse gas emissions. Of this, 28 percent is for heating, cooling, ventilation, lighting, and powering buildings. The remaining 11 percent is for mining, extracting, harvesting, processing, manufacturing, fabricating, and transporting materials for construction. By 2050, emissions from embodied carbon are projected to be more than four times higher than emissions from operational energy. To meet our emissions goals within the next 30 years, architects must rethink our approach to embodied carbon

Today, approximately 75 percent of annual global carbon emissions are a byproduct of the urban environment.[34] But we can combat this ever-increasing problem by choosing and designing materials to stabilize conditions of capture and emittance through mass and flows. For instance, mechanical systems can initially fleece poor judgments in a building design; however, calculated energy usage will expose the disequilibrium over time. Creating models that predict life-cycle performance will lead to better buildings and secure the architect's role as an orchestrator moving into the future. This is imperative to our environment and to the future of our profession.

Mechanical systems use energy and seldom enhance a building's material atmosphere. For the most part, these systems desensitize the threshold and the sensuality, and have played a major role in homogenizing architecture. Instead of incorporating active systems as the default, we should design material-oriented passive systems that can be *augmented* by the active, thereby reducing energy usage and recapturing our sensual relation to buildings.

Our choices must scrutinize energy usage while finding *potential energies* in materials viewed within the context of their entire life cycles. Of course, some materials are better than others. By specifying and computing efficiency and embodied energy in our virtual models, we would begin to advance a more comprehensive understanding of the material and ecological properties of buildings.

## Wood as a Building Material

Modern architects made buildings with concrete. Novel yet old, this material was reborn through experiments by Auguste Perret and later by Le Corbusier, whose Maison Domino enabled new possibilities for expressive formal plasticity. However, the problem of concrete and steel is unavoidable resource depletion and embodied energy in the final product. This embodiment is built up through de-soiling, deforestation, and energy and water usage in manufacturing and transport.

One of the first uses of the word *sustainability* was in a forestry handbook in 1713. The handbook was written in response to declining timber reserves. The

German term *Nachhaltigkeit*, or "sustained yield," meant never to harvest more than the forest can regenerate. This word *sustainability* would eventually evolve to encompass all forests and biological systems. By 1987, *The Brundtland Report* commissioned by the UN redefined *sustainable development* as "development that meets the needs of the present without compromising the ability of future generations to meet their own needs."

According to Kiel Moe, the term sustainability has been misappropriated[35] and made synonymous with *greenwashing*, or providing a false impression that a building has employed environmentally sound principles. Sustainability is a way of thinking. It is about energy efficiency, durability, and economy. It is about understanding culture, context, history, and modes of development. It is also about practicality and pragmatics. Most importantly, it is about design ethics—truth and reason over style and prescription.

With this in mind, using material data in our calculations could equate to the conservation of energy and sequestering of carbon, transforming buildings from negative to positive entities.[36] Few materials readily offer new possibilities for ecological positivity. Wood, however, affords the most expedient and resource-ready opportunity to advance architecture into ecological tectonics.

Today, the use of wood in buildings is an *exaptation*, holding "features that now enhance fitness but were not built by natural selection for their current role."[37] This old material becomes new by adapting to new functions. While adaptations have functions, exaptations have effects. A bird's feather is an example of exaptation; originally evolved for thermal regulation, it soon became adapted for flight. Similarly, wood, initially used in post-and-beam construction, has been adapted and transposed into architectural elements, matured and advanced in new ways through digital design and fabrication processes that impact material capacity and opportunity.

Combining traditional construction logics of wood with new technologies and fabrication methodologies could introduce new ecological tectonics to an old material. Like the concrete of early modernism, the manifold potentials of wood, made possible by software and fabrication technologies, enable new forms of architecture that are boundless in imagination.

Looking to history, we can trace an evolution of modern wood construction in architecture. From the frameworks of Frank Lloyd Wright, to the adaptations of Rudolph Schindler, to the countless construction variations that developed in the United States. In Europe were the structures and furniture of Aalto, and later the advanced material processes invented in Germany. Today, we see innovative uses of wood in the works of Zumthor, SANAA, Kengo Kuma, Shigeru Ban, Heatherwick Studio, and many others.

For Aalto, the use of wood was not only a local vernacular and a national symbol; it was also a symbolic kinship to the forest in a "battle against metal."[38] This commitment, displayed by his observations and various material experiments, framed a point of view that began early in his career.

At 24 years old, he wrote an article, 'Motifs from Times Past,' published in *Arkkitehti* (1922), in which he stated:

> When we visit a medieval church, look at an old manor house, or con-
> template a hundred-year-old vernacular building, we find that there
> is something that reaches out to us, a mood (atmosphere). It may be
> caused partly by hand-crafted surfaces, by the building materials' artistic
> purity, by the simple lines that harmonize with the landscape; partly, it
> is created by the materials' one-hundred-year-old patina, and fine worn
> surface.[39]

In the Muuame Church of 1926–29, Aaltos travels to Italy show influence. As the simple box form moves from Classicism to functionalism, the wood frame and azure blue barrel vault ceiling retain a vernacular tradition.[40] In Viipuri (1935), we see the wood ceiling morphing into a sinuous curve, and in the Finnish Pavilion (1939), into an illusory wall. Much later, this blue finish makes a reprise in Finlandia Hall (1971) and in the Essen Opera House (1988).

Aalto's early commissions for renovations of wooden sanctuaries adopted characteristics of Finland's wooden churches of their unexpected interior vaulting. According to Randall Ott, the timber framing and surface topology of these wooden churches

> inherently encourages an ambiguity of surface and structure since the wall
> membrane of the building simultaneously performs both tasks of enclosure
> and support. The skin and bones in such a building are essentially one in
> the same, and a blending or even total negation of their separate readings
> is inevitable.[41]

With many unexplained offsets of structure and surface, Aalto's early engagement with these structures may explain some of the irregularities of the ceiling forms and beams in his later work.

Sarah Menin describes Aaltos use of wood at Sunila Housing (1936–38) as "in-between" vernacular and modernity. Menin defines wood, with Latin root *materia* closely relating to matter, as mother and maternal love.[42] This sentiment for wood as the primordial material possessing the embrace of mother earth fits well with our conversations about Aalto, who continually expressed his affinity for wood and its elemental and atmospheric qualities.

Menin also writes that "the round-wood trellis is a psycho-spatial episode, functioning, in Aalto's terms, 'to tie the threads of a living present with those of a living past.'"[43] We see this way of 'threading' time, first, in Aalto's House (1935–36), again in the Standard Terrace Housing (1937–38) and the Villa Mairea (1938–39), and in a number of his later houses and small-scale works.

In his larger works, Aalto tested the limits of wood as a structural device and its flexibility as a form-giving material. The Varkaus Sawmill (1945–46) remains one of Finland's most significant industrial projects. As described by Karl Fleig,

> it stands on the ruins of an older industrial development, so that the new and thoroughly rationalized sawmill could be built upon the still solid concrete roofs. The structure consists of timber with a thin steel framework. The pliable architectural forms cover the industrial activity like an organic skin.[44]

The building's exterior shape and details conform to its various functional requirements.

Aalto's Otahalli Sports Center, designed for the 1952 Olympics, is notable for its long wooden truss that spans 45 meters (Figure 3.2). Here, the optimization of the wooden material is expressed in the diagraming of forces by way of

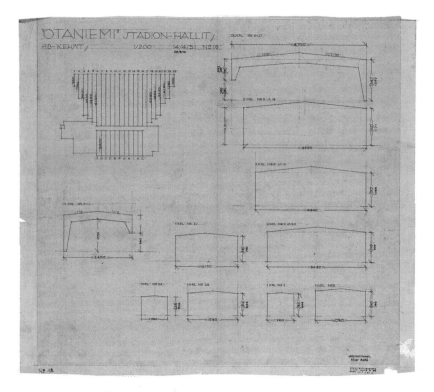

**FIGURE 3.2**   Otahalli Truss Variable Geometry

*(Credit:* Alvar Aalto Foundation 47–287a)

varying thicknesses and repetitious vertical striations—a detailing strategy that Aalto repeated when using wood as structure.

In the essay 'Wood as a Building Material' (1956),[45] Aalto explicated the matters of wood in construction:

> The ease with which wood can be worked technically is the background for most architectural form. In virtually all cultures, early architecture was based on wood, providing a testing ground for later structures and forms.
>
> While the natural weaknesses of wood-fire hazard and the constant maintenance required have reduced its role as a load-bearing or exterior element in architecture, its value has risen as a light structure for roofing wide spans, thus bringing new variation into the rich world of architectural forms.
>
> Wood will probably retain its value as a rich, deeply human material whose resources are not yet even near to being exhausted.

Today, wood structures have become a testing ground for new possibilities generated by ecological thinking, design software, and computer-controlled manufacturing and fabrication. In particular, digital Computer Numerical Control (CNC) machinery and robotic fabrication have made new possibilities for the most elastic of form-structures.

As far as ecological thinking concerned, mass timber construction is most beneficial. With mass timber, we can design sustainable structures using the same material as frame and mass. This material also has low maintenance, provides fire resistance, and sequesters carbon as it carries us to new heights.

When farmed, wood can be a resource that is both socially responsible and economically viable. Sequestered carbon can endure a metamorphosis from log, to lumber, to precise fabrication. As this material structures buildings, it continues to lock carbon, acting in repose to ecological concerns through its natural, biological process. Consider how a beaver used a similar ecological construction model for millions of years—making a home, sustaining the land, and developing an extended ecosystem for a shared environment. With wood as a prototype, we may look to grow more of our building materials in the future, using plants, fungi, or bacteria to enhance performance and pollute less.

## Aalto's Embodiment—An Architecture of Ecology

Many artists and architects have discussed their inspiration for using natural elements. In the early 1930s, Aalto's experiments with wood were parallel with artists Jean (Hans) Arp and László Moholy-Nagy. These two artists each promoted a *biotechnique* design message that called attention to the ingenious qualities of natural forms.

Aalto was aware of Moholy-Nagy's call to use biology as a form of visual communication that could change people's thinking about art and architecture. The trips through Finland that Aino and Alvar made with Moholy-Nagy in the 1930s helped to re-frame the Aalto's views on nature and modernism, which, in turn, helped to re-shape their work. At this time, biological and ecological determinism entered the conversation, as seen in the design evolution of the Viipuri Library and in the human spirit Paimio Sanatorium.

In 1938, Moholy-Nagy wrote,

> Architecture will be brought to its fullest realization only when the deepest knowledge of human life as a total phenomenon in the biological whole is available. One of its most important components is the ordering of man in space, making space comprehensible, and taking architecture as arrangement of universal space.[46]

Underpinning these realizations is a spatial, technical, aesthetic, and ecological concern for a biological material that is a native, practical, and productive resource in Finland. Wood became a material synonymous with Aalto, and it afforded a profound metamorphosis in his architecture. Aalto, according to Göran Schildt, could be called "a pioneer of the modern ecological movement, since he repudiated all the one-sided and, in the long term, disastrous strategies of exploitation that threaten the biological equilibrium of our planet."[47]

## Nature of Elements—The Villa Mairea

The layers of decisions in Aalto's process of designing Villa Mairea, in addition to the various interpretations, have been well-documented. We will focus on the elements that balance the material atmosphere and its built ecology.

The house's contrasting settings start with its column structure, "the fusion of the opposite image of a geometric architectural interior and an amorphous forest space."[48] Although there is a rational grid structure, the columns are made of various materials: steel, wood, and concrete. Moreover, these elements are wrapped, masked, bundled, and distorted, all to hide the inherent geometric regularity. This process transforms the literal structure into spatial negotiations and elemental referents; transmuting the steel into wood "refers to nature by already codified architectural signs."[49] This complex relationship of structure to material is entirely contradictory—modern yet traditional.

The welcoming of the entry canopy starts the script of an experiential journey. Succeeding the path at the entry, handshaking with the door, one enters an interior forecourt, a sunken space that sets up an oblique view towards the exterior. The intentionality of this event is methodical; it is the space that draws you together with the landscape and grounds the positioning of the house within the contours of the forest's clearing. The ascent of the masonry steps, the terracotta floor, and its sinuous connection with the wood floor, symbolically draw the contour, demarcating the space of the idea: *the hall as an "open-air" space.*

With the hall connected both literally and figuratively to the garden and the forest beyond, the house appears representative of "Aalto's 'extended rationalism' and fusion of opposites; the living space of the Villa Mairea merges images of tectonic architectural space and the amorphous forest space, modern utopia, and peasant tradition."[50] As our minds process this metaphor to directly transfer meaning from one domain to another, the space of the hall links separate entities into one. This relationship, not observed directly but present in our peripheral field of vision, feels like an envelopment of a broader cultural experience.

This connection extends to the house's heating and cooling systems. Hidden within the ceiling are 52,000 filter slits that distribute the air, both hot and cool, evenly across the suspended pine ceiling. This conditioning system, joined with the fireplace and garden room, encompasses a larger synergistic arrangement of form and function. In addition, the window system and the movable window wall affords natural ventilation in a complementary interplay between active and passive strategies.

## Nature of Atmosphere—Jyväskylä University

At Jyväskylä University (1951), we can learn how materials give context to one another as literal and phenomenal imaginations or embodied meanings.[51] These thoughts start with engaging the body, understanding scale and movement, imagining the touch of the building, and forming a situated landscape. With these engagements, architects can create a wholeness of experience that begins with a conviction about materials and their ability to envelop a situated context. Aalto's architecture at Jyväskylä University is a topological formation that reconciles the existing context, his conceptual attitude, and material matters.

The campus plan sets up a tracing of movement and human activity. The campus buildings and its central sports field negotiate the contours of the hills and the city grid. This activity develops through a twofold strategy: First, by imagining the boundaries and demarcations set by buildings and the spaces between those masses. Second, a transference of the Greek typological planning conditions— an intellectual transfer of form through history and time, as the buildings are arranged not at 90-degree correspondences but by angular associations.

The campus entry is a forecourt, one that is formed by the arcade of the sunken library building, a classroom block, and the main auditorium hall, also known as a festival hall. The auditorium building entry wall is solid multi-story brick, except for the glass set between the white stone floor and white painted wood ceiling of the lobby. Chunky interior columns clad with fluted Doric-like glossy tile, wood posts around the stairs, and the trees appear through the glass.

Opposing the brick at the forecourt, in stark contrast, is the library arcade of white concrete columns and its white wood canopy. Beyond this is a low brick wall with a roof that is accessible by a narrow space and stair. The library's exterior is not expressed as a building itself, but as a supporting element for the existing buildings beyond. Its accessible rooftop of green grass covers its mostly windowless volume so that visitors can access the classrooms from outside during the warmer months. Inside, the reading room is lit from above by a long, prism-shaped clerestory which is not visible from the court.

Entering the lecture hall from the arcade, one finds a four-story space with deep white gypsum ceilings that are punctuated by deep, large capsule-shaped skylights. This ceiling casts light over a cascading stair made of brick, light-colored stone treads, and dark risers. You ascend alongside the brick parapet and white gypsum walls, delivering you into the lecture rooms on each floor. This interior space reads like the exterior rooms and courts of the broader campus, placed in reciprocity with the contours of the hills and the city's grid and between opposing masses.

For Aalto, architecture is not whole to parts, but parts to a whole, "each element—in this case, space, light, walls, steps, rails and their supports—its independent role while defining its complementarity within the whole."[52] The contrasting materials of brick, natural and painted wood, white concrete, metal, stone, and gypsum form as morphological elements of the landscape (Figure 3.3).

**FIGURE 3.3**   Jyväskylä Auditorium Lobby Situatedness

In the various walls, beam details, claddings, and some of the long and short span spaces, such as the auditorium, café, and swimming pools, the aggregation of parts into a whole is manifest.

In the café, the brick boundary wall does not touch the ceiling, almost like a site wall, receiving a rather tall clerestory of wood members in rhythm with the elaborate wood truss of the ceiling space above. The brick, expressed as a topological element, is married with the ground. It is an element that carries physical weight and makes walls that emerge like ruins from the earth, both inside and out.

The brick module sets up cadences of penetration and framework on the exterior. The lines modulate the material and set the reading and emotion of the building. The mullion lines connect vertical striations through the brick wall. Horizontally the lines change. The brick opening datum variations, the syncopated wooden window mullion grid, and the white cladding compose a moving juncture between earth and sky.

Inside, the wood provides a situated atmosphere, representing the forest and the contours against the sky. Yet, it is transfigured: wooden ceilings are painted white as if an imaginative element, while the window mullions maintain a natural finish. This system engages with nature and material within their specific context. Together, the white tracery around the roof, the interior parapets, and the stair simulate the snow-covered surroundings, forming a conceptual tie with this place, where snow can remain present for one-third of the year. The white concrete and stone floors heighten this experience, drawing on nature to make us "at home" in our place in the world.

## Nature of Ecology—Muuratsalo

Architects and builders experiment with new systems of construction. Aalto considered his experiments' *research* in materials, structure, form, and radiance with nature. In his Summer Home, the "Experimental House" (1952–54) in Muuratsalo, Finland, we see this directly. Aalto's material experiments in form, structure, and material construct an ecological development. The house is made of brick walls, uneven in height, covered on the exterior with whitewash, and left uncovered in the open courtyard. The walls of the courtyard display Aalto's investigation of contrasting material colors, textures, brick types, and configurations.

Interestingly, most of the bricks used were rejects from the nearby Säynätsalo Town Hall, signaling recycling and economics. The mass walls of the structure are situated to protect the courtyard from northern winds coming from the lake and to maximize solar heat gain through the walls and floors. The shaping of the openings around the courtyard creates an internal microclimate.[53] And, the greenery on the trellis provides shade for cooling in summer, whereas solar radiation penetrates in winter.

Like the standard brick wall, the roof wooden frame system is predominantly vernacular; however, its configuration strategy experimented with more with natural relationships. Sarah Menin tells us Aalto

> also tried using an ancient granite-boulder foundation system and even sought to heat the house in the winter with a pump using solar energy stored in the water of the lake. He wrote of the house, "proximity to nature can give fresh inspiration both in terms of form and construction," demonstrating his progressive interest in technology, but always wanting to test such progress against the experience of human frailty.[54]

In the house in Muuratsalo, Aalto followed rules of making architecture that are the fundamentals for design with ecology (Figure 3.4). First, an orientation towards the winter sun led to the asymmetrical building design. Second, he used brick as a thermal mass to control heat energy. Third, natural ventilation strategies

**FIGURE 3.4** Muuratsalo Courtyard Elements & Atmosphere

took advantage of wind and enhanced the natural conditioning apparatus. Fourth, ecologically renewable materials, such as brick and wood, were used in addition to incorporating natural light, air, humidity, and thermal performance. Last, he inspired harmony between our physical and imaginative bodies through memory and material sensation.

These characteristics also provide an atmosphere. The choice of exterior whitewash embeds the building in winter. The exposed brick courtyard is a clearing, a place to dwell, and a representation of a Finnish farmhouse with its central fire pit, emitting energy to clear the snow and ice from the brick (a phenomenal embodiment of warmth and tradition). As Reyner Banham wrote, "the space around a campfire has many unique qualities . . . above all, its freedom and variability."[55] Aalto embodied this premise in his own words:

> We may define the ideal goals of architecture by saying that the purpose of a building is to act as an instrument that collects all the positive influences in nature for man's benefit, while also sheltering him from all the unfavorable influences that appear in nature and the building's specific surroundings.[56]

## Ecological Tectonics—Säynätsalo

In discussing the material in architecture, Nader Tehrani asks, "How could it be that the conceptual task of architecture could become so remote from problems of building, of putting things together, of making—in essence of aggregating?"[57]

Four distinct parts, associated sets, or aggregations suggest ecological tectonics at Säynätsalo. First, is the earthen berm, building massing, and orientation. Second, is the courtyard and its microclimate. Third, is the brick mass and the integrated heating system. And fourth, is the multi-variant, wooden roof truss. Aalto aggregated these parts together into a whole. Concerning 'problems of building,' we review the third and fourth sets as elements of conditioning atmosphere.

The whole building mass and its arrangement of elements, the berm, the court, the brick, the windows, and the wood, are all active participants in developing an embodied material concept in dialogue with the environment. Forms, systems, and materials become interlaced through dependencies of energy and light, *element-systems* and *type-forms* that are both figurative and configured (Figure 3.5). The figures are topological engagements made by mass and light. The configuration of elements and materials captures the varying conditions of material comfort, sensation, and experience, set by what Aalto called *mood* or *atmosphere*.

The system of brick defines an integrated experience. Kenneth Frampton describes atmospheres of mind and body as elements of experiential imagination:

> The architectural promenade leading to the second-floor council chamber is orchestrated in tactile terms. Not only is the staircase lined in raked brickwork, but the treads and risers are paved in brick. The kinetic impetus

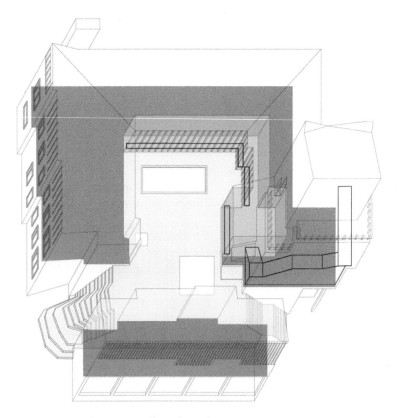

**FIGURE 3.5** Säynätsalo Town Hall Ecological Tectonic

of climbing is thus checked by the friction of the steps. After this "resist-ance," the polished timber floor of the council chamber announces its hon-orific status through sound, smell, and texture, and above all through its slipperiness and its springy deflection under the weight of the body.[58]

The brick also excites a whole-body experience. Frampton continues,

From entry to council chamber, the subject encounters a sequence of con-trasting tactile experiences. Thus, from the stereotomic mass and relative darkness of the entry, where the feeling of enclosure is augmented by the tactility of the brick treads, one enters into the bright light of the council chamber, the timber-lined roof of which is carried on fanlike, wooden trusses that splay upward to support concealed rafters above a boarded ceil-ing. The sense of arrival occasioned by this tectonic display is reinforced by various nonretinal sensations, from the smell of polished wood to the floor flexing under one's weight together with the general destabilization of the body as one enters onto a highly polished surface.[59]

Karl Fleig tells us more about the modified truss system, an expressive and strategic technical device,

> the ceiling clearly reveals the entire supporting structure for the roof whose main members are arranged in such a way that the triangulated struts also support the secondary roof framing. In the harsh winter climate of Finland, the necessary ventilation between the interior and exterior surfaces of the roof has been facilitated by the placement of all the main framing in the interior of the room, avoiding the problem of heavy, built-in roof framing.[60]

These aggregate experiences are conditioned through complex interrelationships of spatial orientation, thermodynamic and material reciprocities, and psychological sensitivity. This overlapping of informed material associations is where the agency of architecture is presented.

## The Agency of Information—Contemporary Embodiment

In an interview titled 'Encounters with Aalto'[61] (2007), Shigeru Ban provides a dialog of how his thoughts on architecture changed after experiencing Aalto buildings in person:

> Until I actually looked at his buildings in Finland, I was not able to understand how he made architecture from the context and used new methods of design with neutral, gentile materials from nature, such as wood and brick. This encounter was a great shock to me.

In 1986, Ban designed an exhibition of Aalto's work. He first considered using wood, then realized using such precious resources for a temporary exhibition would be a waste. He went on to say, "I found cardboard tubes scattered all over my studio . . . leftover rolls from tracing paper . . . I didn't like the idea of throwing them away. These tubes are surprisingly strong, and their neutral color and gentile texture reminded me of Aalto; that's what triggered the idea."

Ban later used these paper tubes to make houses, paper emergency shelters, a church, and a dome. This paper tube soon evolved into a *timber fabric model*, empowered by information and specifications embedded in the digital model, forming new workflows and means of fabrication. This modeling allows for 'real-time' analyses of the properties and representation of material choices and their consequences, leading us towards better decisions and more extraordinary performance with less material and energy usage.

According to Kieran and Timberlake, "Today, through the agency of information management tools, the architect can once again become the master builder by integrating the skills and intelligences at the core of architecture (in order to) uphold a true return to craft."[62] Moreover, the rising digital curve empowers designers with resources to manage more profound attention to the atmosphere of experience and elemental circumstance.

These enhanced optimizations and informed material fabrication potentials move us closer to ecological tectonics. By choosing more responsive materials, we can preserve our environment and make better buildings; the tools of digital and informed tectonics ultimately enable us to have an enormous impact while achieving a smaller carbon footprint.

The Aaltos investigated material fabrication at Artek and in the Atelier. He stressed that his office family of professionals must comprise architects who could resolve a wide range of design problems, a model that most architecture firms emulate today. He also worked with fabricators to see his vision and resolve relationships between formal and material models. Today, we see the same calling as offices value architects with software and fabrication experience solving design issues.

Engaging professionals in material-based design incorporates current technologies to advance ever-present architectural geometry, form engineering, and construction that extends from the fabrication lab. As Rivka Oxman explains, "The structuring, encoding and fabricating of material systems has become an area of design study and the expanded professional knowledge base common to both the architect and the structural engineer."[63]

Optimization is inherent in both digital and ecological tectonics. The engineer, Maturo Sasaki, writes,

> The optimization results emerge within a particular morphological language of form is specific to computational logic (it has adaptive behavior). Structural shapes can be seen as direct expression of the inherent static forces of the systems, with which they share a principle of maximum structural performance generated by the smallest possible mass (mimicking the morphology of biological structures).[64]

These explorations in the collaborations of Sasaki and Toyo Ito present the cultural and ecological designation of tectonics.

Smart materials present a different kind of adaptive behavior. These materials, as Ulrich Konigs tells us, "have the ability to modify their composition independently by reaction with external and internal influences. They react to necessities resulting from the material structure itself just as living organisms do."[65] Smart materials can react to changes in their environment, like phase-changing materials that absorb or release heat.

These materials and methods move us towards a *crossover between art and science*, as described by Cecil Balmond:

> Here, form isn't preconceived. Rather it is driven by forces, mysteriously emerging on its own, echoing experience and future possibility. Investigating and unraveling organizational systems is at the core of this research. This process comes down to considerations of very roots of order from a place of number, algorithm, and pattern. And influences everything we do.[66]

Digital models make for efficient production. Staging and efficiency are essential parts for studying and executing the enveloping of a complete structure. When collaborating with digital crafting companies, digital models are often made at various stages and scales to create each project's unique geometry and engineering. These models can consider material systems using CNC processing for the fabrication, engineering, and organization of all forms and connections of a building's structure. This framework is mathematically precise, using parametric models to afford minute tolerances and maximum quality.

This modified workflow, working from the start with material fabricators, exposes potentials and technics of construction during the design process, is a true design-build collaboration. It is similar to working methods of the past, where an architect's designs outlined and assigned materials, and the builder knew what to do. However, the informed process of today is not quite so simple. With today's technology-driven processes in mind, we might consider the workflow reversing from the past *form-structure-material* process towards a new *material-structure-form* process.[67] In turn, our latest information workflow, where embedded material data manifest inside the software, can help us to structure our decisions better, resulting in more informed, response-driven material architectures.

## The Kunsthaus Bregenz Museum

Peter Zumthor set up a relationship between body and building in the Kunsthaus Bregenz Museum in Bregenz, Austria (Figure 3.6).

> Like the human body, the museum is a hydronic heat and cool system with a decoupled fresh air ventilation system. The concrete surfaces are hydronic, thermally active surfaces (T.A.S.) that temper the thermal comfort of bodies in the space through radiant heat transfer as opposed to the minimal air system in a building for low energy consumption.[68]

This T.A.S., first developed in France in the 1980s, called "Batiso," is a low-energy, thermodynamic mass structure and a performative envelopment system.

**FIGURE 3.6**   Photo, Kunsthaus Bregenz (KUB), Austria, Peter Zumthor, 1997

*(Credit:* Florian Glöcklhofer, CC by SA 2.5)

The thermodynamic mass structure includes the concrete foundation, which serves as a heat sink made possible by the project's adjacency to groundwater and the lake. The loops couple the earth with a storage tank that supplies the hydronic tubing integrated into the concrete pour. In the winter months, a supplemental gas-fired boiler feeds the system. The structural T.A.S. envelops the gallery bodies

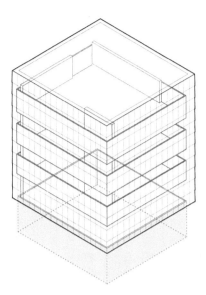

**FIGURE 3.7**   KUB Thermally Active Surface & Mass

on five sides. This strategy minimizes radiant asymmetries perceived in standard air and hydronic perimeter radiation systems. In addition, the heating and cooling supply across the thermodynamic mass requires a lower temperature differential, thereby using less energy (Figure 3.7).

High-velocity ducts cast in the terrazzo topping of the concrete structure distribute supply air while asymmetrical buffer zones flow with return air.

> The thermal loads in the gallery space are decoupled from the air system, allowing for a small volume of air. As the fresh air mixes with the existing air a quarter of the time per hour, the air is heated and rises through slots in between the glass ceiling panels. The minimal fresh air exchange and humidity control allow for the systems in the galleries to be visually concealed.[69]

Cooling works similarly to the heating system, and this system is a third of the cost of conventional HVAC systems (Figure 3.8).

The project mixes three zones: a buffer zone of the exterior envelop described by Zumthor as a lamp; a service zone, organized in section, the ceiling plenum above the galleries, made of a frosted glass light surface; and primary zones,

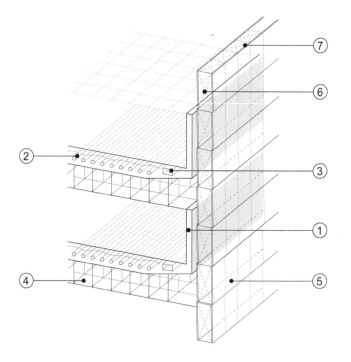

1. Gallery Bodies - Concrete Structure
   Thermally Active Surface (T.A.S.)
2. Integrated Hydronic Tubing - Heating and Cooling System
3. Decoupled Fresh Air - High Velocity Air Ducts in Terrazzo Floor
4. Ceiling Plenum - Frosted Glass Light Surface
5. Etched Glass Façade - Outer Surface "Lantern"
6. Insulating Glass - Inner Façade Envelopment
7. Steel Frame- Outer Surface "Lantern" Frame

**FIGURE 3.8**   KUB Detail—Mass, Surface, & Curtain

for the galleries, the entry, and the underground levels organized by vertical walls supporting the thermally active concrete structure. These zones enhance the T.A.S. In addition, the project acknowledges service as a vital design element, integrating the concrete system into a tectonic defined by atmosphere (Figures 3.9 and 3.10).

"The clarity of the building's zoning in many ways represents an ideal diagram for T.A.S. buildings. It boasts high-performance building envelope decoupled thermal and ventilation systems, abundant daylighting, and exposed surfaces in multiple sides of the conditioned spaces."[70]

**FIGURE 3.9**   KUB Gallery Bodies in Section

Despite the heaviness of the concrete, the gallery vessels provide visual weight-lessness. The etched glass shingle is an exterior rain-screen, light diffuser, thermal buffer, and a curtain that switches its glow throughout the day. The interior ceiling system—a glass lid that closes the concrete vessels—is interconnected with the lamp of the exterior covering and the electric lighting contained in the plenum. These continuously changing illumination surface systems alter our perception, the thermally active structure cradles our bodies, and the continuous light enhances the view of the artworks inside. The concrete and glass detailing are minimal yet provide extraordinary functionality and atmosphere.

## The Maggie Center Leeds

The site of Maggie Center Leeds is situated within a hospital precinct (Figure 3.11). The building is a garden, a partially sunken tree house, risen from the earth in symbolic rebirth. The choice of material enhances this figurative

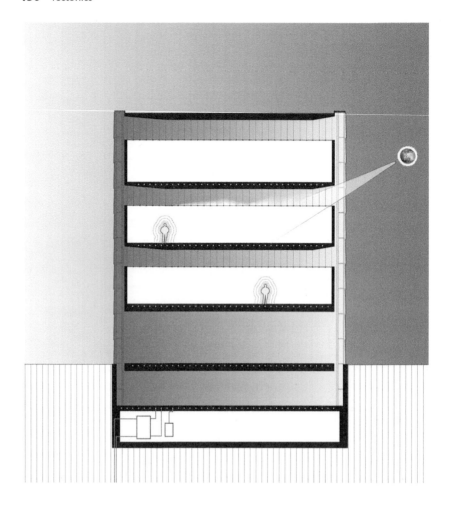

**FIGURE 3.10** KUB Section Light Inversion

concept. Made of prefabricated wood "trunks" and "branches," the structure imbues intimacy with nature and provides a peaceful atmosphere.

The trunks are structural cassettes made of wood composite panels where each of the glue-laminated branch-fins are keyed. Each fin is inclined, then curves outwards, growing into branches. The beam branches extend to the curved perimeter and are supported by a thin hybrid glass window wall and a timber frame system (Figure 3.12).

The recessive element, the frameless structural glazing, is supported by a concrete raft foundation held at the top by a recessed deflection head channel at

**FIGURE 3.11**    Photo, Maggie's Yorkshire Leeds, Heatherwick Studios, 2020
*(Credit:* Hufton + Crow)

the cross-laminated timber (CLT) deck. The perimeter glazing ensures that the gardens and planting surrounding the building can be viewed unobstructed from inside and out (Figure 3.13).

The landscaped roof of plants and trees is made in varying levels that follow the site topography. The stepped levels of each trunk are formed to situate the building as part of the ground, and the earthen roof provides insulation (Figure 3.14).

The load paths associated with the cantilevers and the resulting shear forces are managed by birch plywood, high-stress CLT and appended fins with the CLT roof slab. This innovative approach created an optimized structure (fabricated by CNC) that transfers the heavy loads of the landscaped roof, economically and sustainably. In addition, wood naturally sequesters carbon. With the global warming potential in the embodied energy of concrete being three times that of

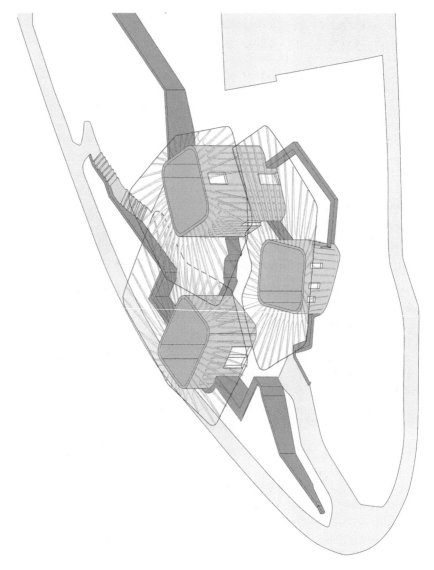

**FIGURE 3.12** Maggie's Yorkshire Isometric of Trunks and Branches

wood, elements of the wood structure incorporate concerns of ecological tectonics (Figure 3.15).

Light is crucial to the experience. About 70 percent of the floor area has a daylight factor (DF) greater than 2 percent, and the areas of most activity have a DF greater than 5 percent, exceeding LEED, BREEAM, and other green building

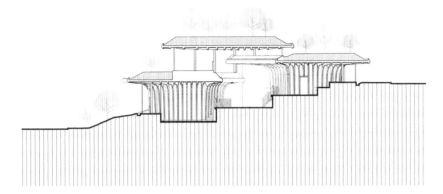

**FIGURE 3.13**   Maggie's Yorkshire Building Section

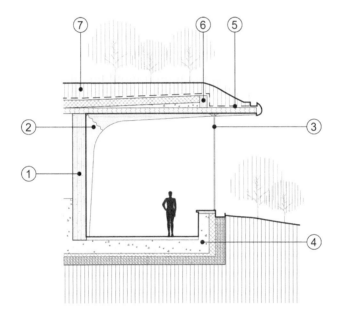

1. Cross Laminated Timber (CLT) - Structural Cassette "Trunks"
2. Glue Laminated Timber - Structural Beam "Branches"
3. Frameless Structural Glazing Perimeter Façade
4. Concrete Raft Foundation and Glazing and Ground Upstand
5. Cross Laminated Timber (CLT) - Structural Deck
6. Glue Laminated Timber - Deflection Head Channel
7. Landscaped Roof - Lightweight Aggregate Soil on Insulation
   and Concrete Topping

**FIGURE 3.14**   Maggie's Yorkshire Detail Section

**FIGURE 3.15**    Maggie's Yorkshire Photo, Wood Structure Fabrication

*(Credit:* Blumer-Lehmann AG)

requirements. The total energy load is calculated to be 76.07 kWh/m$^2$/yr, far better than a standard facility.

In casting nature as the ultimate caregiver, the building is an empathetic resolution that contributes to positive ecology and psychological effects of mind and body, experience, and memory.

## Notes

1  Koolhaas, Rem. *Elements of Architecture*. Taschen, 2018.
2  Aalto, Alvar. 'The Relationship Between Architecture, Painting, and Sculpture,' in *Synopsis*. Ed. Hoesli, Bernhard. Birkhäuser, 1970, p.25.
3  ibid.
4  Aalto, Alvar. 'Taide ja Tekniikka (Art and Technology),' in *Sketches*. Ed. Aalto, Alvar. MIT Press, 1978, p.87 (Aalto—Sketches).
5  Aalto, Alvar. 'The Humanizing of Architecture,' in *Alvar Aalto in His Own Words*. Ed. Schildt, Göran. Otava, 1997, 1940 (Aalto).
6  Aalto, 'Art and Technology,' p.172.
7  Frampton, Kenneth, 'The Case for the Tectonic,' in *Modeling History*. Columbia Books on Architecture and the City, 2017.
8  Schwarzer, Mitchel. 'Ontology and Representation,' in *Karl Bötticher's Theory of Tectonics*. JSAH 52, September 1993, pp.267–280.

9   Sekler, Eduard. 'Structure Construction, Tectonics,' in *Structure in Art and Science*, Ed. Kepes, G. Braziller Books, 1965, pp.89–95.

10  See Leach, Neil. 'Introduction,' in *Digital Tectonics*. John Wiley & Sons, 2004.

11  Oxman, Rivka. 'Informed Tectonics in Material-Based Design,' *Design Studies*, Volume 33, Number 5, 2012, pp.427–455.

12  Bech-Danielsen, Claus. *Towards an Ecology of Tectonics: The Need for Rethinking Construction in Architecture*. Edition Axel Menges, 2015, p.14.

13  Churkina, G., Organschi, A., Reyer, C.P.O. et al. 'Buildings as a Global Carbon Sink,' *Nature Sustainability*, Volume 3, 2020, pp.269–276. https://doi.org/10.1038/s41893-019-0462-4.

14  Tehrani, Nader. 'Aggregation,' in *Material Design*. Ed. Schröpfer, Thomas. Birkhäuser GmbH, 2011, p.48.

15  Aalto. 'Influence of Structure and Material on Contemporary Architecture,' p.99

16  Moholy-Nagy, László. 'Biological Needs,' in *The New Vision: Fundamentals of Design, Painting, Sculpture, Architecture*. W.W. Norton & Company, Inc., 1938, Dover Edition, 2005, p.23.

17  Aalto, 'Art and Technology,' p.174.

18  Kreuger, P.C. 'Ecological Properties of Building Materials,' *Materials and Structures*, Volume 20, 1987, pp.248–254.

19  Le Corbusier. *The City of Tomorrow and Its Planning*. Dover Publications, 1929 (reprint 2013), pp.34–35.

20  Reiser, Jesse, and Umemoto, Nanako. *Atlas of Novel Tectonics*. Princeton Architectural Press, 2006, p.72.

21  Brown, Howard, Cook, Robert, and Gabel, Medard. *Environmental Design Science Primer* (originally published by Advocate Press, New Haven, 1978). Buckminster Fuller Institute, p.5, Accessed in www.bfi.org.

22  Pallasmaa, Juhani. *The Thinking Hand: Existential and Embodied Wisdom in Architecture*. Wiley, 2009.

23  Zumthor, Peter. *Atmospheres: Architectural Environments—Surrounding Objects*. Birkhäuser, 2006.

24  ibid, p.22.

25  Leatherbarrow, David. *Architecture Oriented Otherwise*. Princeton Architectural Press, 2012, p.91.

26  Pallasmaa, Juhani. *The Eyes of the Skin: Architecture and the Senses*. Wiley-Academy, 2005, p.32.

27  Herzog, de Meuron. 'Firmitas,' in *The Complete Works 1989–1991*. Ed. Mack, Gerhard. Birkhäuser, 2000, Volume 3, pp.222–225.

28  Aalto—Sketches, 'Motifs from Times Past,' p.1.

29  Pallasmaa, Juhani. 'Matter, Hapticity and Time Material Imagination and the Voice of Matter,' *Building Material*, Volume 20, 2016, pp.171–189.

30  Frampton, Kenneth. *The Case for the Tectonic in Modeling History*. Columbia Books on Architecture and the City, 2017.

31  Aalto, Alvar. *Second Nature*. Vitra Design Museum GmbH, 2014.

32  Anderson, Stanford. 'Aalto and Methodical Accommodation to Circumstance,' in *Alvar Aalto in Seven Buildings*. Ed. Tuomi, Timo et al. Museum of Finnish Architecture, 1998, p.143.

33  Kieran Timberlake. https://kierantimberlake.com/page/carbon-accounting (Accessed 05 March 2022).

34  For more information see https://architecture2030.org/ (Accessed 05 March 2022).

35  Moe, Kiel. 'Compelling Yet Unreliable Theories of Sustainability,' *Journal of Architectural Education (1984–)*, Volume 60, Number 4, 2007, pp.24–30.

36 For more on Sequestering Carbon in the Built Environment, see https://sustaina blebrands.com/read/product-service-design-innovation/3-advances-in-sequestering-carbon-in-the-built-environment (Accessed 05 March 2022).

37 Gould, Stephen Jay, and Vrba, Elisabeth S. 'Exaptation—A Missing Term in the Science of Form,' *Paleobiology*, Volume 8, Number 1, 1982, pp.4–15.

38 Aalto, 'Karelian Architecture,' referencing his experience in using wood in interior design, p.119.

39 Aalto—Sketches, 'Menneitten Aikojen motiivit (Motifs from Times Past),' p.1.

40 For color scheme—See https://visit.alvaraalto.fi/en/destinations/muurame-church/ (Accessed 05 March 2022).

41 Ott, Randall. *Surface Versus Structure: Alvar Aalto and the Finnish Wooden Churches*, 84TH ACSA Annual Meeting Open Sessions 1996, p.513.

42 Menin, Sarah. *Accessing the Essence of Architecture: "In-Between" Nature and Modernity in Aalto's Engineers Housing in Sunila*, p.49, footnote 21, Macfarlane, J. *Dictionary of Latin and English Languages*. Eyre and Spottiswoode, n.d.

43 ibid., p.49, Aalto used these words to describe Gunnar Asplund's architectural legacy in 'E.G.Asplund in Memorium,' (Aalto), p.66.

44 Aalto, Alvar. *Alvar Aalto—The Complete Works*. Birkhauser Verlag GmbH, 2014, Volume I, p.132.

45 Aalto, Alvar. 'Wood as a Building Material,' *Arkkitehti*, Volume 6–7, 1956, pp.101–102.

46 Moholy-Nagy, László. *The New Vision, and Abstract of an Artist*. Wittenborn, 1947, 1928.

47 Schildt, Göran, 'Alvar Aalto and Human Error,' in *Matter and Mind in Architecture*. Alvar Aalto Foundation/Alvar Aalto Museum, 2000, p.60.

48 Pallasmaa, Juhani, Mallgrave, Harry Francis, and Arbib, Michael A. *Architecture and Neuroscience*. Tapio Wirkkala-Rut Bryk Foundation, 2013, p.14.

49 Porphyrios, Demetri, and Aalto, Alvar. *Sources of Modern Eclecticism: Studies on Alvar Aalto*. Academy Editions, 1982, p.55.

50 Pallasmaa, Juhani. 'Body, Mind, and Imagination,' in *Mind in Architecture: Neuroscience, Embodiment, and the Future of Design*. MIT Press, 2017, p.64.

51 Johnson, Mark L. 'The Embodied Meaning of Architecture,' in *Mind in Architecture: Neuroscience, Embodiment, and the Future of Design*. MIT Press, 2017.

52 Anderson, 'Aalto and Methodical Accommodation to Circumstance,' p.192.

53 See more on this topic in Passe, Ulrike, and Battaglia, Francine. *Designing Spaces for Natural Ventilation: An Architect's Guide*. Taylor & Francis, 2015, p 126.

54 Samuel, Flora, and Menin, Sarah. *Nature and Space: Aalto and Le Corbusier*. Routledge, 2003, p.99.

55 Banham, Reyner. 'A Home Is Not a House,' *Architectural Design*, January 1969, p.58.

56 Aalto, 'Reconstruction of Europe,' p.153.

57 Tehrani, Nader. 'Aggregation,' in *Material Design*. Ed. Schröpfer, Thomas. Birkhäuser GmbH, 2011, p.48.

58 Frampton, Kenneth. 'Intimations and Tactility: Excerpts from a Fragmentary Polemic,' *Art Forum*, March 1981, pp.52–58.

59 Frampton, K. *Studies in Tectonic Culture: The Poetics of Construction in Nineteenth and Twentieth Century Architecture*. MIT Press. 1995, p.12.

60 Aalto, *The Complete Works*, Volume I, p.114.

61 Ban, Shigeru. *Alvar Aalto: Through the Eyes of Shigeru Ban*. Black Dog Publishing, 2007, p.64.

62 Kieran, Stephen, and Timberlake, James. *Refabricating Architecture: How Manufacturing Methodologies are Poised to Transform Building Construction*. McGraw-Hill Education, 2003.

63 Oxman, Rivka and Oxman, Robert. 'Introduction,' *The New Structuralism*, Volume 4, 2010, p.23.

64  Maturo Sasaki, *Fabricate: Making Digital Architecture*. UCL Press, 2017, p.59.

65  Königs, Ulrich. 'Adaptive und selbstorganisierende Systeme in der Architektur,' *Graz Architektur Magazine*, 2005, pp.1–20.

66  Cecil Balmond Studio. https://www.balmondstudio.com/approach.php (Accessed 05 March 2022).

67  Oxman, Rivka. 'Informed Tectonics in Material-Based Design,' *Design Studies*, Volume 33, Number 5, 2012, pp.427–455.

68  Moe, Kiel. *Thermally Active Surfaces in Architecture*. Princeton Architectural Press, 2010, p.132.

69  ibid., p.134.

70  ibid., p.136.

# 4

# TECHNIC—FLEXIBILITY AND THE NEW STANDARD

**Technic** = technical terms, details, and methods; technology
(*Tĕkʰnɛ*: "craftsmanship," "craft," or "art" knowing and making)

As described by Aristotle, *Technic*, or *Techne*, is a true art, craft, or discipline. It is associated with anything made by humans against anything not made by humans. Techne assumes knowledge of making, understanding needs, and optimum practice; those things carefully considered versus those not.

Architecture in the 21st century requires us to deliberate design beyond how a building looks or its tradition but measure how it performs. Buildings are at once representational and operational. In other words, they manifest both an idea and a form of function. However, we cannot fall back on the *form-function* debate of the past. Instead, we must realize program and technic as provisions for inhabitation and how decisions made around these conditions create a performative architecture.

Making architecture is a multi-variant decision-making process. In order to make informed choices, we model our intentions. This process is especially true in the design of large buildings or urban planning; however, the decisions we make as individuals, even at a small scale, multiply in everything we do, so our choices can scale up quite quickly. As a result, our conclusions profoundly impact life on earth and our spaces to dwell.

Today, architecture is made by teams, not individual "Masters." Although we often look back at key individuals in history, we must design together for the

DOI: 10.4324/9781003160571-5

future. As architects, we work with specialists that feed our model-specific parameters to reduce technical errors, realize optimal fabrication methods, perform simulations and input maintenance procedures, and measure life-cycle goals.

Regardless of how software influences our design processes, architects remain the conductors of the many groups, team members, specialists, and decisions involved. This fact is ever more critical in guiding, organizing, and measuring performance parameters. These parameters are fundamentally dictated by circumstances that are either externally governed by regulation or internally administered by design investigation; either way, they require thoughtful analyses of the conditions of place. These conditions by examination are qualified and quantified through modeling. Only after we understand the measures and rules that develop the circumstances of our surroundings can we make informed decisions about building.

During the last years of his life, Aalto discussed 'The Human Factor,'[1] which seems a fitting place to start our discussion on technic. Architects now find themselves in an adaptive state, with offices expanding and being redefined as technology advances. In addition, we encounter the crises of climate and acknowledge the common need for equitable and sustainable growth. These changes have significantly impacted our working methods and way of life since Aalto's time, and more radically over the past decade.

Göran Schildt had said, discussing Aalto and the human factor, "At the time, I thought he was thinking primarily of the fixation on economic growth that has become a nightmare for present-day (post) industrialized society and that threatens to propel our exploitation of the earth's resources to a final catastrophe."[2] Schildt's remark on Aalto resonates today as these issues have reached what might be a tipping point, with consequences that not only have to do with climate but also the countless inequities in our society.

Aalto's late writings and lectures touched on a big picture issue drawing upon his earlier stories, asking his audience to observe past lessons to provide a more meaningful, harmonious life. He reflected upon our central point, *the human factor*, where all our societal ills are contingent upon "two alternatives: either human error or technical failure."[3]

Throughout history, there have been attempts to fix problems by setting standards and policy by authoritative rule, by forms of egalitarianism, or, most recently, by social insurrection through the use of computer networks. Hardware and software technologies are incredible tools for positive revolution. However, like many things in rapid transformation, they are fraught with misguided standards and obsolete policies. The problems of technology have to do with the human factor. In other words, the error lies in how people use technology, not necessarily in the technology itself.

In the case of social media, the question of standards centers upon data sets and computational algorithms used to sort and disseminate data. A common argument is that we must regulate data so that the *correct* information reaches the *intended* audience. The unqualified standard is the authoritarian firewall, the one of singularity, while the qualified is the plurality, as in the *Arab Spring*, the open standard that gave freedom of information to reach the (un)intended audience. In order to maintain equitable and sustainable processes, we must define *flexible* standards while maintaining sets of rules as agreed upon *minimum* standards.

As architects, we rely on dimensional and modular standards, safety standards, building and energy compliance standards, and production standards, to name just a few. Together these standards set minimum measurable outcomes that are widely accepted as essential rules and regulations. In general, standards follow measured science and empirical data that are calculated or passed along through time as common expectations in the design and construction of our buildings.

Today, most standards are transcribed and embedded into digital tools. As we expect that our code inputs are correct, we make decisions that ensure our buildings will remain standing and perform as efficiently as modeled. We also expect the people entering this data to have requisite knowledge and experience that we can rely upon.

Science encompasses the systematic study of the structure and behavior of the natural world through observation and experimentation, and technology is the application of scientific knowledge for practical purposes. Science in architecture requires systematic observing, measuring, experimenting, and formulating, along with adaptive thinking and theory.

Artful resolution is another standard that carries meaningful intention, intuitive composition, appropriate inspiration, and organic or natural selection. Technology is the architect's tool that is used to manage the integration of these disparate matters. Architecture fuses science and art, synthesizing objective measures and subjective intuitions. A sculptor only needs a hammer and mass, a painter, a tool and surface, a musician, sound and color, but an architect in design and building needs all of these and much more.

As stated by Aalto,

> We need an art based on matter, an art that is conscious of its own task. If we leave out the human being from our work, whether art or technology, how are we to protect 'the little man' in today's mechanized world? It is not enough to protect man ideologically. Technology—even standard technology—must seal the same systems of detail, prioritizing the requirements of man.[4]

Can we prioritize humanity yet diminish the human factor with technology? The answer depends on whether machines or digital tools can take over and perform our service equally, equitably, and sustainably. Take, for instance, the self-driving car. This would indeed, once perfected, remove the human error of accident, in addition to being more efficient. However, this does not reduce the automobile's burden on our infrastructure or the inequity in who can afford to drive.

Perhaps a better example is the autonomous truck currently in exploratory service. With a promise to afford encouraging possibilities for producers and consumers, the autonomous truck will not only remove human error, but provide an improved social condition, with added opportunity for the operator to consume less and deliver more.

One might ask, how does the truck afford the driver? Much like architects, where 24 percent are sole proprietors, a significant percentage of truck drivers are also independent operators who own their rig. So, why is this an advantage? The owner of an autonomous truck can allow the truck to continue operating during downtime, affording the benefit of more income and better time management. The advantage of technology is when new standards are adopted for the benefit of all.

Software development that drives autonomous vehicles affords efficiency, excellent pattern detection, and more predictable modeling and measure. In addition, the algorithms, artificial intelligence, and deep learning required by computers to provide safe travel with minimal interference could also help architects and fabricators. First, however, we must remember that the truck is pure science; it doesn't need to be beautiful or provide comfort for more than its single passenger. On the other hand, architecture is required to respond to concerns of aesthetics, comfort, and performative variation. As architects, could software and its accompanying advancements augment our intuitive design-thinking processes by helping to drive efficiency as an "automatic" process?

Aalto was critical of automatic processes in architecture. Since human error is ever-present, we must scrutinize computations. In 1972 Aalto wrote, These accurate calculations contain just as much human error as earlier planning methods based on faith and emotion . . . thus as important as ever today to take the human factor into account . . . we must therefore be extremely cautious." He added that "technical error is more easily eliminated . . . human error, however, can never be neutralized; it is an eternal problem that cannot be changed by tackling its consequences."[5]

In latter-day disparagements about using computational formulas, Aalto criticized the profession and academia:

> There is an increasing tendency to believe that man can avoid the difficulties associated with individual quality by drawing up formulas and making calculations, producing some kind of recipe for the problem of how to make good "building art." This is increasingly leading to systems, computations, formulas, that are believed to lead automatically to the right kind of housing and the right kind of public buildings.[6]

Contrasting, yet markedly accompanying Aalto, Nicholas Negroponte, cofounder of the MIT Media Lab, in the 1969 essay '*Towards a Humanism through*

*Machines*,[7] defined three possible ways of having machines assist in the design process:

1.  Current procedures can be automated, thus speeding up and reducing the cost of existing practices [CAD/CAM and BIM as Performance-based Design];
2.  Existing methods can be altered to fit within the specifications and constitution of a machine, where only those issues are considered that are supposedly machine capable [Parametric and Robotics];
3.  The process, considered as being evolutionary, can be introduced to a mechanism (also considered evolutionary), and a mutual training, resilience, and growth can be developed [Generative Design, Simulation, and Artificial Intelligence].

Negroponte considered the third alternative an "intimate association between two dissimilar species—man and machine—and two different processes—design and computation." This assertion directs computation that balances the human design process towards a new humanistic approach. Machine learning and design parameters merge to form a new automatic association with the body and mind's needs.

In making architecture, we go through varied processes in developing successful outcomes. Sometimes these procedures involve experiments, analytical methods in developing or reinforcing an idea; other times, these are intuitive, using experience as a guide. Yet, in all circumstances, the measure of architecture involves the review of information.

## Performative Tools

Computational analysis involves reviewing information to find the most economical, efficient, and optimized structure by using measures and parameters developed by architects. Among other things, this can be used to measure efficiency, material impacts, methods of organization, and code compliance. There are four general computational categories or strategies:

The Stele of Hammurabi, an ancient Babylonian code, decreed that a house should not collapse or the builder face consequences.[8] Following this, performance today must go beyond finite code prescriptions and accurately predict how a structure will respond to its environment and inhabitants' comfort.

Throughout the design process, choices and collaborative reviews are made through experience or perhaps by convincing others that your intuitions are correct. Still, most require a more methodical approach that requires specific calculation and consultation with experts. An example might be the choice of window placement and how that decision will result in less heat gain or enhanced passive ventilation. To know this, we can rely on experience, having done it before, or more accurately, model and simulate the condition, thereby proving our choices through scientific calculation.

Considering the human factor in the equation is essential. For example, a person chooses not to open or close the window as modeled, how does this impact the whole system? To err is human; therefore, there is no perfect solution. The lesson here is that if a building calculated to specific compliance equations with all decisions predetermined without an ability to adapt or change has a human error, you may as well have not followed any standards. Therefore, we must include human psychology in design, not only towards the air of our work but into its parameters of performance.

In 1971, the architect Luigi Moretti (1907–73) defined parametric architecture as the study of "the relationships between the dimensions."[9] The Oxford English Dictionary defines parametric as "a numerical or other measurable factor forming one of a set that defines a system or sets the conditions of its operation."

Parametric Design and Building Information Modeling (BIM) have become the mechanisms for delivering accurate measures of defined standards and flexibility in production. These tools allow us to embrace topological and dimensional variation in the simulation of forces, energy flows, and systems. The resulting model allows for the study of optimal design strategies to help reduce material usage, energy consumption, and human error.

Buildings, especially large-scale urban structures, require complex coordination. BIM establishes shared data sets in a virtual domain to simulate an actual building project. The gathered information can process material parameters of force, energy, cost, and fabrication. Although already widespread, these technologies are still in their early stages, and we (and the machine) still have much to learn.

Algorithms perform computations to solve a set of inputs. One example of this is a search engine, which uses weighted sets of algorithms that are designed to "look at many factors, including the words of your query, relevance, and usability of pages, the expertise of sources, and your location and settings to generate [the best results]."[10] In general, as defined by the Cambridge Dictionary, an algorithm is a "set of mathematical instructions or rules that will help calculate an answer to a problem." Algorithms can assist in managing complex information, revealing patterns, and generating new spatial arrangements.

In architecture, as we know, our problems are manifold, which can present difficulties when we attempt to employ algorithms that design for us. It is more appropriate for software to be designed with our working methods in mind as a way to augment our intuition, working like a close partner or consultant. To be complete, codes need to recognize the human factor—people's feelings, equity, and other social conditions surrounding our work. These tasks require computers to process relevant instruction; therefore, we can expect trained architects, the code's authors, to be the ones designing the software.

In 1977, the architect William Mitchell (1944–2010) defined generative design as an operation "to produce a variety of potential solutions."[11] It is exploratory and used to iterate the parameters needed to derive optimal solutions to problems that are analogous to evolutionary processes in nature.

When exploring optimal design solutions, various iterations made through the generative process produce viable solutions through variable outcomes. In addition, predetermined design parameters help generate the results. Therefore, these tools would be useless if human designers were not there to strategize, define the parameters, and script the algorithms needed for each variation to run effectively.

Like the preceding CAD/CAM processes, these computational types will become standard in practice, but only when the relationship between humans and computers becomes more seamless and intuitive. As Negroponte says, "a designer, when addressing a machine, must not be forced to resort to machine-oriented codes." Design therefore should "respond to a natural language," and that language, built into code, should be programmed to respond to underlying conditions of material, body, and place. Once set, the assigned parameters can produce a series of solutions for the designer to choose from. This process is repeated until the optimal solution has been *evolved* by a series of human and machine judgments. This process is no longer about *expressing* the digitization of architecture. In the words of Negroponte, "the Digital Revolution is over—we are now in a digital age . . . being digital will be noticed only by its absence, not its presence."[12]

Today, we have advanced devices for measuring, testing, and evaluating our intuitions, experiments, and data through computational analysis and simulation. In addition, digital modeling enables architects, fabricators, and manufacturers to seamlessly integrate experimental systems into the construction process. Making a new model standard requires a critical examination of how we transcend procedural and pattern-based production and move towards ecological acts. Digital design should not be a separate parametric, generative, or algorithmic process. Instead, we should use tools to augment our intuitions and better guide us through the technological metaverse.

Aalto reminds us that

> the problems of architecture cannot be solved at all with the methods of modern technology. Of course, architecture uses technology, but it does so by applying various technologies simultaneously, and its principal goal is to bring these technologies in harmony. Architecture is thus a *supra-technological* form of creation, and the harmonization of many disparate forms of activity is central to it.[13]

As technological simultaneity is far more evident and necessary today, one of many lessons from Aalto is that we must direct our use of technology towards a collective, responsible future.

## Alvar Aalto and Standards

When Aalto was emerging on the international scene, methods of manufacture and the fundamental discourse on architecture remained entrenched in considerations about mass-production and technological solutions that intended to standardize architectural production. Throughout modernism, rationalism replaced traditional styles. One of its goals was to economize methods of production through rational, modular standards, whereby technical and practical goals replaced traditional philosophical and aesthetic arguments.

Standardization was one of the critical tenets of Taylorism and Fordism in the early 20th century, which became dominant in the burgeoning technocratic society that drove mass-production, economics, and eventual social upheaval. The airplane, automobile, and other technological manifestations of this period became the preoccupations of architects, namely Le Corbusier, who was a proponent of mass-produced housing.

Much of this was a moral aim to focus on social housing and the needed methods to advance those goals. Mass production and standardization were the mechanisms to create more equitable and healthy advancements for housing.

At this time, Aalto fully subscribed to this notion of standardization. He and his wife Aino made several trips to Central Europe, and he participated in CIAM Conferences in 1929 and 1931, where he got to know all the leading modernists personally. He visited villas designed by Le Corbusier, the Bauhaus school in Dessau, and the Weissenhof-Siedlung in Stuttgart. It is also likely that he and Aino visited the just completed Zonnestraal Sanatorium by Johannes Duiker in Hilversum, which influenced the design of the Paimio Sanatorium competition entry of 1929.

In that same year, Aalto made comments regarding standardization:

> The use of standard elements is the manner of the industrial age; it is the only means to achieve scientifically sound results and raise quality . . . the architect creates the standards . . . he may himself use these units in several buildings or someone else may use them. The architect creates an entity, a system of these units.[14]

During the design and construction of the Turun Sanomat building in Turku (that followed the Le Corbusier *five points*), the Aaltos began to produce office standards made official by a new stamp applied to drawings. The first was laid in April 1929 and continued through August 1932, albeit his attitude towards mass-production and standardization was beginning to change.

After Alvar and Aino exhibited their *Minimum Apartment* in 1930, Aalto reformed his attitude about functionalism and rationalism. At the Nordic Building

Conference of 1932, Aalto called for *scientific standardization*. In 1935, he discussed what he learned from his time designing Paimio and Viipuri, saying,

> My aim was to show that real rationalism means dealing with all questions related to the object concerned, and to take a rational attitude also to demands that are often dismissed as vague issues of individual taste, but which are shown by more detailed analysis to be derived partly from neurophysiology and partly from psychology. Salvation can be achieved only or primarily via an extended concept of rationalism[15]

or as Pallasmaa describes as, "Synthetic Rationalism" or "Holistic Rationalism."[16]

Hannes Meyer's *Building*[17] in 1928 at the Bauhaus promoted the architect as "a social condenser," the artist specializing in order; in this light, building was mostly organization: social, technical, economic, and psychological. Through his work at the Paimio Sanatorium, Aalto adopted this approach as the designer and social administrator. Aalto worked on the core building construction details, mechanical systems, and all aspects of the building. In addition, he and his wife Aino designed, developed, and administered the manufacture of furniture, door handles, lighting, and plumbing fixtures, including the central heating plant, kitchen, and the crematorium.

The Aaltos considered technical solutions to resolve the functional, ergonomic, physiological, and psychological factors in the daily life in the hospital environment. They designed light fixtures to eliminate glare, and others enclosed in glass to protect them from dust. In the patient rooms was a draft-less heating and natural ventilation via the double-window system, and other details, such as radiant heating panels, spittoons, and 'noiseless' washbasins, suspended wardrobes, 'catch-less' door handles, all based on the care of the body.

The range of fixtures, furniture, and equipment designed and constructed for Paimio initiated experimentation and methods of production that went beyond the standard architect's practice. A local experimental workshop was set up to test bent and pressed wood, and to fabricate the first bentwood structures. The Artek Company, a moniker for Art + Technology, was formed in 1935 and enabled more measured experimentation and fabrication of the lighting fixtures and furniture. The fixtures and furniture developed around "flexible" mass-production standards hinting at what is now known as mass-customization.

Aalto soon immersed himself in developing a new standard for architecture. This standard was to be flexible, forward-looking, and include nature and humanism in a holistic, synthetic, artful, technological environment. He wrote and spoke about his new *rationalism*, the proper meanings of *function*, and the ideal *flexible* standardization in two insightful documents.

In 'The Humanizing of Architecture' (1940), he wrote,

> During the past decades, architecture has often been compared with science, and there have been efforts to make its methods more scientific, even efforts to make it a pure science. But architecture is not a science. It is still the same great synthetic process of combining thousands of definite human functions and remains architecture. Its purpose is to still bring the material world into harmony with human life. To make architecture more human means better architecture and it means a functionalism much larger than the merely technical one. This goal can be accomplished by only architectural methods—by the creation and combination of different technical things in such a way that they will provide for the human being in the most harmonious life. Architectural methods, on occasions, resemble scientific methods; in architecture you can adopt a research process similar to those used by science. Architectural research can be more and more methodical but substance of it can never be solely analytical. Always there will be more of instinct and art in architectural research.[18]

Reinforcing this in 1941, 'The Reconstruction of Europe is the Key Problem for the Architecture of our Time,' he discussed standardization and the need to view architecture, not as a set of standards or practical methods, but as something elastic that brings those many disparate elements into harmony.

> It is clear that architectural standardization should not be applied to complete buildings or inflexible, uniform entities, but on a deeper level to its constituent parts—building materials and components—organized in such a way that the main emphasis is on giving these components properties enabling them to form an unlimited number of different combinations, giving rise to a system in which identical parts can be used to produce an almost unlimited variation function and form.[19]

He went on to say, "The most important thing, of course, is to a devise a system that will enable us to make buildings at the field of specific function and are adapted to different natural conditions."[20] and that "harmonization . . . will require a period of direct supra-technological work, in other words, a period of laboratory experiments and harmonizing the various technical elements used as a raw material."[21]

Standards were developed by Aalto and his Atelier into internal office models later applied in appropriate variation and adjustment, advancing a flexible form-system-material combinatory methodology. Many architectural offices have since emulated this strategy and working technique as a standard practical model.

## Elastic Form Production

The historian Charles Jencks tells us,

> When one sees an architecture, which has been created with equal concern
> for form, function and technic, this ambiguity or tension creates a multi-
> valent experience where one oscillates from meaning to meaning always
> finding further justification and depth. One cannot separate the method
> from the purpose because they have grown together and become linked
> through a process of continual feedback. And these multivalent links set up
> an analogous condition where one part modifies another in a continuous
> series of cyclical references.[22]

To understand this multivalent experience, we compare Aaltos accommoda-
tive form-system design strategy to his discussion on the uniformity of the vernacular Karelian House. Aalto tells us that "wood dominates almost one hundred
percent both as material and joining method" while its "inner system of construction results from a methodical accommodation of circumstance." But, he went on,

> the Karelian House is in a way a building that begins with a single mod-
> est cell or with an imperfect embryo building, shelter for and animals, and
> which then figuratively speaking grows year by year. "The expanded Kare-
> lian House" can in a way be compared with a biological cell formation.[23]

Aalto's studies for low-cost dwelling, the AA Type House, were conceived
as research in standardization, involving flexible planning and elastic production
strategy as compulsory responsibility (Figure 4.1). As Aalto wrote in a document
titled, 'Flexibility in Standardization,' the idea

> is based on something more than sociological needs—one that includes
> a moral basis. The design must exploit technical progress certainly, for
> unlimited numbers of shelters must be produced, but mechanics cannot be
> allowed to dominate, to produce the 'limited house.' From the factory must
> come thousands of types, each one based on actual want, and solving cor-
> rectly specific shelter needs. This is the moral solution.[24]

Aalto developed parameters for the *ultimate form* of the house:

> 1) Nature. This does not mean a study of terrain but more the surround-
> ings, i.e., the view, trees, etc., 'good influences.' 2) Orientation. The house
> should be placed to take normal advantage of the sun, i.e., living to the
> south, service to the north. 3) Seclusion. As against the 'good influences'
> of nature, there are 'bad influences,' that is street traffic, proximity to neigh-
> boring houses, etc., which must be screened off.[25]

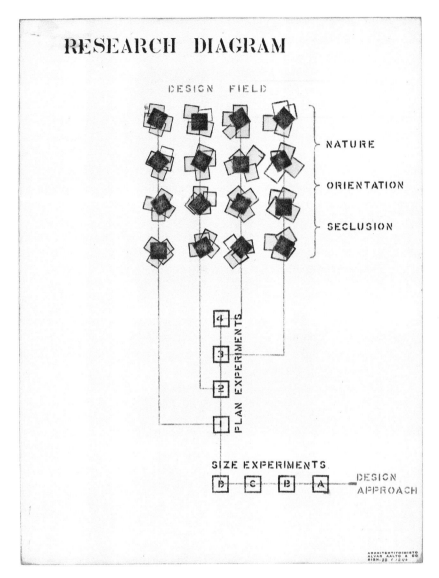

**FIGURE 4.1** AA Houses Research Diagram
*(Credit:* Alvar Aalto Foundation 88–1246)

Describing his experimental work with students at MIT, Aalto stated,

> The result was a set of tables containing entries for the main direction in which the site slopes and the angle of gradient are entered according to a certain scale. This yields the site's general morphological type; its orientation and the general effect of unfavorable external factors are also marked.

By using these "variables of circumstance," we arrive at a primitive but fully viable site description. These elements can form a variety of combinations, providing a rather exaggerative idea of the vastly different conditions that a standard unit of housing may face.[26]

These A.A. Housing Types imagined evolving types made by simple standard modules. These modules would be added to or reconfigured around a central court or hall according to the parameters. The plan and the parameters, not the standard modules, afford the house flexibility and variation. He furthered this development by diagramming relationships between types, medical, technical, and human beings as the fields of influence required for town planning, stating, "development in the next phase will be the adoption of recommendations of medical research specialists."[27]

The houses were not mass-production (rigid recurrent standard) but a semi-mass-customization strategy (flexible modulated standard), and they demonstrate Aalto's position as an architect, accentuated by Shigeru Ban:

> Architecture is not only for privileged people but also for ordinary people, including disaster victims . . . this project demonstrates Aalto's concept of flexible standardization in the most compassionate way: even for low-cost temporary housing, the architect should endeavor to maximize the quality of housing for its inhabitants.[28]

Following Aaltos lead, we could consider this house using contemporary tools to iterate form more in tune with its circumstance and situation by optimizing performance through specified input parameters. We could also imagine a 3D printed house, with its inherent topological structure, accommodating change without altering the production process. A new standard typology arrives at its formation through the same parametric influence described by Aalto, suggesting an elasticity of form and planning that affords variation and optimal performance.

## The Elastic Plan

Today, the shape of an automobile is almost identical, due primarily to the aerodynamics required to meet fuel consumption standards and mass-production. Unfortunately, this kind of standardization does not work in buildings. Buildings need to reach similar standard goals; however, buildings exist in particular sites and locations with unique parameters—climate, orientation, social condition, among other factors. Unlike a car, mass-produced to be the same in any place, architecture made according to variables present in a particular site is mass-customized at its best.

Aalto experimented with differentiation and similarity, not sameness. "With what Aalto called '*elastic standardization*' he opened the monotony of a global '*International Style*' towards site- and user-specific geometrical differentiation and apparent visual divergence."[29] We can see this elastic standardization in the High-Rise Apartments in Bremen, Germany, where the building form is an attempt at resolving his "ideological conflict: the contradiction between the imperative of homogeneity dictated by industrial production and the need to celebrate the values of individualism."[30]

Holger Hoffman compares Aalto's *Neue Vahr* in Bremen to Hans Scharoun's *Julia* Tower in Stuttgart as a "seemingly similar approach to '*irregularity*'—at least when assessed by a '*formalist*' point of view." He notes that the plans are "conceptually identical, yet geometrically different." For example, Scharoun's plan is standardized, with a fixed set of rules, whereas Aalto's plan is a "locally adjusted—or elastic—version of a generic set of rules." Likewise, we may compare the Neue Vahr plan to the Royal Crescent at Bath (1774) by John Wood, where the great public space, or open-air "room," with its repeating colonnade gives way to flexible interior planning and garden. Here, the plan variations are mainly a consequence of formal exteriority with little regard to the interior. In Aalto's work, the variable planned interiority is measured regarding the exterior.

The Neue Vahr building plan is oriented conspicuously towards the west-south-west, with an elevated ground floor and shared roof terrace similar to Le Corbusier's Unite d'Habitation. However, unlike the Unite, its facade undulates and develops variation that enables controlled indirect southern light to enter most units, allowing residents to enjoy maximum daylight without excessive glare and heat while at home in the afternoons (Figure 4.2). The southerly side was primarily blank except for the shared living room at the southeast corner and punched windows. The service core is placed towards the northwest, creating a foil to the prevailing winds.

The deformation of the plan presents opportunity and optimization in the arrangement of the joint connecting space and its interrelationship to the 'fan' shape. "The floor plan resulted from an effort to avoid the depressing, closed-in feeling that one often experiences in small apartments."[31] The interior room planning unwinds to accommodate the fan shape, which opens the deep apartments up, like a blossom, towards the light and the setting sun. Aalto believed that "architecture and its details are in some way all part of biology."[32] His empathetic "flexible standardization" is based on various types in architecture and analogous variety in nature.

The placement of voids in the inset terraces molded a type of embedded brise soleil, affording a remarkable degree of privacy. As written by Karl Fleig, "As a consequence, the window wall is more subtly expressed, and space is provided for balconies withdrawn from the neighbors' view. In this manner, too, the interiors receive wide windows and window niches."[33]

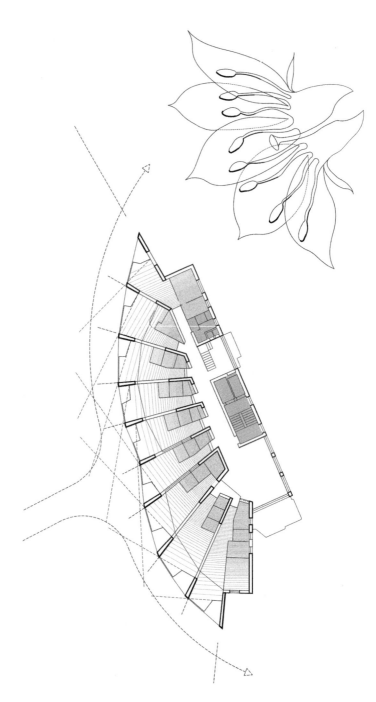

**FIGURE 4.2** Flower Anatomy and Neue Vahr Bremen Associative Geometries

The gently curving facade gradually morphs and reshapes the formal familiar towards the formal responsive. Its elastic deformations are opportunistic to its position in the local context. For Aalto, the mechanism of the ideal plan is not geometric order or precision but how it accommodates itself to its location and function. As we saw in the Baker House, in the Berlin Hansaviertel, and later here in Neue Vahr, he emphasizes the interconnecting room. This flexible device utilized in most plans helps overcome typological boundaries of functional use.

We see that the plans and structures of Aalto are not geometric but associative. Altering the grouping or orientation of elements does not change the sum of the parts, and in most cases, a quotient is net zero or greater. In other words, the differentiation adds, not subtracts.

In the words of Rivka Oxman,

> Associative geometry may support a design approach in which a geometrically or tectonically defined series of dependency relationships is the basis for generative evolutionary design process. Geometric variants of a class of structures can be generated parametrically by varying the values of its components, for example, the folds of folded plate, the grid cells of a mesh structure. Parametric software—are media for the generative and iterative design of structuring that can produce the geometric representation of topological evolution.[34]

The associative rule-based differentiation system of Aalto is remarkable when contrasted with an analogous programed rule-based system of parametric modeling. We imagine digitally shaping a form-system evolving the architecture entirely elastically to match the concept and its structure with the nature of the place.

## Elastic Design and Flexible Fabrication

Systems of manufacture and production were continuing research for Aalto. In 1970, he wrote,

> We could make standards which raise the level not only of the living standard but the spirit too. One very important thing would be if we could create an elastic standardization, a standardization which did not command us, but one which we would command.[35]

He also discussed the elastic standardization of flower petals, how each is standard yet different, and how we must follow the shapes of nature as the only way to standardize the elements of architecture.

Elasticity is a way to describe a form-system that realizes flexible standards through a concept of *difference and repetition*. This differentiation is a cornerstone of parametric design and part of open systems that consider elements of assemblage theory within material production in the built environment. This flexibility in production and amalgamation of material can help us arrive at an architecture that relies on thermodynamic materialism.[36]

Materialism for Aalto was a concern that comprised matter with psychophysical forces. According to Kenneth Frampton, "Perhaps the most distinguishing initial aspect of Aalto's career was his meditation of functionalism through ergonomic and psychosocial considerations."[37] We can find these in combination most succinctly in Alvar and Aino's fixtures, furniture, and lighting experiments.

This exploration began with the stool for Viipuri Library and later in the design and construction of the Paimio Sanatorium. These were simultaneous experiments, researching the possibilities of laminated striations of wood and plywood to make bentwood configurations and discoveries of rational form developed for comfort and ergonomic concerns. Many of these items are still produced in Finland today.

Aalto admired yet questioned the work of other modernists. He saw the potential flexibility of cradling steel tubing in a chair's function, which later informed his wood experiments. He was a critic of the tubular steel-framed chairs developed by Marcel Breuer (1902–81) (he owned two Wassily Chairs). He described them as cold, mechanical, and lacking feeling, stating that "psychophysically these materials are not good for the human being."[38] Of course, steel furnishings would not do in a building to house patients suffering from a bodily affliction.

At the Paimio Sanatorium, the Aaltos needed a new type of chair with a thermodynamic embrace and comfort to provide healthful well-being for the body. With inherent properties more suitable to the needs of a thermodynamic body, wood became the material of choice. In 1956, Aalto wrote,

> The biological properties of wood, its limited thermal conductivity, its affinity with man and living nature, its pleasing tactility, and the many different surface treatments available have preserved its dominant position in the interior design sector of architecture despite all the recent experiments with other materials.[39]

How to make wood, a rigid material, more flexible to form an ergonomic reclining seating apparatus was the question. To solve this, Aalto developed a new bent plywood production method that would resolve the constraints and parameters desired for ergonomics and standard technical production. The Paimio Chair used curved plywood for the seat and steam-bent birch for the supporting frame. Aalto operated within the constraints of handcraft and repetitive industrial production. As a result, the wood fabrication process depended on both and used standard elements differently.

The crafting of the chair reconciled a traditional outline with an anthropomorphic form through material research. Aalto was confident that wood could match tubular steel's structural potential and spring. As a result, the chair is formed and structured by lightweight, natural, thermally sensible material, removing all the steel tubing. The body-molded plywood seat affixed at four points hovers between the bentwood frames. Unlike combinatory material designs, the all-wood chair, as it changes with age, temperature, and humidity, remains in balance. This attunement with body proportions was revolutionary, made by elastic thought, research, and modeling.

In 1933, Alvar and Aino developed the laminated "bent-knee" leg that would prove essential to creating the three-legged stackable stool, of which a million or so have sold since the mid-1930s. The #60 stool is a model development that merges elastic design with flexible fabrication.

Experiments with laminated plywood ultimately led to z then y structural bending forms that became chairs, stools, tables, and so on (Figure 4.3). Similar procedures occurred with lighting fixtures, and both involved tradespeople and industrial manufacturers. Aino Marsio-Aalto, in 1935, as the artistic director of Artek, continued these experiments with various materials and designed many furniture components with Aalto.

Later, the component leg has four sizes used in over 50 different furnishings with only slight modification. As a result, the stool standard attained a flexible configuration where elements serve whole and vice versa. This elastic

**FIGURE 4.3**   Photo, Bent Knee Fabrication Paimio Chair

standardization was emblematic of the Aaltos view towards extended rationalism; all considerations harmonized into a thinking whole.

Technical and practical concerns and goals replaced traditional aesthetic arguments and theoretical discourse of architectural history. The inherent flexibility and practicality of its form, a seat, a table, stackable, and so on, were combined with its simple construction—a round top with three bent legs. The art historian Gustaf Strengell saw the leg as a leitmotif for a new tectonic element comparable to the classical column.[40]

Aalto's intuition was that this newfound elastic standardization could enable mass-customization through augmentation and variation with minimal incremental cost.[41] These developments parallel today's exchanges with trades and digital fabrication design and methodology. Moreover, the contemporary technic of mass-customization allows us to customize products with the economy associated with mass-production techniques of the past.

## Material Modular Standards

In 1936, Ernst Neufert advanced his *Bauentwurfslehre* or *Architects' Data*, a reference guide to design and planning a building project. In its introduction on "The human scale in Architecture," he wrote, "Architectural design remains largely about man and his spatial needs. The aim of *Architects' Data* is to bring together in a convenient form dimensional and spatial planning information relating to most human activities."[42]

In 1948, attempting to reconcile the dimensional incongruities in standards used in different localities, Le Corbusier published *Le Modulor*. It was focused not so much on *standards* but on the measure of the body, illustrated by anthropomorphic data and ancient proportional systems assembled in diagrammatic form. In its formal purity, flexibility was not essential to the system, nor was the anthropomorphic woman.

Aalto and Neufert knew each other personally and admired brick, but they wanted to reform it, albeit for different reasons. Much like Le Corbusier, Neufert focused his efforts on developing a standardized measuring system called *Octametric*. He claimed that his modular system resolved the missing link between house, room, furniture, and body. In contrast to Neufert, Aalto used brick for effect and a material unit of his *flexible standardization*. He compared brick to the living cell:

> in nature, standardization appears . . . only in the smallest: units, the cells. This results in millions of elastic combinations in which there is no trace of formalism. Furthermore, this gives rise to the enormous wealth of organic growing shapes and their eternal change. Architectonic standardization must follow the same path.[43]

In architecture, the parts and their materiality must be particularly *conscious of the whole*.

In 'Art and Technology' (1955), Aalto emphasized the localness of material production:

> An ordinary brick is for all appearances a primitive product, but if it is made correctly, properly processed from the country's own raw materials, if it used in the right way and given its proper place in the whole, then it constitutes the basic element: in mankind's most valuable and visible monuments and is also the basic element in the environment that creates social well-being.[44]

The brick of the House of Culture (1955–58) in Helsinki demonstrates an organic use of brick through an elastic standard. The brick follows standard modular production except for one parameter; it is not squared. This slight augmentation, shaping the brick, provides a simple, flexible arrangement of a customarily non-flexible material. The standard details of construction didn't change much. However, an elastic imagination formed a technique ascribed to flexible fabrication.

The building is a formed juxtaposition between the orthogonal and the curvilinear. A solution of opposites and paradoxes, the office block is rectangular, clad with flexible copper, while the auditorium is a sinuous fan shape clad with rigid brick. The bricks are non-rectangular, ensuing the *fan-shaped* plan and adjusting to varying radii. In addition, rounded corners made it easier to assemble and remove the human factor of imperfect alignment while enhancing the surface texture.

Pallasmaa describes Aalto's realization of multivalent architecture and its technical and psychological matters. Aalto,

> instead of aiming at conceptual and formal purity, sought to reconcile opposites such as nature and culture, history and modernity, society and the individual, tradition, and innovation, standardization and variety, the universal and the regional, the intellectual and emotional, the rational and the intuitive.[45]

Before the brick at the House of Culture, Aalto launched his idea of flexible standardization. In 1942, to research more about flexibility in construction standards, Aalto formed the Finnish Standardization Office modeled on the German Institute for Standardization's Construction Standards Committee that Neufert oversaw. Aalto wrote in 'The Flexible Stair,'

> The architect is a person who makes use of technology, among other things, when doing his work. He is like a painter with a palette in which

technology may represent the blue color, or perhaps even black, but that which contains many other ingredients that must be included in the result. The goal is to make the little man a little happier by offering him a setting which suits him exactly, and does not make him a slave to standardization. In other words, I am advocating unbridled individualism. The password is *flexible standardization*, the adaptability of details to innumerable different human needs. The difference between technological and architectural standardization is that the technological path leads to one single type, whereas sensible standardization leads to millions of different types.[46]

Soon after, Neufert became a supporter of Aalto's *sensible*, flexible standardization concept.

He was particularly taken by a Building Information Card detailing the "Flexible Stair,"[47] which codified Aalto's view that building systems should never be based on standard modules. The Flexible Stair may be understood today as a forerunner to parametric design because it showed how architects could use algorithms to standardize construction and yet still customize their designs.[48]

Digital design methods and computer-controlled fabrication technologies can cut and assemble various shapes and spans in construction. As a result, every member can be different but fabricated without substantial added cost. In addition, differences designed to optimize energy transfer or enhanced levels of light or comfort might offset the cost differential by fuel savings or increased worker productivity.

Parametric design and digital fabrication technics enable mass-production of non-standard, highly differentiated products. Difference no longer compromises the efficiency or economy of manufacture, thereby permitting variable production, presenting a robust new standard that arises derived as it would be in nature through evolutionary optimization.

Swiss timber construction company Blumer-Lehmann AG writes,

Modern timber construction starts in a virtual space, where a 3D digital model, also known as a parametric model, enables different versions of highly complex construction projects to be digitally programmed and tested. Creativity has almost no limits here. Thanks to parametric planning and programming, we can successfully harmonize even the most unusual forms, functions, and constructions and produce these on our systems at competitive prices.[49]

Observing and reintegrating architectural handcraft through advanced fabrication techniques is now readily available. The effect can be a fabrication process influenced by ecological parameters and optimized yet flexible material production. Through observing, crafting, and experimenting, Aalto learned and now teaches about the nature of materials and the potential in flexible fabrication and advanced material optimization.

*Material Intelligence* is the new password that empowers flexible fabrication techniques and promises employing inherent ecological parameters. Each material is born with a particular set of parameters with which we can analyze through a meaningful process of iteration to develop knowledge through progressive differentiation. Like a spider web, all our material choices can be optimal and natural to a specified condition.

We observe this material intelligence by informed tectonics and advanced optimization through digital modeling and computational analysis. Gramazio and Kohler describe this where "data and material, programing and construction are interwoven. This synthesis is enabled by the techniques of digital fabrication, which allows the architect to control the manufacturing process through design data. Material is thus enriched by information: material becomes informed."[50]

Architects and builders' experiment with new construction systems, and it takes time to adopt these methods and standards into building and model codes. CLT is a recent example. Product use did not become widespread until assembly methods became flexible enough to permit various modes of production, which in turn allowed for an adoption of the system into model codes. Digital modeling and testing helped to advance these compliance mechanisms.

Engineered wood products exemplify a synergy between Material Intelligence and Mass Customization by crafting elements that may be prefabricated but are not solely a catalog of products. We can see this in the projects engineered by Blumer-Lehmann AG and others whose pioneering wood structures represent timber construction's performative and ecological prospects.

The Urbach Tower in Germany is a recent example that advances an innovative self-forming process for complex curved components. Like the bentwood experiments by Aalto, the tower uses curved load-bearing elements, albeit at a building scale.

> Existing forming processes are very expensive and energy intensive, and require heavy pressing tools. But with the new self-forming method, the material curves by itself. This is attributable to the natural swelling and shrinking of timber under the influence of moisture.[51]

The fabrication process created self-forming, pre-calculated drying timber components, thus naturally forming the shapes and eliminating costly production tools.

## Natural Standardization

Bodies have the capacity to affect and be affected by other bodies. The body of a building affects our bodies and our environment more than our bodies on it. Therefore, considering how a building can affect change in our environment is vital to our physical and psychic realms and to the ecology in which it resides.

Aalto reminds us that "In architecture, the role of standardization is this, not to aim at a type but, on the contrary, to create *viable variety* and richness which is an ideal situation is comparable to nature's infinite capacity of nuance."[52]

Viable variety is a form of speciation in nature where species evolve to accommodate changing circumstances in an environment or place. It is a functional change adapting from one type into another. Aalto understood this reference to morphology as he argued that "singular cells give rise to varying formal configurations" and that "nature herself is the best standardization committee in the world."[53]

Discussing production and standards helps to remind us that buildings we produce must be beautiful, artful, and technologically viable, performing beyond expected standards and considering "natural standardization rather than the standardization borrowed from the domain of pure technology."[54]

In comparing architecture with animal constructions, Juhani Pallasmaa attempts to reunite reason and beauty, advocating for an eco-functionalist realism while supporting advanced practices: "Animal architecture teaches us that a proper way towards an ecologically sound human architecture . . . is not through regressing back to primitive forms of construction, but through extreme technological sophistication."[55]

Biomorphism in architecture adopts form from nature as an associative symbolic device that does not necessarily increase the performance of a building. On the other hand, biomimicry adapts forms from nature to optimize structural systems and mimic natural energy performance—hence, the declaration that "biomorphism is a formal and aesthetic expression; biomimicry is a functional discipline."[56] Using technology to emulate natural evolution reinforces biological thinking to aid in building in harmony with environment. Furthermore, by developing and testing simulations to optimize our design intentions, we can get closer to the standards of nature.

We observe sophistication in nature by how plants, some insects, and animals have adapted to their environments and optimized structures they make. A spider is a prime example. Many have evolved to develop an externally structured device for catching prey through a web.

This web is formed as an affordance to the spider. The spider uses energy to construct the web; however, the web sets up a condition to catch food without using energy. The strength, weight, stickiness, and internal production of material for the web are optimized as part of the spider. The relationship of optimization and performance is an attunement to the spider's situated environment, which forms natural reciprocity between the spider, its construction, and the environment in which it lives. Most spider species have their own standard web structure. However, each web is different, and it is the environment that necessitates adaptation and has evolved elastic variation in the making of webs in different ecosystems (Figure 4.4). The concept and material geometry of the web is uniform, but its structure varies.

The web device is a lesson in a functional form that affords the spider a tool for catching its food. The metaphor of buildings as biological processes reminds us that entities work together in nature. Designing a building that looks like a web (or a spider) is not productive, but modeling the *system* used by the spider to make its web strong and lightweight is. The spider has evolved ways to live using the least amount of resources in the most effective ways. We still have much to learn from nature.

**FIGURE 4.4** Spider Web Typologies and Technics—Sheet, Cob, Funnel, and Orb Webs

Since the shape of our work tends to add cost and time to a project, we should look to nature to take structure and material optimization seriously. "In nature, materials are expensive, and shape is cheap,"[57] therefore, to obtain the forms and shapes we desire, we must document the economic and ecological advantage that those forms and shapes provide. Using fewer materials requires more design, and if our plans become more economical and productive, our designs become much more valuable. To optimize is to minimize; therefore, we must optimize the form of our buildings to minimize the use of material and the consumption of energy.

Aalto's concept of *universal substance* reminds us that design is a natural process where all decisions occur together synthetically, joining disparate ideas and structures into one unifying whole. In 1938, Aalto stated, "The very essence of architecture consists of variety and development reminiscent of natural organic life."[58]

Optimization is a function of life. Living things survive as they adapt to the circumstances of their surroundings and the energy exchanged between their body and the environment. In architecture, technics combine studies of the human body with the body of a building. This measure starts with material structure and light. Material, as in how we can do more with less or *lightness* and light, as in how we form and shape our buildings towards maximizing daylight or *light-full*. One is tectonic, the other topological; both optimized using parametric and generative design tools. We use these tools to improve circulation patterns in floor plans, reveal passive air flows, and develop more adaptive standards.

When considering energy in a building, light and heat are two primary considerations. Controlling light will avoid heat gain, and thermoregulating heating and cooling will provide greater comfort and consume less energy. The architect's job is to equalize these conditions so that the human body and the body of the building co-exist in harmony.

In the early 20th century, environmental data began to take shape; however, architects did not have the sophisticated tools we have today, nor ecological ethics as we now understand them. Largely unaware of the adverse effect that fossil fuels were having on the climate, "architects instead sought to analyze how psychological norms, social behaviors, and atmospheric patterns were intertwined, and how the built environment could optimize these interconnections."[59] These interrelated conditions were concerns associated with equilibrium and comfort.

Le Corbusier delivered his idea of equalization through his *les techniques modernes* (the modern techniques). These included five performative elements: natural ventilation (*aération naturelle*), natural lighting (*éclairage solaire*), solar control (*brise soleil*), thermally active facade in opaque or glazed walls (*mur neutralisant*), and internal air conditioning (*respiration exacte*). Le Corbusier made many diagrams, analyses, plans, and sections for this idea. The first three elements, considered passive mechanisms, worked well when devised and appropriately distributed. However, the latter two mechanical systems were not proven by adequate scientific calculation or recognized performative metrics, especially the hermetic double "neutralizing" wall, which was not executed due to cost.[60]

In 1926, published in the magazine *L'Esprit Nouveau*, Le Corbusier illustrated his *Five Points of Architecture*. Its ribbon window diagram demonstrating optimized daylighting was known by Aalto; however, the free facade was not in his intentions. From Le Corbusier's diagram, we understand that a window placed in the middle of the room creates shadow at the edges, or if the window were at the border, the opposite edge would be dark. Although Aalto used the ribbon window in the Turun Sanomat (1930) in Turku, and later in the Finnish Public Pensions Institute (1956) and a *window wall* in the Rautatalo Office Building (1955), he preferred the ordinary window in a typical wall complemented by the window in the roof. To make the standard window effective and form dimensional quality, he promoted the *side-lit room* accompanied by the skylight, making progressive transitions from space to space and from function to function. This situation would celebrate light space through light-dark syncopations and dynamic energy.

Aalto experimented early on with light and energy in multiple environmental schemes. Beginning with the windows of the Paimio Sanatorium, there was an attempt to eliminate the need for artificial ventilation while maintaining a thermo-conditioned environment. Here, a passive airflow is slightly warmed as it enters between the three-part, double-glazed, double window panes. In addition, the ceilings in the patient room have radiant heating panels. The passive flow of preheated air passes over the panels. It heats the room through convection in combination with the window radiators, which simultaneously, by conduction, warm the floor and mass of the building.[61]

The skylights in Viipuri are deep, producing no glare or direct view of the sun. The roundness also prevents shadows. Aalto explained, "This system is humanly rational because it provides a kind of light suitable for reading, blended and softened by being reflected from the conical surfaces of the skylights."[62] This system marks the beginning of Aalto's "simultaneous solution of opposites," where the opposing forces of use, form, and structure are all resolved together. According to Aalto,

> It is possible in a scientific way to ascertain what kinds and what quantities of light are ideally the most suitable for the human eye but constructing a room the solution must be made with the aid of all the different elements which architecture embraces. Here the skylight system is a combined product of the ceiling construction and special technical limits in horizontal glass construction. An architectural solution must always have a human motive based on analysis, but that motive has to be materialized in construction.[63]

Aalto's skylight was later expanded to form a *roof-window-wall-skylight-system*. This condition is topological, the building form is modeled to create the optimal condition for daylighting, thereby acclimatizing its situation requiring little or no added energy.

## Towards an Ecological Standard

The ecological turn in architecture started many decades ago. Discourses by Frank Lloyd Wright, Buckminster Fuller, and Le Corbusier opened the conversation for Norman Foster, William McDonough, and Ken Yeang to progress new approaches in ecological building.

In 1938, Frederick Kiesler, in his essay 'On Correalism and Biotechnique,'[64] proposed that in design, we "must include science dealing with the fundamental laws which seem to govern man as a nucleus of forces" and that only this "new science can eliminate the arbitrary divisions of Art, Technology, and Economy, and make architecture a socially constructive factor in man's daily activities." He discussed a *technological environment* that is no longer a two-fold condition of biology and geography, but a three-fold environment comprised of nature, humans, and technology. This *total* environment includes a whole technic, which man has developed to regulate nature better.

Kiesler stated, "No tool exists in isolation. Every technological device is co-real: its existence is conditioned by the flux of man's struggle, hence by its relation to his total environment." As we use tools, they and we evolve. Along the way, our tools and products become standard, variation develops to optimize specific tasks, and later a simulated type often triumphs as an "image" of the working type (Figure 4.5).

> The *Standard* grows out of scientific knowledge. The *Variations* are a natural adaptation of the *standard* to specific conditions and are therefore valid. The *Simulated* product and its temporary survival is only made possible by a lack of knowledge within its social environment.

Today, tools grant knowledge beyond simulacra or imagery, producing real simulation.

Aalto met Kiesler in 1938, and they maintained a relationship throughout the 1940s.[65] In 1941, Aalto wrote, "a building is the act as an instrument that collects all the positive influences in nature for a man's benefit, while also sheltering him from the unfavorable influences that appear in nature and the building's specific surroundings."[66] Therefore, following Kiesler, a building is a total environment made by instruments for better synergy with nature.

Architecture, and any form of construction, requires standard practical methods, communications, and techniques. As our tools and communications have evolved, today's standards of representation, computation, and fabrication methods have changed. We have an opportunity to reconsider the 'simulated' dynamic of the architect *create problem* | engineer *solve problem* paradigm that has existed in practice for too long. Using building information models can enhance our collaboration and arrive at design solutions that incorporate a topology of energy

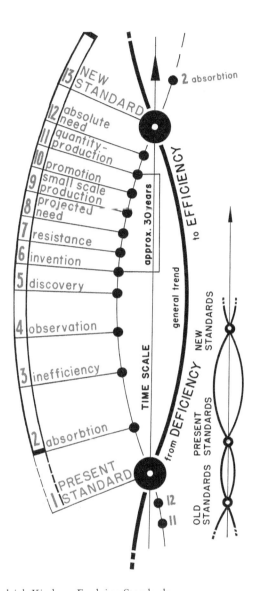

**FIGURE 4.5** Fredrick Kiesler—Evolving Standards

*(Credit:* Frederick Kiesler Foundation)

and material systems as a natural process, but only if our considerations deal with performance, not prescription.

Design methods rather than mechanical systems remained the abstract method for architects until the 1950s and early 1960s. In 1963, the Olgyay brothers produced in their book, *Design with Climate: Bioclimatic Approach to Architectural Regionalism*, climactic analysis, charts, diagrams, and sample projects to demonstrate ways to mitigate negative forces of the environment. The 'Schematic Bioclimatic Index' was most notable, which sought to reconcile the imbalance between the built environment and psychophysical comfort. As the caption reads, "These relationships are imagined as a dome of protection—'the project of man's needs'—should be the shelter with calculated surfaces of transmitting, absorbing, filtering or repelling characteristics of the environmental factors," a premise that Victor Olgyay later called the 'Theoretical Approach to Balanced Shelter.'[67]

These examples of calculated passive comfort strategies help us understand that our first design decisions can be better interrelated with our environment to be supplemented by active mechanisms only when necessary to arrive at a state of equilibrium.

Late 20th-century efforts to quantify data and create rating systems have promoted energy efficiency and more healthy environments. Two of the most well-known of these started in the 1990s—the LEED rating system by the U.S. Green Building Council and Passive House Institute. In addition, the Living Building Challenge, WELL Building Standard, Minergie-P, and others add requirements for living in harmony with nature and human health. These all acknowledge that since we spend almost 90 percent of our time indoors, managing natural air flows is essential to human health.

However, the mere following of checklists and prescriptions to solve our ecological crisis or make us healthier is not enough. Many of these instruments have become detrimental to the very sustainable building strategies sought to be engendered by these schemas.

Today, much thinking in making buildings has become a race to meet the new compliance standard. Architects once sought to create buildings tuned between idea, place, and use. Today, buildings are out of tune, caught somewhere between fantasy, trade-offs, and prescriptive policy guidance that has forced architects to comply with an artificial standard, not a natural standard that accounts for living, breathing systems.

The quest for energy conservation over energy equilibrium described by Kiel Moe has had an *iatrogenic effect*. "Architects from Berlin to Dubai deploy the trope of 'sustainability' without any comprehension of the profound energetic misfit of the technique, its ecological cost, or its actual thermodynamic work."[68] This unintended consequence leads to "greenwashing." As stated by Moe,

> What constitutes sustainability is a set of commonsense set of decisions that should be at the core of any design practice, a basic fiduciary assumption. It no longer makes sense to differentiate sustainable practices from presumably unsustainable, yet taught, practices but rather to integrate these theories and practices directly into pedagogy and practice.[69]

We cannot substitute energy conservation or calculated environmental performance for quality. Aalto told us 50 years ago, "The victory of formulas would not be so dangerous if it were not a kind of lifebuoy which every architect wants to use to achieve good results."[70] Unfortunately, too many architects have subscribed to formulaic certificate achievement that greenwash deficiency in design. What happens in a building when we turn off the energy grid? Is it still habitable? Can we still breathe? Perhaps this is a good measure.

It has taken many years of deliberation to arrive at this point on the curve. It is time to ramp up and speed up our ecological response in designing and constructing buildings. If we do not, we will slip back down the embankment and float out to sea on the broken ice. Transforming the professional scope of architects towards modeling *wholeness*—not just an image of a building but an integrated fabrication that rewards *performance* (energy) and *optimization* (production)—is essential.

*Praxis* is the act of practice (including political action). *Praxis* + *Techne*, or production of that practice = *Poiesis*, or new production practice. This equates to an *Enviro-Poiesis* made available by transforming the relationship between craft + material and technology + optimization to create an ecological production standard that is measured and calculated by computational analysis.

One way of using a computer is for validating results. For example, consider a word processor automatically checking your spelling and grammar as you write your ideas. *Might we similarly use our design software?* Not to make our designs, but to check our parameters as we work towards a more thoughtful performance-driven architecture. Drawing science into architecture has always been difficult. However, computational design frameworks can install more accurate parameters to make quantitative adjustments around our qualitative design decisions.

With enhanced computer models of buildings, we can simulate realities that can be varied and actuated by understanding the worlds they serve. In addition, artificial reality will help expose how augmented reality architecture can stimulate our environment, body, and mind by moving away from representations.

Digital modeling enables architects, fabricators, and manufacturers to seamlessly integrate experimental systems into the construction process. As written by Mario Carpo, "Digital tools can be powerful allies of design-by-making because digital simulations can make or break more models in an instant than a physical craftsman could in a lifetime. And when a model works, whether a physical model or its digital equivalent, there may be no need to understand why."[71]

Methods of communication and architecture development require a return to a functional form that considers the environment, culture, social conditions, equity, the human condition, and physiology. We now have the opportunity to utilize simulations of environments to predict the performance and experience of architecture like never before.

Economic realities in construction and litigation make it difficult for architecture firms to experiment to the same degree as the architects of early modernism

**FIGURE 4.6** Photo, International Olympic Committee (IOC) Headquarters, Switzerland, 3XN, 2019

*(Credit:* 3XN, Adam Mørk).

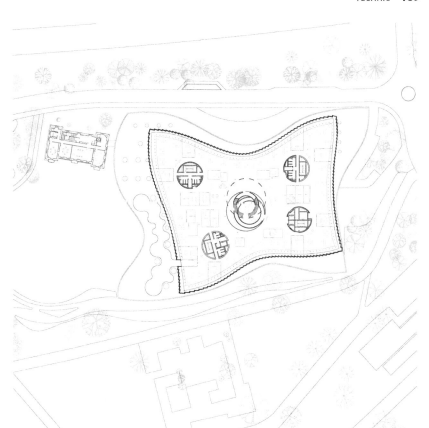

**FIGURE 4.7**   IOC Flexible Floor Plan

*(Credit:* 3XN) (3)

and before. However, with the advancement of technology and computational software, we can explore and test in a virtual setting. Kai Strehlke, Head of digital CAD/CAM processes at Blumer-Lehmann AG, tells us that "testing and developing the idea using a mock-up in the design phase with the client and manufacturer provides architects and designers with important insights for production and assembly logistics, quality, and costs. Or, in one word: certainty."[72] Enabling architects to maintain an exploratory practice requires digital competency. Architectural education precedes and advances this new paradigm.

## The International Olympic Committee Headquarters

In Lausanne, Switzerland, 3XN worked to consolidate the functions of the Olympic Committee into one new building campus at Louis-Bourget Park (Figure 4.6). The IOC HQ is designed around transparency, flexibility,

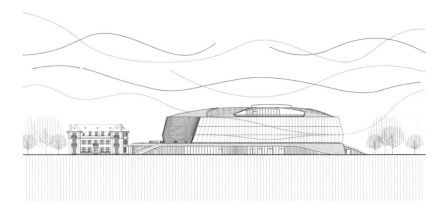

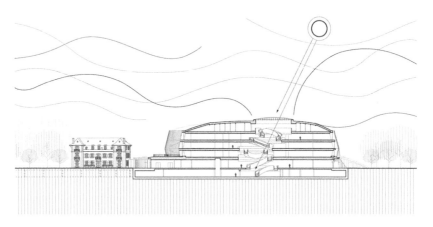

**FIGURE 4.8** IOC Elevation and Section

*(Credit:* 3XN) (3)

sustainability, and collaboration. It provides excellent lake views, and it is a metaphor for transparent, open organizational values. Its configuration and grounding provide the same amount of green space previously on the campus (Figure 4.7).

Jan Ammundsen, Head of Design at 3XN, said,

> With its dynamic, undulating facade, the building appears different from all angles and conveys the energy of an athlete in motion. Its interior is designed with as few structural constraints as possible. This open and flexible environment will adapt to multiple work styles now and in the future.

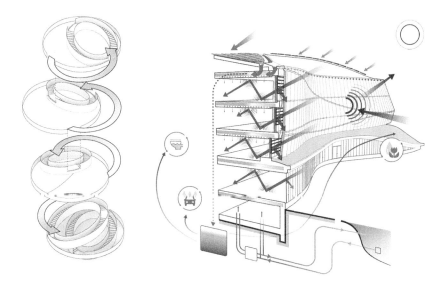

**FIGURE 4.9**   IOC Topological Stair and Façade System

*(Credit:* 3XN) (3)

The interior is a standard open office type with flexible planning and a non-standard interconnecting stair (Figure 4.8). The 'Unity Staircase,' evoking the interlocking rings of the Olympic emblem, supports opportunities for social interactions as one must transit half-arc of the central atrium to enter the next stair ring (Figure 4.9).

The main feature is the undulating, transparent, double-wall facade, designed using BIM and algorithm-aided parametric tools to anticipate and resolve the complex curved geometry. The high-performance parameters required a testable standard component system, but the assembly was formed using various elements; it is a flexible standard system. In addition, the double-wall enhanced energy management and integrated the sun-shading devices. Due to the compliance parameters, the entire wall assembly, whether rectilinear or curvilinear, is a mass-customization assembly (Figure 4.10).

The IOC HQ adopted and adapted three sustainable building certifications—LEED v4 Platinum with the highest score ever given, SNBS Platinum, and Minergie-P—making it the most sustainable office building globally. Minimized environmental footprint and maximized sustainable features represent the IOC's commitment not to compromise workplace quality or the environment. For example, the green roof, terraces, fitness center, and natural environment afforded by the built form and floor plan provide an opportunity for employees to become re-energized throughout the day. In addition, rainwater capture and other features significantly reduce water usage while solar panels located on

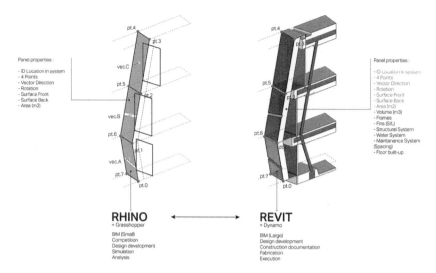

**FIGURE 4.10**  IOC Parametric Panel System Software Diagram

*(Credit:* 3XN)

the roof (and out of sight) reduce electricity consumption from the city grid (Figure 4.11).

## The Swatch Headquarters

The Swatch Headquarters in Biel, Switzerland, is composed of a stacked, four-story concrete building covered with a wooden grid-shell roof. By testing the limits of wood, Shigeru Ban reminds us that wood is our only truly renewable construction material (Figure 4.12).

The shell structures are made of spruce timber from Swiss forests. "A total of just under 1,997 cubic meters of this was needed, a quantity that regrows in the Swiss forest in less than two hours."[73] Considering ecological tectonics in viewing Ban's portfolio of work, we see many experiments with wood. For Ban, wood is simultaneously structure and finish (Figure 4.13). He remarks that "when fabrication is done off-site, building with timber is quiet, fast, and precise. It can make finish materials unnecessary—and it has a pleasant smell."[74]

Parametric and computation tools along with CNC fabrication machines enabled this project to successfully transition from design to construction. According to Hermann Blumer, founder of the engineering firm Création Holz, the roof is an arched bridge, its forms are familiar and well understood. Compound curves made with wood present little fabrication difficulty; the problem was integrating the building infrastructure (Figure 4.14).

**FIGURE 4.11**   Photo, The Swatch Headquarters, Switzerland, Shigeru Ban Architects, 2019

(*Credit:* Blumer–Lehmann AG)

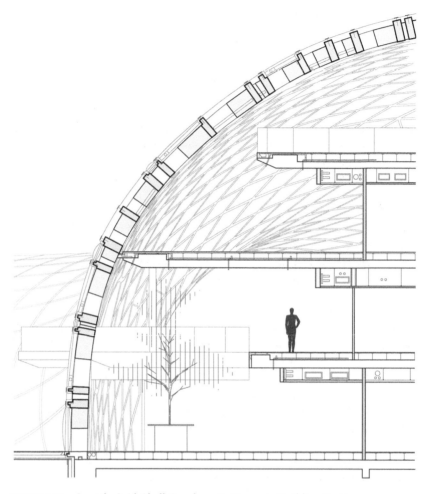

**FIGURE 4.12**  Swatch Grid-Shell Envelope & Concrete Building Section

The building's infrastructure includes lighting, sprinkler, ventilation for radiant heating and cooling in the ceilings, and the thermal performance and photovoltaics on the exterior skin. A number of cut-outs and channels are made in layers to accommodate these systems. Noise and acoustic control were also factors. This assembly had to be lightweight and thin, which required significant design engineering that could only be accomplished using BIM and parametric three-dimensional planning. Groundwater is used as a supplemental heat source to reduce heating and cooling significantly (Figure 4.15).

The state-of-the-art skin material assembly was carefully designed and configured to achieve low-energy construction. The complex integration of metal panels, with retractable shading, and transparent ethylene tetrafluoroethylene

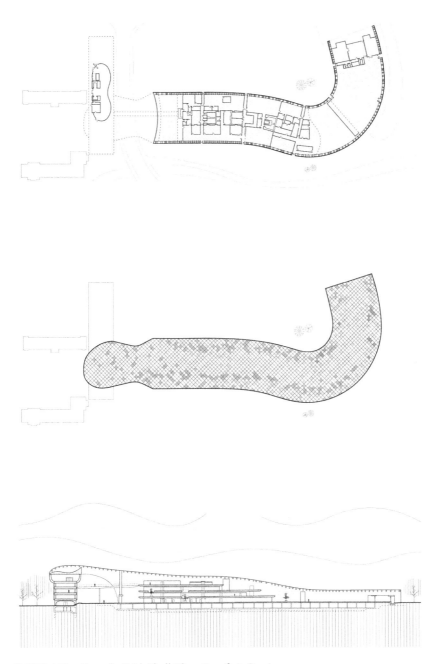

**FIGURE 4.13** Swatch Grid-Shell Plan, Roof, & Section

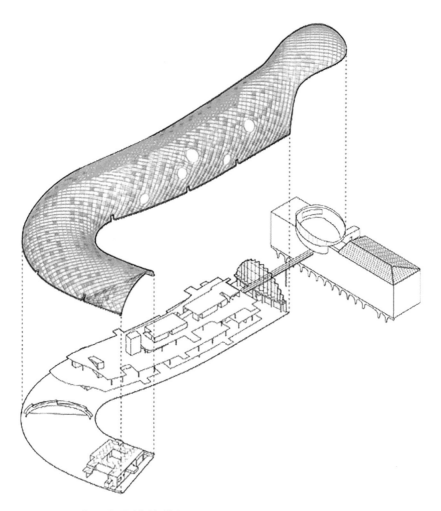

**FIGURE 4.14**  Swatch Grid-Shell Axonometric

(ETFE) cushion assembly (a plastic polymer to reduce weight) were made to clip into cut-outs designed and fabricated in the wood structure. The digital model helped calculate the overall geometry and optimize the interfaces and material connections (Figure 4.16). In all, over 7,000 different shapes make up this assembly. Without the use of wood, the design and its fabrication would have been implausible.

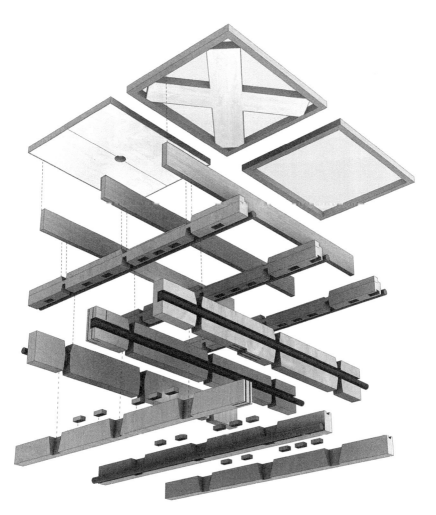

**FIGURE 4.15**   Swatch Integrated Components Exploded Axon Diagram

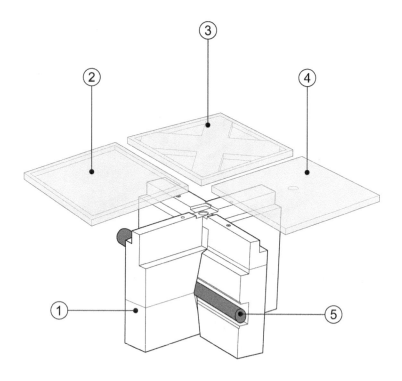

1. Grid-Shell - Timber Framing System
2. Grid-Shell - Transparent Panel
3. Grid-Shell - Shading Panel
4. Grid-Shell - Infrastructure Metal Panel
5. Grid-Shell - Embedded Infrastructure Piping

**FIGURE 4.16**  Swatch Integrated Components Diagram

## Notes

1  Aalto, Alvar. 'The Human Factor,' *Alvar Aalto in His Own Words*. Ed. Schildt, Göran. Otava, 1997, p.280 (Aalto).
2  ibid.
3  ibid.
4  Aalto, Alvar. 'Taide ja Tekniikka (Art and Technology),' in *Sketches*. Ed. Aalto, Alvar. MIT Press, 1978, p.174 (Aalto—Sketches).
5  Aalto, 'The Human Factor,' pp.281, 283.
6  Speech at the Helsinki University, by Alvar Aalto.
7  Negroponte, Nicholas. 'Towards Humanism Through Machines,' *Architectural Design*, Volume 6–7 September 1969, John Wiley & Sons Ltd.
8  https://avalon.law.yale.edu/ancient/hamframe.asp. Code #229 "If a builder builds a house for someone, and does not construct it properly, and the house which he built

fall in and kill its owner, then that builder shall be put to death." And #230 "If it kills the son of the owner the son of that builder shall be put to death."

9  Moretti, Luigi. 'Ricerca Matematica in Architettura e Urbanistica,' *Moebius*, Volume 4, Number 1, 1971, pp.20–53.

10  https://www.google.com/search/howsearchworks/algorithms/ (Accessed 05 March 2022).

11  Mitchell, William. 'Ch. 2: The Computer's Role in Design,' in *Computer-Aided Architectural Design*. Van Nostrand Reinhold, 1979, p.29.

12  Negroponte, Nicholas. *Beyond Digital*. https://web.media.mit.edu/~nicholas/Wired/WIRED6-12.html (Accessed 05 March 2022).

13  Aalto, 'The Reconstruction of Europe,' p.154.

14  Pallasmaa, Juhani. *Alvar Aalto: Between Humanism and Materialism*. MoMA, 1998, pp.34–35.

15  Aalto, 'Rationalism and Man,' p.92.

16  Aalto, Alvar. *Artek and the Aaltos: Creating a Modern World*. Bard Graduate Center, 2016, p.195. A great resource on Aalto and Standardization.

17  Schnaidt, Claude. *Hannes Meyer: Buildings, Projects and Writings*. Niggli, 1965.

18  Aalto, 'The Humanizing of Architecture,' pp.102–103.

19  Aalto, 'The Reconstruction of Europe,' pp.154–155.

20  ibid, p.155.

21  ibid.

22  Jencks, Charles. 'Semiology and Architecture,' in *Signs, Symbols, and Architecture*. Wiley, 1980, p.16.

23  Aalto, Alvar. 'Architecture in Karelia,' in *Karjalan rakennustaide*, Uusi Suomi, 2 November 1941, Citation from Frampton, Kenneth, *Modern Architecture*, 1980, chap. 22, opening quotation.

24  Aalto, Alvar. *The Architectural Drawings of Alvar Aalto*. Garland Pub, 1994, Image #88/1244.

25  ibid.

26  Aalto, 'The Reconstruction of Europe,' p.156.

27  Aalto, *The Architectural Drawings of Alvar Aalto*, Image #88/1244.

28  Ban, Shigeru. 'The Architect and Society,' in *Alvar Aalto: Through the Eyes of Shigeru Ban*. Black Dog Publishing, 2007, p.98.

29  Hoffmann, Holger. 'Alvar Aalto's Associative Geometries,' in *Alvar Aalto Researchers' Network Seminar—Why Aalto?*, Jyväskylä, 9–10 June 2017.

30  Porphyrios, Demetri, and Aalto, Alvar. *Sources of Modern Eclecticism: Studies on Alvar Aalto*. Academy Editions, 1982, p.106.

31  Aalto, Alvar. *The Complete Works*. Birkhäuser Verlag GmbH, 2014, Volume I, p.262.

32  Aalto, 'The Reconstruction of Europe,' pp.149–157.

33  Aalto, *The Complete Works*, p.262.

34  Oxman, Rivka. 'Introduction,' *The New Structuralism*, Volume 4, 2010, p.20.

35  Aalto, Alver. 'The Influence of Construction and Material in Modern Architecture,' in *Synopsis: Painting, Architecture, Sculpture*. Birkhäuser, 1970, p.23.

36  For additional context, see Abalos, Iñaki. 'Thermodynamic Materialism,' in *Essays on Thermodynamics*. Architecture and Beauty, 2014.

37  Frampton, Kenneth. *Aalto in Retrospect Six Foci for the Next Millennium*. Domus, 1998, pp.45–56.

38  Aalto, 'The Humanizing of Architecture,' p.104.

39  Aalto, 'Wood as a Building Material,' *Arkkitehti*, Volume 6–7, 1956, pp.101–102.

40  Frampton, *Aalto in Retrospect Six Foci for the Next Millennium*, pp.52–53.

41  An elaborate description by the Aalto Foundation of the design and fabrication process of the chair and stool can be found here https://artsandculture.google.com/exhibit/a-stool-makes-history-alvar-aalto-museo/QRQs-mBx?hl=en (Accessed 05 March 2022).

42 Jones, Vincent, Neufert, Ernst, and Thackara, John. *Architects' Data*. Granada, 1980, p.1.

43 Aalto, 'The Influence of Construction and Material in Modern Architecture,' p.13.

44 Aalto, Alvar. 'Art and Technology,' in *Aalto, Sketches*. MIT Press, 1985, p.127.

45 Pallasmaa, *Alvar Aalto: Between Humanism and Materialism*, p.21.

46 Aalto, 'The Flexible Stair,' p.165.

47 ibid., p.166, for Standardization Office Building Card.

48 Vossoughian, Nader, Aalto, Alvar, and Neufert, Ernst. 'Architectural Standardization in Germany and Finland, 1933–45,' *The Journal of the Society of Architectural Historians*, Volume 79, Number 2, June 2020, 202–212.

49 https://www.lehmann-gruppe.ch/en/timber-construction/free-form.html (Accessed 05 March 2022).

50 Gramazio, Fabio and Kohler, Matthias. *Digital Materiality in Architecture*. Prestel Pub, 2008, p.7.

51 https://www.lehmann-gruppe.ch/en/news/allgemein/urbach-turm.html (Accessed 05 March 2022).

52 Pallasmaa, *Alvar Aalto: Between Humanism and Materialism*, p.35.

53 Aalto, 'The Influence of Construction and Material in Modern Architecture,' p.100.

54 Aalto, 'Reconstruction of Europe,' p.154.

55 Pallasmaa, Juhani. *Architecture of the Essential: Ecological Functionalism of Animal Construction*. https://www.animalarchitecture.org/juhani-pallasmaa/ (Accessed 05 March 2022).

56 Pawlyn, Michael. *Biomimicry in Architecture*. RIBA Publishing, 2019, p.4.

57 Julian Vincent as quoted in Pawlyn, *Biomimicry in Architecture*. RIBA Publishing, 2019, p.9.

58 Aalto, 'Wood as a Building Material,' pp.101–102.

59 Barber, Daniel A. *Modern Architecture and Climate: Design Before Air Conditioning*. Princeton University Press, 2020, p.14.

60 Taylor, Brian Brace. *Le Corbusier, the City of Refuge, Paris 1929/33*. University of Chicago Press, 1987, p.80.

61 For more details see, Ford, Edward R. *The Details of Modern Architecture*. MIT Press, 2003, pp.120–127.

62 Aalto, 'The Humanizing of Architecture,' p.106.

63 ibid, p.107.

64 Kiesler, Frederick. 'On Correalism and Biotechnique. *A* Definition and Test of a New Approach to Building Design,' *Architectural Record*, Volume 86, Number 3, September 1939, pp.60–75.

65 Charrington, Harry. *An Agency of Endless Play: Alvar Aalto & Frederick Kiesler*. Working papers—Alvar Aalto Researchers' Network, 12–14 March 2012, Seinäjoki and Jyväskylä.

66 Aalto, 'The Reconstruction of Europe,' p.153.

67 Barber, *Modern Architecture and Climate*, pp.236–237.

68 Moe, Kiel. 'Iatrogenic Architecture "Compelling Yet Unreliable Theories of Sustainability",' *Journal of Architectural Education*, Volume 60, Number 4, 2007. pp.24–30.

69 ibid.

70 Speech at the Helsinki University, by Alvar Aalto.

71 Mario Carpo, 'Digital Indeterminism: The New Digital Commons and The Dissolution of Architectural Authorship,' in *Architecture in Formation: On the Nature of Information in Digital Architecture*. Ed. Lorenzo-Eiroa, Pablo. Taylor & Francis, 2013.

72 https://www.lehmann-gruppe.ch/en/timber-construction/leistungen/parametrische-planung-programmierung.html (Accessed 05 March 2022).

73 Courtesy of Swatch PR International and Shigeru Ban Architects.

74 Courtesy of Shigeru Ban Architects.

# 5

# THERMODYNAMIC—HEALTH AND INSTRUMENTS OF SENSATION

---

**Thermodynamics** = the interaction between forms of mass and energy, and our perception.
(*Thermós*: "warm, hot" + Dúnamai "I am able" thus, the capability to exchange hot or cold)

---

As architects continue to use technology and science to inform their work, parametric design and subsequent digital fabrication tools have assisted by delivering considerable leaps forward. Bioscience and neuroscience are the sciences needed now to advance our work. We need to consider a more symbiotic balance between buildings, ecology, and bodies. Flows of energy, heat, and air need to be better managed and predicted. Stimulus between building and our body should be more tuned and enhance our perceptual system. We can make buildings more responsive to environmental and temporal change by developing a more thermodynamic architecture.

There are two realms considering thermodynamic responsiveness: *Literal* (Active) and *Phenomenal* (Perceived). The literal or active sensations derive from conduction, convection, and radiation thermodynamic forces. The phenomenal or perceived are those sensations experienced through corporeal impressions. Together these heighten somatic pleasure and influence neurobiological perceptions.

DOI: 10.4324/9781003160571-6

In the 1963 essay 'Transparency: Literal and Phenomenal,' Colin Rowe (1920–99) and Robert Slutsky (1929–2005) described the double reading of the word transparency as both literal, like seeing through a window, and phenomenal, as in layered readings or positions within a work of art or architecture. The purpose was to describe how architects see things differently.

These phenomenal notions play with our awareness and reading of a work of art or architecture. However, there is a third notion of transparency: exposing the fact of a situation, a phenomenal hyper-literal state where we have someone see what is before us, define what to see, and feel what is physically present; to work between that part of our mind that looks for order and information and the other part that looks for meaning and feeling.

In this reading of the literal and phenomenal, architects deal with the transposition of elemental facts and atmospheric imaginations. The physical qualities of material thereby correlate with the atmosphere, the mood, and the subsequent perception of a work. Measures of perceived fact and feeling are through body and mind in how the material of our work shapes physical and mental qualities. These psychophysical associations form sensory experiences detected through innate and imagined neurological connections when bound together.

Maurice Merleau-Ponty (1908–61), in *Eye and Mind* (1964), conditioned that it is by "lending his body to the world that the artist changes the world into paintings."[1] The artist's body is within the work, and the paint projects matter of the world. In this, we can "touch" the world of the artist by "seeing" through their envisioned image. In addition, through fundamental matter, the artist can evoke sense and sensation by guiding our mental imagination and psychological perception. This "intertwining" or "overlapping" is the situated embodiment of the artist's work, and it is true of painting and sculpture as well as architecture.

In *Intertwining* (1996), Steven Holl tells us:

> the experience of material in architecture is not just visual but tactile, aural, olfactory; it is all of these intertwined with space and our bodily trajectory in time. Perhaps no other realm more directly engages multiple phenomena and sensory experience than the haptic realm.

He also reminds us that "our body moves through and, simultaneously, is coupled with the substances of architectural space [and matter]—the 'flesh of the world' (Maurice Merleau-Ponty)."[2]

In discussing *Embodied Experience and Sensory Thought* (2007), Juhani Pallasmaa wrote, "an artistic work has an impact on our mind before it is understood" and "the foremost skill of the architect is, likewise, turning the multi-dimensional essence of the design task into an embodied image; the entire personality and body of the architect become the site of the problem."[3] Sarah Goldhagen writes, through a notion of *embodied rationalism*, Aalto and his body of work are situated in time and place such that a "sensitivity to site, season, place, and memory inevitably, naturally, figures into a phenomenologically grounded modernist architecture."[4]

These thoughts on intertwining matter and perception bring us back to the beginning of our discussion, to the purpose of architecture as a topological body of elements and atmospheres formed and assembled as literal and phenomenal experiences.

Observing sensations and perceptions has always been the way of attunement between our body and mind and the environment. The baths of Rome, the Finnish sauna, the Japanese irori, and the hearth develop social bonds through rituals, ceremonies, and shared experiences around different places and cultures. The situational experiences augment through a technic of material and spatial arrangement by which we experience a thermodynamic delight.

Kiel Moe writes,

> The ancient Roman bathing complexes represent a compelling example of an architecture that is thoroughly thermodynamic in its conception, design, and use but one that resists modern—if not to say reductive—social, formal, and technical characterizations . . . as its form is based on a composite reading of space, matter, energy, and time.[5]

Peter Zumthor's Therme Vals (1996) resists Moe's remark that modern architecture cannot have a thermodynamic conception. Therme Vals situates thermodynamics by establishing a relationship to the mountain and its hot spring. The building becomes part of its natural setting. Zumthor stated,

> there was a feeling for the mystical nature of a world of stone inside the mountain, for darkness and light, for the reflection of light upon the water, for the diffusion of light through steam-filled air, for the different sounds and water makes in stone surroundings, for warm stone and naked skin, for the ritual of bathing.[6]

We learn from Zumthor that engaging the body in space and observing the body's boundaries is an empathetic way of *seeing* the wholeness of our choices. These boundary decisions develop demarcation, threshold, sequence, and sensation, primarily by thermal change and bodily experience, not merely aesthetics or theoretical discourse.

Aalto, too, understood this empathy in building through haptic thermodynamic sensation. The sauna is a whole shared experience of Finnish culture. There are five million inhabitants and over three million saunas in Finland—an average of one per household. For many Finns, a sauna is a sacred place. In many buildings, including his home, and Muuratsalo, Aalto endowed the sauna with a memorable if not ritual identity. The sauna at the Villa Mairea anchors the body of the building through traditional expression to the phenomenal abstraction of the forest. The space of the forest is drawn in by the position, material, view, and formal character of the sauna. It is an existential association where the *body of building* conforms to the *body of man* as the image of the forest situates both the building and one's metaphorical imagination.

The forest in Finland is a provincial and cultural atmosphere. In the Kalevala, the national epic poem, adventures, beliefs, and rites of the forest-dwelling, where the space of nature is a critical aspect of Finnish identity. As written by Richard Weston,

> This conception of *'forest space'* provides a key to understanding Aalto's intentions in the Villa Mairea. Walking around the living room, one experiences . . . something very much akin to the feeling of wandering through a forest in which spaces seem to form and re-form around you: in a forest. The individual feels himself to be the moving center of its spaces. For Aalto, such *'forest space'* provided both a means of *'naturalizing'* his architecture and also of achieving a *'democratic,'* non-hierarchical organization conceived around 'the small man' for whom he wished to build.[7]

The situatedness of the forest inside the Umwelt of Aalto displays how an association with nature can constitute the entire concept of dwelling and the experience necessary to dwell.

Underlying provincial and cultural undertones aside, the sauna and the baths require pure physical thermodynamic action for conditioning the body for sensual pleasure. In describing thermodynamics, Philippe Rahm states,

> The problem of global warming has placed the relationship between climate and architecture at the center of current preoccupations. In order to assume our responsibility in the face of these new ecological concerns, we must make the most of the moment in order to reappraise the field of architecture in a broader way, extending it to other dimensions, other perceptions, from the physiological to the atmospheric, from the sensorial to the meteorological, from the gastronomic to the climatic.[8]

As our understandings of society, ecology, capital, science, and the dissemination and use of information have evolved, so should architecture. As we look to trade old models for new ones, we should learn from examples that relate to the now continuous flow of people, energy, capital, material, and data in a thermodynamic exchange.

## Thermodynamical Systems

Thermodynamics studies the relationship between heat, work, and associated energy flows. In physics, according to Enrico Fermi, "Thermodynamics is mainly concerned with the transformations of heat into mechanical work and the opposite transformations of mechanical work into heat. . . . The first law of thermodynamics is essentially the statement of the principle of the conservation of energy for thermodynamical systems. As such, it may be expressed by stating that the variation in energy of a system during any transformation is equal to the amount of energy that the system receives from its environment."[9]

For purposes of our discussion, the second law of thermodynamics conditions that "if we bring two bodies at different temperatures into thermal contact, heat flows spontaneously by conduction from one of these bodies to the other"[10] and that conversion of energy can never reach 100 percent efficiency. In other words, energy cannot be created or destroyed. It can only change its form or transfer from one object to another; lamps convert electricity into light, or better, how plants convert sunlight into energy, or how our body reacts to the body of a building. It also states that heat moves from warmer to cooler, air moves from higher pressure to lower pressure, and moisture moves from wetter to drier. Most of the unusable energy takes the form of heat (like a lamp), and in buildings, heat is a nemesis or a redeemer.

There are three types of systems in thermodynamics: open, closed, and isolated. *Open systems*, like those in biological systems, exchange both energy and matter with their surroundings. Like a mechanical system, *closed systems* exchange only energy with their surroundings, not matter. Finally, like a beverage cooler, *isolated systems* separate the inside from the outside, exchanging very little energy with the outside environment.

Thermodynamics refers to the work and transformation or transduction of this energy. The system stores, exchanges and gives off energy and information. We consider how these flows pass through or block energy from entering the system in buildings. Our surroundings provide helpful energy that can interact with mass and void. We can make architecture that accounts for thermal performance by choosing materials and passive and active systems that synergize energy flows.

In biology, thermodynamics is metabolism, transduction of energy into life. Bodies in nature take energy from their environment and transform it into valuable energy. Unlike a mechanical system, natural systems exchange energy and entropy together. As an organism is a system,[11] might we reevaluate buildings as biological, open systems rather than closed and isolated environments?

In architecture, thermodynamics is the fundamental relationship between forms of material mass and its integral void. Likewise, our bodies partake in thermodynamical systems, constantly exchanging energy with the material we touch and the air we breathe. Choosing how energy gets produced and consumed, how to place matter, arrange voids, and how the system opens and closes to its environment comprises thermodynamic architecture.

## Thermodynamic Materialism

The three primary forces considering the thermodynamic performance of a material entity are as follows. 1) Conduction, transfer of heat between objects when in contact, 2) Convection, transfer of heat by flows, 3) Radiation, transfer of heat from a warm entity through space to a cooler entity.

A fireplace is the archetype of thermodynamics in architecture. It is a conductor of heat energy into surrounding material, a convector that moves air through cold and hot flows, and a radiator as we feel the warmth from the body of the fire. As a warm body, a fireplace attracts, and its gentle illumination invites. It is an example where elemental matters of earth, air, water, and fire (atmospheres of energy and light) thermodynamically manipulate the conditions of the body and excite the mind. For Semper, this was a tectonic element, while Frank Lloyd Wright adds that "the hearth is the psychological center of the home."

Thermodynamics plays a vital role in sensory physiology and sensation. Human comfort and perception are essential to architecture. Material and form choices can produce a psychophysical impact as architecture equally shares mental and physical qualities. This thermodynamic effect is contingent upon material and enhancing the haptic experience of the five senses and reactions to stimuli.

Psychophysics is the analysis of perceptual relationships between physical stimuli and mental phenomena. The qualitative aspect measures the probability of a particular judgment of a catalyst. "From this, we are able to precisely quantify what stimulus information observers are able to perceive, remember, and use to guide their actions."[12] Therefore, we can consider the measure of thermodynamics as a literal balance of hot and cold that assimilates phenomenal material perception.

The essence of *Thermodynamic Materialism* is a synergistic design process that gathers materials and masses required to organize spaces as conductive, convective channels integral to the architectural concept. It is a topology of experience where cognitive and physical converge through embodied perception. This concept of materialism accounts for energy flows and responds to orientation, use, material, and physiology. Using thermodynamics as a principle form generator can be a potent agent in developing more sensory-rich buildings. Using Philippe Rahm's suggestion, thermodynamics in "architecture should no longer build spaces, but rather create temperatures and atmospheres."[13]

Perception of convection, conduction, and radiation is determined by scheduling how the body inhabits, moves through, and perceives an environment. The effect is an everyday body of experience enhanced by intelligent concepts and engaging forces of nature. J.J. Gibson's concept of *affordance* can help us contemplate affective perception. Affordance implies that person and environment are complementary. A natural environment provides a place (habitat) to live, but the built environment affords a place (shelter) to dwell. We perceive architecture in terms of what it affords in complementing sensory experience. The affordances we encounter in architecture are active and real, not abstract, and the emotions they arouse are active, too, not just the result of imagination.

Understanding a thermodynamical system related to the body and the body of a building is a material relationship that forms the elemental or atmospheres in architecture. Using response-driven formations, porous envelopments, productive materials, and synergistic fabrications, we can make buildings perform better respecting our metabolism, thermal sensations, and circadian rhythms.

For Aalto, this completeness of material and function is an organic process where various parts become fully integrated like organs in a body. This living form, a thermodynamic system, is evidenced in his later works. Juhani Pallassma describes Aalto's architecture not as assemblies of building components but as "creatures." The buildings live in their environment. Through an embodiment of landscape and *archi-technical* form, a proto-thermodynamic architecture emerges.

## The Healthy Body and its Sensory System

According to Sarah Robinson, a body metaphor opens a more complex yet subtle understanding of architectural potentiality:

> Like our body, the building is a series of interrelated systems, each possessing its own identity and offering a particular array of affordances. The mind is nested in the body, and the body is nested within the contexts of a room, building, city, earth, universe. We could say that our body has, nested within it, at least four bodies: our physical body, and the more ephemeral, but equal the real, emotional body, mental body, and social body.[14]

In 1925, Le Corbusier wrote that "feeling perceives and reason confirms," and later in 1931, that "joys of the body are interdependent to intellectual sensations in a symbolism having strong, sober, even basic roots: physiology and lyricism."[15]

In 1926, Rudolph Schindler (1887–1953) wrote a series of essays titled "Care of the Body" for the *Los Angeles Times*, describing how technical aspects of building construction: ventilation, plumbing and health, heating, lighting, and furniture provide feeling and how these design elements naturally purpose our healthy body.

In 1940, Aalto wrote in 'The Humanizing of Architecture,'

> It is not the rationalization itself that was wrong in the first and now past period of modern architecture. The wrongness lies in the fact that the rationalization has not gone deep enough. Instead of fighting rational

mentality, the newest phase of Modern architecture tries to project rational methods from the technical field out to human and psychological fields . . . Technical Functionalism is correct only if enlarged to cover even the psychophysical field. That is the only way to humanize architecture.

The Paimio Sanatorium completed in 1932 provides an example of this *human body* approach to architecture incorporating the body in the design through technical strategies required to serve it. Here, the building designed to comfort the body is the central focus, a *somatic* plan.

Aalto was sick at the time of the Paimio design competition. As a result, he stayed in bed for an extended period, and this influenced many of his decisions. The patient room exemplified his attention to mind and body (Figure 5.1). The patient in bed was the dominant figure in the room, and around was a series of organized events and compassionate considerations. The ceiling detail, window, floor to wall curvature, lighting, plumbing, heating system, occupancy symbols, and even the door handles—bent so a coat pocket wouldn't catch—were innovations designed for functionality to support both the patient and nurse.

In 1956, Aalto later explained,

> The main purpose of the building is to function as a medical instrument . . . one of the prerequisites for healing is to provide complete peace . . . The room design is determined by the depleted strength of the patient, reclining in his bed. The color of the ceiling is chosen for quietness, the light sources are outside of the patient's field of vision, the heating is oriented towards the patient's feet, and the water runs soundlessly from the taps to make sure that no patient disturbs his neighbor.[16]

The instrumentalization continues in the collective and utility rooms. The spaces have empathetic arrangements that affect our somatic psychology; Aalto's elemental form combined psycho-function with the atmospheric. Aalto, in 'The Humanizing of Architecture,' also described experiments combating what he described as "dysfunctional architecture," starting at Paimio:

> I was able to discover that special physical and psychological reactions by patients provide good pointers of ordinary housing. If we proceed from technical functionalism, we shall discover that a great many things in our present architecture are unfunctional from the point of view of psychology, or a combination of psychology and physiology. To examine how humans, react to forms and constructions, it is useful to use for experimentation especially sensitive persons, such as patients in a sanatorium.[17]

The bright yellow stairs and the terraces with colorful and minimal functional surfaces are still used today, not just here at Paimio, but as a model for healthcare

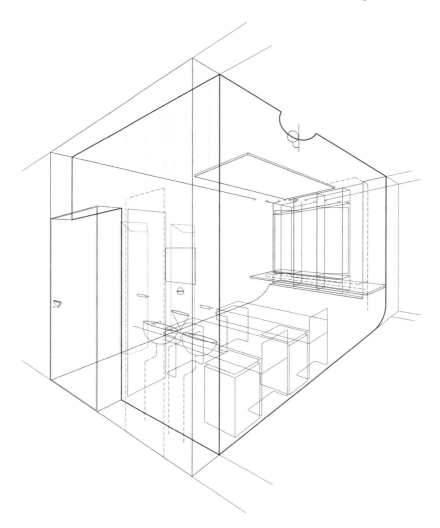

**FIGURE 5.1** The Paimio Room

in general. The bright spaces nested in the building provide views of the trees and offer a peaceful atmosphere. The terraces are oriented and, positioned towards the sun, afford thermodynamic experience by basking in the light—at the time, the only prophylactic for tuberculosis. This responsiveness is now expected in any caring environment.

During and after Paimio, the Aaltos designs took on an atmosphere of health. His terms of psychology, psychophysical, extended rationalism, and technical rationalism, continued to inform and extend into bioscience, neurophysiology, and mental well-being. As written by Pallasmaa, "Alvar Aalto's Paimio

Sanatorium is not only a metaphor of healing; even today, it offers the promise of a better future."[18]

## The Conditions of Atmosphere

According to Javier Garcia-German in his book *Thermodynamic Interactions* (2017), thermodynamics in architecture can develop *territorial atmospheres*, how a building is situated to take advantage of flows of energy from its environment; *material atmospheres*, the interaction between the indoor atmosphere and its material system; and *physiological atmospheres*, the somatic and perceptual exchange of an energy experience between the body and the body of a building.

A territory is an area of control that governs and is governed by its environment. Consequently, buildings influence immediate surroundings, and collections of buildings impact a region. For example, the Villa Rotunda is visually stimulating and climactic. The building is positioned in optimal orientation, approximately 45 degrees north. The bi-axial quadrants annex outdoor seasonal activity. Flows of air pass directly from one side to another, utilizing window and door alignments, and air currents from the lower level—cave-like in section—flow to cool the building by convection.

A building or grouping of buildings can also govern an environment. Describing microclimates, weather, and dynamical systems, Philippe Rahm tells us: "architecture is a thermodynamic mediation between the macroscopic and the microscopic, between the body and space, between the visible and the invisible, between meteorological and physiological functions."[19] The architect Luis Barragan makes courtyards with fountains and reflecting pools, developing evaporative cooling and enacting a meteorological architecture. The water devices use thermodynamic phenomena with evaporation, reflection, color, light, and sound to cool the air and the mind through somatic sensation.

The saliency of this thermodynamic experience comes from the courtyard gradient made by evaporation and the surrounding walls containing air and pressuring its flow into the surrounding rooms. This cooling effect is enhanced by the precinct walls' shadow, influencing a micro-weather system by changes in hot and cold. Air flows over the courtyards create eddies by stirring up the cool air and driving its passage through permeable boundaries.

These thermodynamic conditions design weather events. In *Atmosphere Anatomies: On Design, Weather, and Sensation* (2021),[20] Silvia Benedito describes this conditional environment as an immersive journey that leads to a spatial organization attentive to the body's episodic psychophysiological entanglement with the surrounding environment. Thermal thresholds between indoors and outdoors, liquid and vapor, private and public, architecture and landscape, establish thermal zones that offer climatic amelioration or amplification. These boundaries create microclimatic conditions that enhance psychological metabolism or activities and become program thresholds. They have shared situations that create spaces mutually dependent upon culture and climate to afford thermo-dynamic variation.

Returning to Rahm, "architecture should no longer build spaces, but rather create temperatures and atmospheres." Buildings can resolve temperature gradients, imaginations, and psychophysical engagements experienced through time and space. Our choice of materials sets up memory, emotion, and perception. Our arrangement of space sets up efficacy, encounter, and delight. We can use these to measure and impact expectations.

When conditioning the atmospheric quality of architectural space, we should imagine *touch*, in an existential sense, the experience of being-in-the-world, or more simply how the building *touches* us. Often, one's perception of material first comes through sight and expectation of touch, however, touch awareness is faster than sight recognition. The phenomenal touch amplifies the expectant sensation of the touch of the body. For example, sensing warmth is linked to tactility; it is a corporeal feeling.

Thus, as the philosopher Gernot Böhme suggests, atmospheres are *tempered spaces*. He describes,

> synaesthetic qualities such as course or cold, are so called because they are experienced using different sensory qualities that can mutually substitute for each other, for example, a room can seem cool because its painted blue, or because it is completely tiled. It is again corporeal feeling that drives the synaesthetic experience.[21]

Aalto intuitively comprehended the corporeality of architecture and how perception can drive synaesthetic experience. We can see this in the atrium piazza space of the Rautatalo Office Building (1955). The piazza is a three-story hollowed court inside of an eight-story office building (Figure 5.2). The material experience is quite striking; ceramic, marble, leather, bronze all invite sensual touch and visual delight, but it is the way that the light, lighting, color, and furniture suggest a feeling of the outside that makes this space so appealing. The design alters our perception through its built form, skylights and lighting, and through its provisional elements—the plantings, chairs, and tables.

Behind the planter is the interior café. One area has upholstered chairs and wooden tables. Beyond this are the blue-colored serving counter, ceramics, and light fixtures. Imagine the smell of your favorite dish moving across the piazza, possibly reminding you of an outdoor café in the Mediterranean. Each space produces different atmospheres, with elegance and reminiscence of faraway places in one, and provincial memory of azure sky, forest shadows, and blue of the flag of Finland in the other. Color and the varied tactile and visual relationships with changing intensities and types of illumination light up different areas of our minds, provoking a psychological atmosphere.

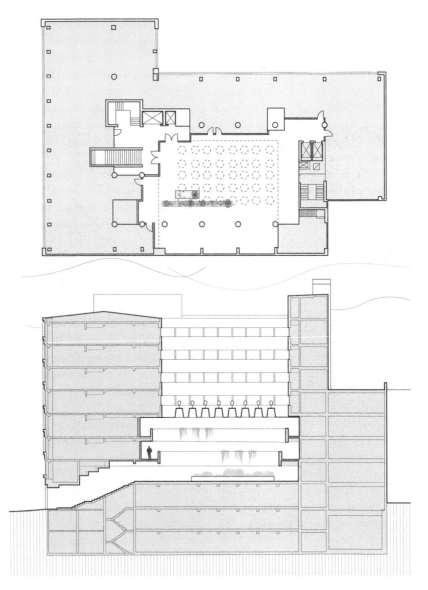

**FIGURE 5.2** Rautatalo Courtyard

For Barragan, space and atmosphere are principally outside, whereas for Aalto, space and atmosphere were wholly inside, with an illusory feeling of outdoors. Nevertheless, these architectures from different places had similar engagements with comfort and pleasure in a total sense. Thermal comfort, health comfort, sound comfort, and phycological comfort synergistically arrive by thermodynamic perception.

## Aalto's Instruments—The Super-Technical Creation

Aalto's *super-technical* approach embodied traditional architecture's sensory experience while assimilating a modern technic. His form-system combinations move us towards a more complete, potentially thermodynamically active, experientially influential form of architecture. He used instincts and experiments to resolve technical interrelationships. Viipuri Library is a compelling example of this complete comprehensive design thinking through technical reconciliation in service of the mind and body.

Aalto described the library as "the soul of the town's cultural life." Finland was liberated from the Russian Empire ten years before Aalto won the competition. It was important for the Aaltos to express ascension and enlightenment of culture both literally and metaphorically in the project. The design went through iterations, beginning with a principally neoclassical scheme, referencing the Stockholm Public Library by Gunnar Asplund, then a glass-covered reading room before gradually arriving at the final built form. Aalto said that he had the luxury of five years (the building completed in 1935) to develop ideas, designs, and details, revealing a process of evolution from a neoclassical past into a present future of architecture.

Like at Paimio, he and Aino Marsio-Aalto at Viipuri invested a great deal of time understanding the relationship of architectural form, material, furnishings, and interior conditioning. Through its many iterations, the project landed on a scheme that fulfilled Aalto's goal of creating a "fantastic mountain landscape with cliffs lit up by suns in different positions." His imaginary sketches developed into an interconnected flow of plan and section sequencing and functional rationality, joining the metaphor of landscape and light with technical precision.

A functional library, according to Aalto's conjunction—*reader, book, light*—must be connected with the human eye in that "the main human function in the building is that of reading a book. The eye is only a tiny part of the human body, but it is the most sensitive and perhaps the most important part." We discuss this further in the *phenomena of light*, but feel it would be remiss not to mention Aalto's point of view that light must be adapted to suit "the physiology of the eye and, going one step further, to the psychological needs of human beings."[22]

In developing satisfying illumination, skylights were shaped, arranged, and constructed so that daylight is indirect. According to Aalto, this "is humanly rational because it provides a kind of light suitable for reading, blended and softened by being reflected from the conical surfaces of the skylights." We can reference the influence of Asplund's rotunda and its embodied light within Aalto's round skylights.

Aalto's approach towards integrating daylight systems began at Turun, then at Paimio before being wholly fulfilled at Viipuri. The *super-technical* attention, in his words, involved human motive:

> The skylight system is a combined product of the ceiling (a room almost sixty feet wide needs a ceiling construction with beams high enough for

the erection of deep cones) and special technical limits in horizontal glass construction. An architectural solution must always have a human motive based on analysis.[23]

Advancing this description, Aalto provided a technical brief:

The main library section was built mostly without the use of interior walls, a rectangular shape, with an exceptionally strong wall laid of brick. The ventilation systems circulate in the windowless, 75-cm thick walls. The ceiling consists of one span of 17.6 meters. It is iron-concrete with special crossing formations, fitted thus due to the system of ceiling lights. In the ceiling, there are 57 conical holes (1.80 meters in diameter), which create the skylight system. The main premise of this lighting system is that the depth of the cones is so deep that 52-degree sunlight cannot freely access it, and the sunlight remains indirect throughout the year. This has made it possible to solve two architectural functions, protecting books from excessive sunlight, and creating such eye-hygienic general lighting conditions, that reading in the main hall, despite the position between the book and the person, will always remain free of shadows and reflections.[24]

An integrated radiant heating system was placed in the ceiling around the skylights and in regularly occupied locations that housed books. Since it was impossible to fit standard radiators in bookshelves, this customized system was considered rational.

The cellar contains a ventilation plan connected to ductwork that is distributed through floor channels at the perimeter and up into the upper reading room walls. The thick walls provide space for the ventilation system, insulation, and acoustic value, protecting readers from outside cold and noise. For this reason, the building retains heat very well and has a minimal need for cooling.

The radiant heating system in Viipuri is reminiscent of Roman hypocaust systems, with their warm floors and ventilated walls. As in the great baths, the building is thermodynamically active. The ventilation system supports this strategy by including enhanced air and heat exchange between the heating chamber and the mass walls. When cold, the air circulates. When warm, the air exhausts. "The heating in the ceiling was certainly supposed to keep the breathing space inside the double slab roof in a salubrious condition and prevent condensation of the skylights, a kind of 'active' insulation of the roof."[25]

The somatic sensation of heat from the ceiling advances Aalto's metaphoric *"many suns,"* perceptually making the building feel more open to the outside world. Connection with nature is presented by installing plants inside the entry hall's glass. Aino wrote in her diary a list of items needed for Viipuri including, "large pots for flowers, green vine in numerous places, and flowers for the children's library window plant holders for the windows."[26]

The Aaltos understood the effect that views of nature have on the mind. Plants were included in almost all projects, demonstrating a commitment to the idea of communing with nature. Vines and flowers were hung to make surfaces on walls or grown from planter boxes to make screens while also providing much-needed color radiance. Besides the scenic nature, the plantings create functional privacy, help reduce glare, and purify the air.

In 1984, Edward Wilson described *biophilia* as the human tendency to interact (or to be closely associated) with other forms of life in nature. Corroborated with neurological evidence, green surroundings and natural materials have beneficial impacts on our health. This biophilic response is not limited to plants and views of nature; it is also how we see our built environment in relation to the natural world.

Since buildings and cities now constitute our *natural habitat*, it makes sense to create environments that better develop and adapt to our living memory and thermodynamic bodily engagements. Connecting with nature is about topology and integrated landscapes. As explained by Nikos Salingaros, "Human beings connect psychologically and physiologically to structures embodying organized complexity more strongly than to environments that are either too plain or present disorganized complexity."[27]

Viipuri presents ordered complexity through its dynamic section. The building made of two simple offset rectangular blocks is deceptive. The internal organization progresses a field of overlapping boundaries, and the transitions are remarkable. The section changes create a topography of horizontal and vertical contours in a seamless, meandering journey, like that of climbing a mountain.

In the essay, 'Alvar Aalto's Open Plan Architecture as an Environmental Technology Device' (2012), Ulrike Passe describes the open section, resultant spatial system, and climactic envelope. She argues that the composition:

> gave Aalto the freedom to elaborate his free-flow open section and to create a well-tempered space for books and people (with thermal comfort during all seasons and no glare, while still perfectly lit), while no books were exposed to direct sunlight, thus enabling conditions for reading as close to nature as possible.[28]

Through analyzing the unique spatial system and its heating and ventilation strategy, Passe detects that "the only effective tool to visualize and quantify the cooling and ventilation potential of air movement in these complex interlocking spaces was a three-dimensional CFD (Computational Fluid Dynamics) simulation of the whole building."[29]

The incidental venturi effect exposed by the simulation may validate Aalto's intuitions but not his intentionality. Hypothetically speaking, if Aalto had the latest digital design tools and analysis techniques, a model simulating the flow of air and situated energy could have accomplished a more deliberate, entirely passive conditioned environment. Without this model, we can only speculate intuitions and intentions. Yet, the fact remains that the building's spatial organization, metaphor, and mechanical systems all work together, in connection with the mass and spatial arrangement, to condition our bodies and our mental perceptions.

## Conditioning the Mind

Throughout history, architects have described, made devices, and made drawings to help us see ideas for and in our world. Planimetric illustrations, perspectival images, isometric projections, and even digital models have one thing in common: they convey specified information intended to help us read the idealized, simulated reality of a work.

Until recent virtual models, drawings were crafted with outlines that convey impressions of depth and three-dimensional shapes. These drawings are revisions of mental images or sketch *views* that we express by impulse from our mental ideas or intentions. Studies have shown that the mind can understand the contour of a line drawing in much the same way that it perceives photographs; therefore, the sketch is a direct flow to project the images seen in our minds.

Physiological investigations of neural response to contours by neuroscientists David Hubel and Torsten Wiesel in the 1960s led to a transformational discovery that neurons in the primary visual cortex are tuned to the orientation of contours, responding to edges. This recognition of outline works similarly in responding to natural biological systems. These realizations fit precisely with artists' and architects' traditional instruments of representation.

Aalto developed a working method with contours that intuitively recognized the understandings of our visual minds. His drawings consisted of contouring, blending landscapes, building form, and detail. These drawings are representational considerations that, according to Aalto, architecture is a form of nature and conceived with organic intent. This type of drawing is not a ruled line but one of flexibility, allowing him to explore variation in his experiment with possibilities of surface, shape, boundary, and material. Thus, for Aalto, the act of drawing was *drawing out* and *bringing forth* from natural content and its contour; the continuous boundary surface as a representative topology of a site.

Accordingly, Pallasmaa tells us, "All art articulates this very boundary surface both in the experience of the artist and the viewer. In this sense, architecture is not only a shelter for the body, but it is also the contour of the consciousness, and an externalization of the mind."[30]

Aalto formed this mode of drawing early. His father was a land surveyor who worked in the forest industry. In his writings about his childhood, he described his father and his apprentices working at "the white table," where he would observe his father and later make his own drawings with all the maps surrounding him. Aalto tells us that "I learned—at the age of four, I believe—the philosophy of pencil and paper." To Aalto, the white table was "a neutral plane in combination with man, so neutral a plane that it can receive anything, depending on man's imagination and skill." The whole of his life was spent on that table. So we can imagine how these early experiences developed into the intuitive and practical methods used by him and his studio.

Intuitive cognition, one of two types of awareness for decision making, involves judgments and decisions based on unconscious situational pattern recognition. This kind of cognition exhibits large capacity and fast responses independent of conscious *executive* control. Intuition affords the ability to understand something immediately, without need for conscious reasoning. To be cognitive is the mental action or process of acquiring knowledge and understanding through thought, experience, and the senses.[31]

This review leads us to questions: How do architects maintain this drawing of information and representation (not speaking of photo-real renderings) within the realm of the digital model? And how could this virtual world, constructed without contour and edge, provide similar cognition?

Forms, like contours, are geometric and topological choices that architects work with, which are, in most cases, involved in defining spaces. For example, in lessons on art and design, the artist Paul Klee makes lesson #1, "let's take a line for a walk." The direction of the line infers movement and results in volumetric positioning—a similar drawing action can take place within most vector-based digital design tools. Fundamentally, points connect lines, lines join into shapes, and shapes extrude to solids. The difference is we when use tools not for *drawing* but for *coding* information. We then need to *process* encoding objects with data. It is not about geometry and edges; it is about topological interrelationships. The boundary or surfacing is still a contour, but not an edge—except when represented as such in a two-dimensional image.

When viewed in this way, form-making through digital processing can bring together *perception* (contour) and *action* (coding) into an action-specific and action-oriented perception, enhancing our perceptions of possibilities in the forms we create by endowing them with data. Like a baseball player who senses a ball differently than the average, we can gain similar prowess by using tools to enhance our ability to effectuate perception.

Perhaps this informs us about how a thinking process could embed itself within our working parameters or present circumstances in a given condition. Modeling these parameters provides opportunities to test and make form-systems and use elements that develop around the needs of a place, purpose, and people. We can also imagine how decisions are enhanced via modeling to discover how the form of a building can work within an existing ecology, perhaps develop a new ecology, and even make us feel better.

The mind perceives our modeling of space through a combination of systems. For example, the hippocampus learns and stores memories, the basal ganglia instrumentally resolves good and bad, and the cortex processes literal and phenomenal impressions to simulate real or imagined worlds.

With informed intuition, perceiving and doing are reciprocal acts. We know this to be accurate by understanding how mirror neurons react to both performed actions and observations in our minds. Mirror neurons respond to actions that we observe in others. This function has two parts: first, *WHAT* action is being done, and the second, *WHAT FOR* or *WHY* (Intention) the action is being done. Understanding our intentions is essential to acknowledge as this directly involves our actions, what is meant and experienced in our work.

Mirror neurons may also be involved in emotions and empathy. Our imagination helps us rectify the differences and consequences of our choices and actions. According to Pallasmaa, there are "two kinds or levels of imagination: one that projects formal and geometric images, [and] the other that simulates the actual sensory, emotive and mental encounter with the imagined entity."[32] The formal imagination deals primarily with sight through a topological, factual reading of form, shape, and objects. The empathic imagination involves other senses (touch, auditory, olfactory, etc.), which engage psychophysical feeling, reading of our sensory systems, and mental imagery, including qualities of experience, judgment, and mood.

We use these imaginations in design to evoke experiences of emotion or sensation. This mirroring is an embodied simulation, or a projected meaning of form made by simulating experiences and memories of a place before objectifying that simulation in material form. As explained by Pallasmaa, "A sensitive designer places him or herself in the role of anonymous user and tests the validity of the ideas through this imaginative personal projection."[33]

Aalto did not theorize but instead followed a holistic line of reason within a developed intuition and subconscious recall of *environmental memory*. This recall was about associating elements of our world into shape, figure, and sensory compositions. The assemblage of these elements was not only about *space*, but about the way mind and body perceive interconnectedness and how our senses interact with the immersive journey.

For instance, at Paimio, mind and body are psychologically and thermally sensitized:

> Thermoception relates to the discernment of temperature and the sensory response to it, imagined or real. Aalto painted the staircase floors bright yellow and encased the handrails of his metal banisters in wooden sleeves because he correctly intuited that people need only look at a wooden handrail in a sunny yellow stairwell to feel warmer. Perception is intersensory.[34]

This yellow color "evokes sunny optimism even in cold, cloudy days."[35]

The multi-sensory design processing intertwines hapticity, kinesthesia, and synesthesia. *Haptic* is our ability to experience by touching; we can think about climbing a stair or holding a handrail. *Kinesthesia* is our awareness of position and the movement associated with proprioception, the sense of your body and its parts in space. Visual cues and one's relative proximity to objects create aesthetic power, crossing thresholds or experiencing changes of light and heat can drive this sensation further. Finally, *synesthesia* is how our bodies produce impressions around these stimuli; associations of sound with shape, words with colors, producing "cross-sensory" phenomena. Together these present a *sixth sense* or what Pallasmaa defines as "our capacity to grasp qualitative atmospheric entities of complex environmental situations, without a detailed recording and evaluation of their parts and ingredients."[36] This sixth sense is our innate intuition and *super-perception* that, for architects, is likely our most important sense.

## Aalto's Sensibility—The Phenomena of Light

Contrasts define light. It is physically a particle and a wave, a measure of speed and distance, yet infinite, and perceived against darkness. Light is also metaphysical and associated with consciousness. Expressions like *Beginning to see the Light*, *In Light of . . .*, *To Bring to Light*, and countless others shed light on seeing the truth and being enlightened.

Otto von Simson perceives that

> the Gothic wall seems to be porous: light filters through it, permeating it, merging with it, transfiguring it . . . Light which is ordinarily concealed by matter, appears as the active principle: and matter is aesthetically real only insofar as it partakes of and is defined by the luminous quality of light.[37]

Louis Kahn tells us, "The sun never knew how wonderful it was until it fell onto the wall of a building."[38] Light distinguishes architectural form, by defining surface with shadow, and shadow formation made with combinatory elements. Light is also a source of heat as energy. It can be measured, monitored, and manipulated. It is also sensational. Too often, light is portrayed only as an optical phenomenon, but it also reinforces our haptic perception.

Discussing visual perception and chronobiology, Sarah Robinson reminds us that

> Gibson's fifth perceptual system is the visual system in which the eye, the brain, and the body function together inseparable. The visual system registers constantly varying intensity of multidirectional light. The cells in the retina do not signal absolute levels of light; they signal the contrast between light and dark. The brain derives meaning from quickly surveying a visual setting, not by recording the scene passively like a camera would—perception is inherently creative.[39]

Our multi-sensory minds actively synthesize observations of our surroundings, and this all begins with our perceptions of light. Psychologically, light can deliver warmth and feeling. Bright light induces an illusion of warmth that intensifies a person's positive and negative responses. Insufficient lighting can alter our circa dian rhythms, while the level and temperature of its color can affect our moods and activity. Intense white light activates our brains, and warm lighting reduces stress.

One thing that attracts people to Aalto's buildings is how light and elements interact with the user. Through his living experience, Aalto negotiated his surroundings by drawing light into affective and effective realities. He seemed to work as a sculptor and as a psychiatrist. His work absorbs psychological and physical aspects of light, resulting in beautiful forms and an enhanced well-being while acclimating social, political, and cultural encounters that came with functioning in everyday life.

According to Sarah Williams Goldhagen, as cited by Eeva-Liisa Pelkonen, Aalto was "schooled in the basic insights and findings of proto-phenomenological experimental psychology" and was "exposed to empathy theory, and probably also the basic precepts of environmental psychology, during his basic training in Jyväskylä." His propensity to discuss physiology, psychology, and neurophysiology brought this to light in writings and lectures over any theory or language outside the realm of architecture and building. For Aalto, architecture was corporeal, made for the human body. Consequently, biological rhythm and the sensation of light are fundamental concerns in architecture, as they are for all living things.

Daylight as a form generator was a principal element that informed Aalto's design decisions. Experience of daylight was harnessed and distributed in various ways. Aalto used a multitude of topological forms and apertures developed to manage light, including window walls, skylights, cloud-like ceiling forms, clerestory lines (high and low), downward glow, cleft surface light, double layer light walls, and light baffles (stepped or applied) to complete the view of the sculpted space. His flexible daylighting system suggested that light is a *material* just as it is an energy force that "dissolves" figures from nature into built form.

Christian Norberg-Shultz described the unique Nordic experience of light: "The sun does not rise to a zenith but grazes things obliquely and dissolves in an interplay of light and shadow."[40] As Robert McCarter writes of Aalto, "his ability to both enrich and extend the thin Nordic light and draw the buildings directly out of the landscape as if they were natural geological formations."[41]

At the Kunsten Museum (1972) in Aalborg, Denmark, we see a technical imagination of light. Metaphorically, the light baffles can appear like roof ice of a snowbank, suspended, sculpted, or melted by light (Figure 5.3). These forms appear to scoop the changing light throughout the day, directing it into the galleries while preventing glare (Figure 5.4). These baffles are mood-enhancing technical devices, nesting mechanical and lighting systems, and intended to "accommodate a service corridor allowing adjustment of the electric lamps."[42]

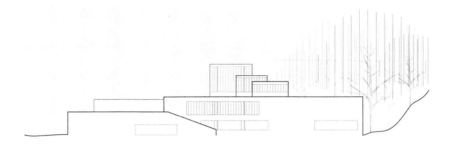

FIGURE 5.3   Kunsten Museum Formation

Daylight and nightlight affect the physiological atmosphere. The daylight in the northern latitudes of Scandinavia is characterized by a high/low, long/short solar dialectic. This effect is unique by what might be called *seasonal dimorphism*, a zoological term defined as two distinct varieties that appear in different seasons. Aalto, knowing this dialectic, used the technics of light to improve optics, reduce glare, increase lux, and influence psychological perception. Various spatial and aperture positions afford a multi-variant experience that enriches basic lighting needs during different seasons.

*Seasonal Affective Disorder* (SAD) is a phenomenon prevalent in most northern climates. Aalto was intuitively aware of SAD symptoms well before Norman E. Rosenthal established the term in the 1980s. The lack of sunlight in the winter is a principal factor in developing seasonal depression. Vital to any neurological discussion of light is the *circadian rhythm*. A mashup of the Latin words for *approximately*, 'circa,' and *day*, 'diem,' the term refers to the 24-hour period of the earth's rotation.

Research suggests that people with SAD overproduce melatonin, a neurotransmitter involved in regulating circadian rhythms. The overproduction of melatonin could lead to idleness and unhappiness. We now know that we can help alleviate these symptoms by introducing light variation therapy, and by creating more social interactions during the dark of winter. Aalto's mood-enhancing architecture sought to achieve this organically. Aalto denoted these rhythms by placing forms around an interconnecting room that created varied light zones.

The Rovaniemi Civic Center (1965), located at the Arctic Circle, has a library with a similar fan-shaped reading room to Seinäjoki. However, the Rovaniemi Library faces the opposite direction, responding to the latitude.

Aalto developed varying light zones focusing more light in specific functional areas. This zoning is essential to creating dynamic variation. Merete Madsen documents this condition in *Light-zone(s): as Concept and Tool*,[43] which displays a daylight diagram for the central reading room where these variations occur

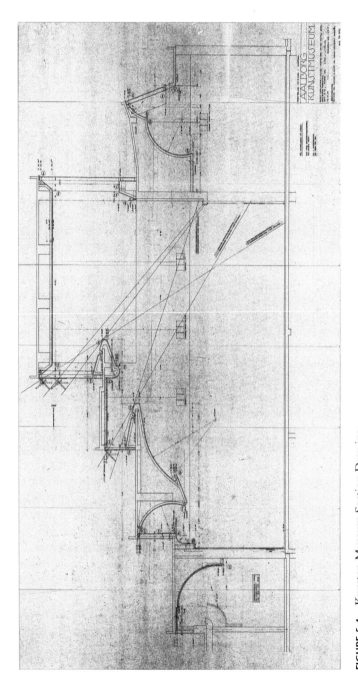

**FIGURE 5.4** Kunsten Museum Section Drawing

*(Credit:* Alvar Aalto Foundation 44–1056)

(Figure 5.5). One light zone is at the control desk, made by a 'scoop' skylight facing south. The second is by the conical skylights in various locations. Last, the canted clerestory windows of the north-facing reading room are most significant. The daylighting systems present indirect light described by Aalto as rational light for a library.

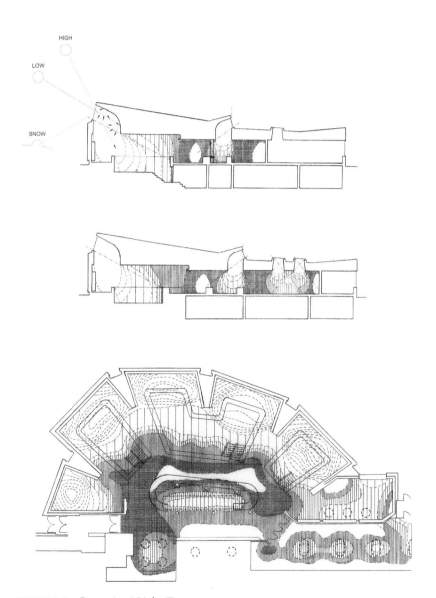

**FIGURE 5.5**   Rovaniemi Light Zones

*(Credit:* Merete Madsen)

Aalto was particularly sensitive to the combination of natural and artificial lighting in a room. As such, lighting was a primary area of exploration. Aalto's daylighting through various forms of window and skylight, electric lighting inventions, and experiments in material, color, and use of plants were not just aesthetic or rational; they influenced the psychological well-being of the inhabitants. Aalto went to great effort to understand combinations of natural and artificial light to provide a conducive median of light levels required throughout the day to create better lighting for people.[44]

He often used artificial lighting structures to simulate the summer sun in winter. We see this in many of his buildings across different typologies, with round skylights often with luminaires within them or mounted above on the outside. Aalto placed lighting between layers of inward and outward facing skylights, in coves and recesses for indirect bands of light, and in most fixtures where the lamp is hidden.

These various lighting strategies and integrations demonstrate a technical understanding of lighting and its effects not seen in many other buildings of his time. There were also hanging lamps, wall lamps, floor lamps, table lamps, and, of course, a multitude of ceiling fixtures. The range and positioning of light made for architectural effects with the illumination of tables, walls, and volumes of space, often delineating lightness and darkness to "screen" spaces from one another.

Aalto did this to affect our minds. In 'Rationalism and Man' (1935), Aalto pronounced,

> My aim was to show that real rationalism means dealing with all questions related to the object concerned, and to take a rational attitude also to demands that are often dismissed as vague issues of individual taste, but which are shown by more detailed analysis to be derived partly from neurophysiology and partly from psychology. Salvation can be achieved only and primarily via an extended concept of rationalism.[45]

The experiential process surrounding architecture is *in* and *of* the world, not simply *about* the world. These illuminations bring forward the *whole* of the world, not just our intellectual imaginations. Aalto understood this in arriving at design solutions, devising forms and using materials that resolved situations of the environment for the body. His primary form-making strategy resulted in material choices and modes of expression that contribute to the health and wellness of people.

These form-system instruments were not accidental. They were achieved by careful measure, analysis, and experiment. Today, we can simulate the effects of climate and daylighting of a place. Using our tools to evaluate and uncover the natural logic surrounding buildings in their places can lead us to new, more responsive environments.

## The Conditions of Building

Buildings designed as closed systems fail to consider the climate or the people dwelling inside. Buildings constructed in the past made opportunities to exchange flows. These flows were manifest by the interaction of material and space, light and air. However, from the close of WWII until changes mandated after the 1970s energy crisis, buildings were typically made of steel and glass, with little regard for energy usage throughout a building's life, or of material mass, consuming large quantities resources and energy during construction.

The mass of Chartres Cathedral in France is quite immense. It is built of solid stone and has existed for many lifetimes. Because of this long life-cycle, the initial embodied energy is divided over time. Here, longevity is clemency for consumption, and the building will continue standing for many lifetimes to come. Yet, the embodied mass affords sensation beyond visual and factual justification. It provides a complete psychophysical experience.

Crossing the threshold of the narthex is a boundary of sensation, a thermodynamic delight, as the cooling climate developed by the building mass arouses the human senses. As the somatic sensation moves through one's body, the light catches one's eye. Provoking an imaginative event as if moving through time, one senses the hand and the stonemason's hammer. This stone touches us back. *Beyond* beautiful, the building is a body full of life.

Through Aalto, we see that building mass and specific spatial arrangements can affect thermal performance and bodily sensation while using little energy. However, from the viewpoint of ecological tectonics, we can no longer build with immense mass and must use less energy. Therefore, under today's circumstances, we rely on material spatial arrangements and calculated technics to property condition our buildings.

From a technical point of view, as described by Fitch in *American Building: The Forces That Shape It* (1947), consideration in design and construction is "the function of a building to control the rate at which heat is lost." Since buildings are no longer laden with mass and their inherent temperament but with air, material choices and their associated technics are critical. For comparison, to achieve an R-value of 30, a masonry wall without interior insulation would need to be 150 inches thick. To achieve the same R-value with polyisocyanurate insulation, we need only 4 inches. With glass, the best R-value that one can expect is 6, and this comes with a cost. These measures mean something to our design considerations, and they should be resolved through considerations that surpass applications of tiny windows or simply adding more insulation.

For Aalto, environmental tempering was part of a building's instrumentalization. When understanding the building as a body of embedded natural forms, it is not possible to separate the apparatus of thermal comfort and visual sensation from the overall form-system-dynamic.

In his lecture, 'The Influence of Structure and Material on Contemporary Architecture,' Aalto discussed, "the question of insulation . . . is understood broadly as ranging from ways to provide shelter from natural forces to ways to separate people and groups of people from one another . . . (the only provisions for insulation in the early days was choice of a building site)."[46] He also discussed insulation and material methods of roofing, surface treatments, and central heating systems. In 'The Humanizing of Architecture,' he wrote: "Study of the relation between the individual and his quarters involved the use of experimental rooms and covered the questions of room form, colors, natural and artificial light, heating systems, noise and so on."[47]

Designing with thermodynamic considerations provides an opportunity to create wholly ecological buildings and interact more precisely with climate, matter, and the human body. Moreover, this deliberation affords a phenomenological reading attained through formal relationships and measured science.

Kiel Moe writes, "The apparatus of insulation—and its co-determinant air-conditioning apparatus—developed more universally applicable heat transfer theories first and later asked questions about human comfort and physiological response."[48] A significant problem of much of the mid- to late 20th-century architecture was that spaces were filled with artificial air inside sealed containers disassociated with physiology. Moe continues, "The physiological apparatus of the human body might better serve as the starting point of an architectural agenda for energy and heat flux than the historical contingencies of conductivity and refrigeration research." Only when we place body and mind at the center of our discourse can we fulfill the promise of a thermodynamic architecture.

The idea is to activate the building's passive body, saving energy by using less active systems and enacting somatic psychology. Developing this method, we need to understand a few things: 1) A building resides in an environment and must respond to that environment, 2) A building must perform efficiently and consume less, 3) Because the body of a building is in service of our bodies, it should sense our needs and desires.

## The Healthy Building Sensory System

With normal functioning physiology, one is considered in tune with their body, but considered out of tune when sick. Why should this be different for the physiology of a building? How do we know if our building is in good health and in service of our health?

Buildings should no longer be considered *machines for living* but a living *apparatus for health and sensation*. To accomplish this, we look to studies on comfort with a thermodynamic measure of varying activities. Past and current efforts to develop accurate human comfort modules and models help apportion naturally conditioned spaces and implement more thermally active materials.

Measures of comfort in dynamic buildings play a role in providing healthy environments. We are susceptible to sudden temperature changes, which could impede cognitive performance and result in antagonism on an emotional level. A well-balanced temperature is essential for creating comfortable surroundings.

In 1957, discussing the module of man, Victor Olgyay wrote,

> the module stems not from visual proportions but is correlated with the movements of the sun and formulated to satisfy Mans's biological needs. Man, with his intimate physical and emotional needs, remains the module— the central measure—in all approaches. The success of every design must be measured by its total effect on the human environment.[49]

The Olgyay brothers, Victor and Aladár, later defined the dynamics of comfort for architecture as *The Bioclimatic Index* (1963), which was developed to comprehend this total effect and define a measured zone of comfort. Although it does not deal with the senses as a whole or the qualities of an environment, the bioclimatic index helps measure pleasant or unpleasant temperatures and co-determinant humidity.

Studies suggest that we spend 87 percent of our time indoors. Knowing the health impacts of being indoors, we must design buildings to be responsive to the needs of inhabitants. First, we must review the way a building responds to its environment. Second, we must determine spatial demarcations and provide porous boundaries that develop adequate air flows both indoors and out. Third, we must analyze materials under varying conditions and look to provide sensual experiences. Finally, we must measure these systemic elements, not merely to meet code compliance, but to create a heightened sense of comfort, pleasure, and health.

The United States Environmental Protection Agency defines the term "indoor air quality"[50] as the air quality within and around buildings and structures, primarily in relation to the health and comfort of a building's inhabitants. Understanding and controlling common pollutants indoors can help reduce the risk of health concerns. Yet, there are many ways to measure air quality. For architects, the equation is to design with proper passive ventilation, acutely moderate how air flows, and maintain quality by sensing temperature, humidity, and contaminants.

Many strategies in maintaining indoor air quality rely upon artificial mechanical systems to perform the work of the building breathing apparatus, but this is not a sustainable practice. If a building is to naturally respond to its environment, it must be made to breathe on its own.

How a building consumes energy and maintains comfort is determined by many factors—how it is formed in its place, its material construction, and its mechanics. Living organisms have evolved systems to conserve energy in harmony within specific habitats. Likewise, we can mimic natural formations and compress evolution through our insights, experiences, and tools that enable the testing of many variables at once. Considering multiple inputs and their significance allows us to look to past experiences, historical precedents, and natural processes.

Buildings designed with ecological responsiveness require direct sensing capabilities. Architects can integrate intelligent devices to coordinate literal and phenomenal atmospheric analysis of spaces. Instruments can acquire real-time data used to measure and adjust the body of a building as the weather changes or per our inhabitation. These sensors monitor wind speed, solar radiation, relative humidity, air and surface temperature, occupancy, daylighting, and biologic or toxic contaminants. Using these devices more comprehensively can aid in developing greater energy efficiency and healthier environments.

Systems and Apps can be developed to enhance the emotive side of sensory experience. Eye and heartrate monitors, and possibly body language readers, can be made with an intelligent assistant to provide real-time (dynamic) system adjustments. Using a touch screen device for these activities is not consistent with a comprehensive design. Manual input devices are impulsive and are often subject to human error. Smart technology sensors and assistants can automate efficiently to regulate and help expose unconscious perception in a building. Designing material interrelationships that combine dynamic sensing systems and computational analysis makes the instrumentality of architecture more valuable and effective.

For architects, computational processes are becoming part of a data reception framework used to analyze the constraints and components of systems. Architects are the agents in developing new values and providing outlines that employ phenological computing and biomimicry to affect thermodynamic performance, helping to optimize built form. To make this whole, we must also include the field of neuroscience.

## Neuroscience and the Future of Architecture

Existential threats of climate, depleted resources, global pandemic, social upheaval, and political megalomania have heightened the way we observe our surroundings and each other. As a result, more respectful analysis is necessary for designers to protect our physical and mental health.

Aalto used the terms *neurophysiology* and *psychophysical field* to relate designing and building to the mind. Today, expectations on the collaboration between architecture and neuroscience are promising. Measurements of psychophysiological reactions (sensors) can give more precise readings of experiences and uses of architectural space. In addition, these measures and scientific experiments can help us design and realize better environments by matching the psychophysical needs of occupants.

In *Neuromorphic Architecture* (2012), computer scientist Michel Arbib writes "on the attempt to answer the question: What if a building had a 'brain' or, more accurately, a nervous system?"[51] Arbib calls for building design with an "interactive infrastructure,"[52] as a system that would cognitively resemble the function of our hippocampus and "keep track of people within the building and perhaps communicate with them to provide a whole new, adaptive level of human support."

Neurophysiology is vital to conceptualizing new forms of architecture. For example, biological systems affected by environmental stress trigger the same neural response to pain and emotion. Likewise, psychological perceptions of light are responsible for the correct functioning of our circadian rhythms and, consequently, our moods and comfort levels. Therefore, we should study and create architecture according to measured form-system-material responses through empathic imaginations.

When thinking about form, our visual imaginations are guided by topological[53] or geometric readings. On the other hand, our empathetic imaginations generate psychophysical experiences through sensory memory systems. These are brought together in architecture by embodied simulation, visualizing the meaning of built form by activating hypothetical and mnemonic experiences of places in our minds.

In 2017, Palassmaa wrote, "I believe that neuroscience can reveal and reinforce the fundamentally mental, embodied, and biological essence of profound architecture against current tendencies toward increasing materialism, intellectualization, and commodification."[54] He continued by stating,

> Our entire being-in-the-world is a sensuous and bodily mode of being. The body is not the stage of cognitive thinking, but the senses and our bodily being as such structure, produce and store silent knowledge. We, therefore, understand architecture through our bodies and metabolic systems.[55]

As a metabolic system monitoring and responsiveness towards the body and comfort, the digital presence goes beyond questions of design, fabrication, and energy efficiency. Conditioned to the senses, the building's "brain" adjusts the body of the building as it touches our human bodies through material design. Likewise, the building augments our perceptions by dynamically responding to the conditions surrounding our well-being.

We hope that in time, digital design and building information systems will also imbed parameters to help us provide more informed *neurocentric* (brain) and *thermodynamic* (body) measures. Academic pedagogy and professional undertakings can then develop more equitable design and reward. Imagine how tools used in neuroscience could help measure comfort and experience? What would be the ultimate measure of our buildings? What might we learn? How would we then award buildings for excellence?

As soon as we can use virtual reality in the design process to simulate the atmospheric elements of environments, neuroscience may become an exciting line of inquiry for architects. Through this merger, architects would have actual data to predict and demonstrate what is working and what is not.

We suspect that neuroscience studies may also help produce better aesthetic decisions. Once the building is complete and we are able to evaluate the impacts of this merger, we will be able to make better judgments as to whether neuroscience technics can *phenomenally* impact architecture. If, for example, we imagine a post-occupancy neurological survey that measures the impacts of perceptual comfort—acoustics, daylighting, thermal comfort, indoor air quality, and so on—compared with our projected design parameters, we could not only evaluate energy performance as we do now but appreciate and anticipate all the psycho-physical impacts of our designs and material decisions.

## The Löyly Sauna

Sauna bathing is an essential part of Finnish culture and national identity. Löyly comes from the old Finnish word for spirit or soul,[56] the envelope of heat and steam that surrounds you in the sauna as water is poured on the hot rocks. The Löyly Sauna in Helsinki, Finland, looks to capture this concept in mind and body (Figure 5.6).

The idea is formed with a conventional rectangular glass box containing warm, heat-absorbing materials, covered with a free-form wooden *cloak* enveloping the sauna and restaurant (Figure 5.7). The horizontal lamella permit views from the inside but shields the outside and creates seating pockets between the inner and outer envelopes. It protects the interior from the coastal climate in winter, admitting low sun while reducing summer cooling loads by blocking the high sun. The material conditions create various sundecks and stairs, simultaneously enacting the thermodynamic boundary.

Computer-aided design helped to coordinate the welded steel substructure and to fabricate the thermo-mechanically modified wood planks milled on CNC machines. The spacing of the planks follows dimensional Finnish standards that allow these lines to remain in continuity with the stair (Figure 5.8).

The building is made with a low profile not to obstruct views. It presents an atmosphere of relaxation that is conditioned by the surroundings. Inside, a raised platform in the restaurant divides the space into two areas, as the wall, used for seating, positions views out to the sea. Outside, the sloping surfaces create intimate terraces and an outdoor auditorium for viewing marine sports activities (Figure 5.9).

The building uses black concrete to absorb heat, light local wood, blackened steel, and wool. These materials create an interplay of light and dark, warm and cool, and they contrast the dimly lit sauna with the naturally lit restaurant. In addition, these materials are durable and long-lasting. The wood, for example, is

**FIGURE 5.6**  Photo, Löyly Sauna, Finland, Avanto Architects, 2016

(*Credit:* www.kuvio.com/#/lyly/ Anders Portman & Martin Sommerschield)

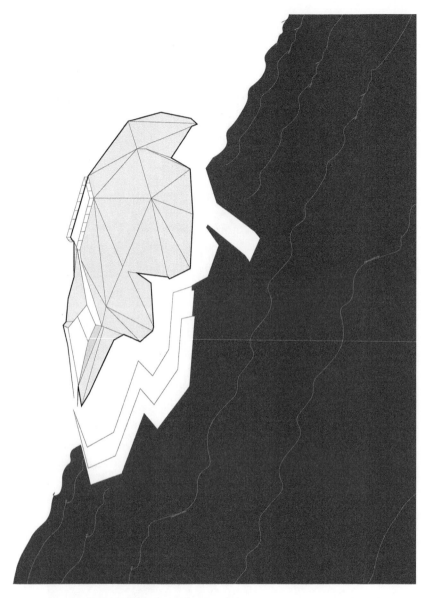

**FIGURE 5.7** Löyly Sauna Cloak & Site Condition

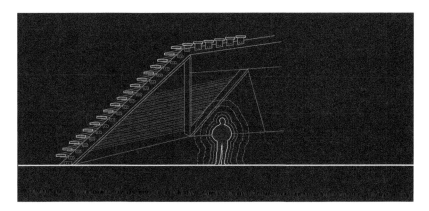

**FIGURE 5.8**  Löyly Sauna Boundary Details

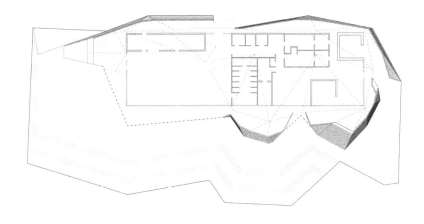

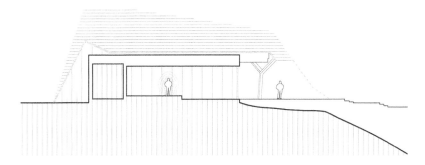

**FIGURE 5.9**  Löyly Sauna Section & Site Situation

**FIGURE 5.10** Minna no Mori Gifu Media Cosmos, Japan, Toyo Ito & Associates, 2015

(*Credit:* Alexis Sakatis)

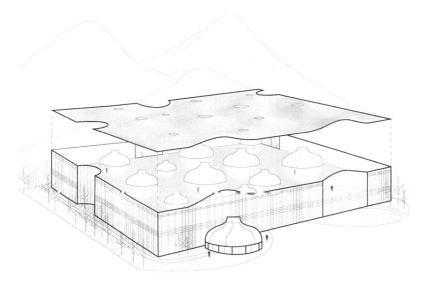

**FIGURE 5.11**  Gifu Roof and Lantern Isometric

pressed, glued, and slightly heat-treated birch—a sustainable Finnish innovation made using leftover plywood industry materials. Löyly Sauna is the first Forest Stewardship Council (FSC)-certified building in Finland.

The thermodynamic building system comprises three different saunas: a continuously heated sauna, a once heated sauna that stays warm through the evening, and a traditional smoke sauna. In addition, a spa with a cold-water basin and a fireplace is placed between the saunas. The bathing experience extends through a stairway leading into the sea for summer swimming or plunging into the winter ice.

Like many Aalto projects in Finland, the building is heated with district heating, and its electricity is produced using water and wind power.

## The Minna no Mori Gifu Media Cosmos

The Minna no Mori Gifu Media Cosmos is a two-story building that contains a central library, community activity spaces, and an exhibition gallery beneath a continuous timber roof (Figure 5.10). The building directly views the symbolic Mount Kinka and was designed to be in harmony with the surrounding forest (Figure 5.11).

Ito's *Home-for-All*, a project made to house displaced people after the 2011 tsunami, established parameters for a new way of thinking about architecture.

**FIGURE 5.12**  Gifu Clearings Plan

This project incorporates three tenets to "revive connections between the hearts of one another, to nurture energy to live, and to be created and built by all." According to Ito, buildings "might offer not only a new community architecture but also . . . a new kind of society." During the design process of Minna no Mori ("forest for all"), workshops were held with local citizens to discuss the building's functions (Figure 5.12).

The floor plans are open to *gather under one roof*. With demarcated clearings made by 11 globes and lanterns suspended from the roof, zones are defined for reading, resting, and studying. The lanterns are made of a white polyester fabric that creates compartments for conditioned air and filters natural and artificial light, ensuring optimal lighting conditions. The changing light environment affords a peaceful atmosphere imbued with nature's presence. The tranquil light and temperature control under each lantern provide empathetic arrangements that are sensorial and psychophysical (Figures 5.13 and 5.14).

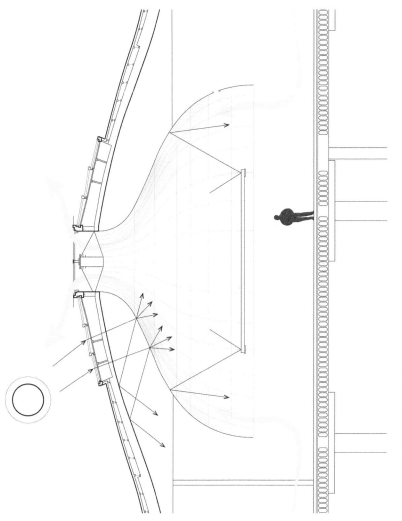

**FIGURE 5.13** Gifu Day Section

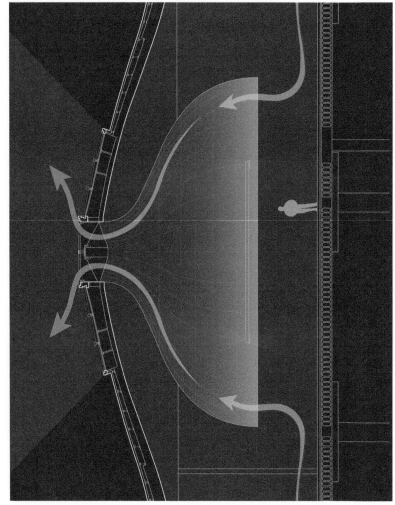

**FIGURE 5.14** Gifu Night Section

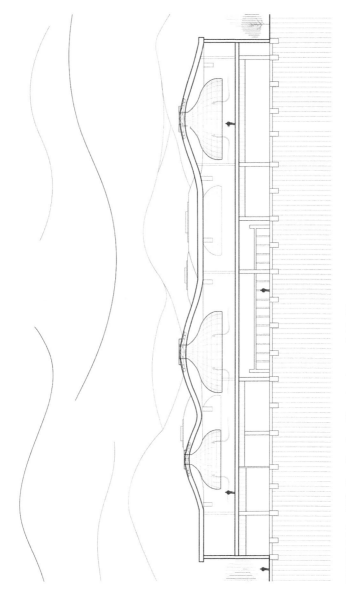

**FIGURE 5.15** Gifu Day Section Illumination and Air Flow

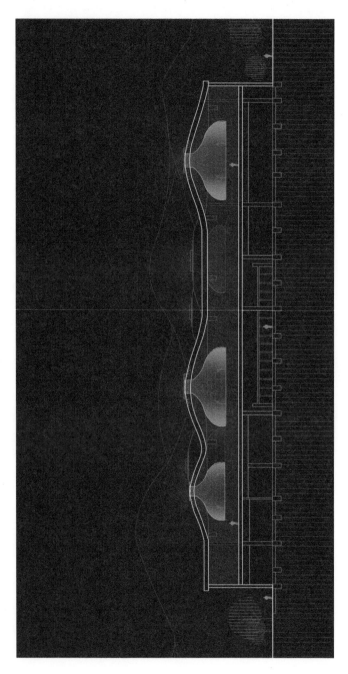

**FIGURE 5.16**   Gifu Night Section Illumination and Air Flow

A wooden lattice grid-shell roof curves to accommodate the lanterns, amplifying the effects of the light and wind, and recalling the shape of the surrounding mountains. Above each lantern is a skylight and an air damper for passive ventilation. The geometry of the 'bell mouth' enhances airflow inside the building, and experiments showed that this passive design would reduce the building's energy consumption by 40 percent.[57] This strategy is advanced with a radiant floor heating and cooling system that is connected to underground water, solar energy, and evening air purging. With its operable skylight system, the entire building can be opened to nature. Considering its imaginative energy and natural lighting strategy, the building is a model for public space in the 21st century (Figures 5.15 and 5.16).

Ito has said,

> before Japan's modernization, we used to think of ourselves as part of nature, and also of architecture as part of nature. We understood humans, architecture, and the environment as part of one interrelated system . . . to get beyond modernism, we probably need to look for new approaches.

The building's planning suggests a new paradigm; a free plan with open regions, interconnected yet segmented for climatic purposes across its open field. This plan type limits energy consumption and establishes intimacy in its public space. It is made with natural and lightweight materials, and it relies on contemporary design and fabrication technology. It is a new typology that embraces the future, enhances our neurophysiology and psychology, and delivers social equity.

## Notes

1  Lefort, Claude. *Merleau-Ponty, Maurice. L'oeil et l'esprit.* Gallimard, 1985, p.16.
2  Holl, Steven. *Intertwining: Selected Projects 1989–1995.* Princeton Architectural Press, 1996, p.16.
3  Pallasmaa, Juhani. *Lived Space: Embodied Experience and Sensory Thought.* OASE#58, 2002.
4  Goldhagen, Sarah Williams. 'Ultraviolet: Alvar Aalto's Embodied Rationalism,' *Harvard Design Magazine*, Fall 2007/Winter 2008, pp.38–52.
5  Moe, Kiel. *Insulating Modernism: Isolated and Non-Isolated Thermodynamics in Architecture.* Walter de Gruyter GmbH, 2014, p.209.
6  Zumthor, Peter. *Peter Zumthor Works: Buildings and Projects 1979–1997.* Princeton Architectural Press, 1999, p.156.
7  Weston, Richard. *Villa Mairea: Alvar Aalto.* Phaidon, 1992.
8  Rahm, Philippe. *Thermodynamic Architecture*, Proceedings, ACADIA 08 › Silicon + Skin › Biological Processes and Computation, 2008, pp.46–50.
9  Fermi, Enrico. *Thermodynamics.* Dover Publications, 1956, p.30.
10  ibid., p.58.
11  See Michel Serres for conversation on systems, imbalance, equilibrium, and time, in Serres, Michel. 'The Origin of Language: Biology, Information Theory and Thermodynamics,' *Oxford Literary Review*, Volume 5, Number 1–2, pp.113–124. https://doi.org/10.3366/olr.1982.008.

12 Albright, Thomas D. 'Neuroscience for Architecture,' in *Mind in Architecture: Neuroscience, Embodiment, and the Future of Design*. MIT Press, 2017, p.202.

13 Rahm, Philippe. *Digestible Gulf Stream, Architecture as Meteorology, Architecture as Gastronomy*. http://www.philipperahm.com/data/projects/digestiblegulfstream/index.html (Accessed 05 March 2022).

14 Robinson, Sarah, 'Nested Bodies,' in *Mind in Architecture: Neuroscience, Embodiment, and the Future of Design*. MIT Press, 2017, p.142.

15 Rüegg, Arthur, Ed. *Polychromie Architecturale: Le Corbusier's Color Keyboards from 1931 and 1959*. Birkhäuser, 1997, p.221.

16 Schildt, Göran. *Alvar Aalto: The Complete Catalogue of Architecture, Design, and Art*. Random House, 1994, p.69.

17 Aalto, Alvar. 'The Humanizing of Architecture,' in *Alvar Aalto in His Own Words*. Ed. Schildt, Göran. Otava, 1997, pp.102–107 (Aalto).

18 Pallasmaa, *Lived Space*.

19 Rahm, *Digestible Gulf Stream*.

20 Benedito, Silvia. *Atmosphere Anatomies: On Design, Weather, and Sensation*. Lars Müller Publishers, 2021, pp.15–16.

21 Böhme, Gernot, *OASE 91 Building Atmosphere*. NAi010 uitgevers, Nl/Eng, 2013, ISBN 978-94-6208-107-9 19,95.

22 Aalto, 'Rationalism and Man,' p.91.

23 Aalto, 'The Humanizing of Architecture,' pp.106–107.

24 Aalto, Alvar. Finnish Architectural Review, 1935, 152. As quoted in The Building that Disappeared, The Viipuri Library by Alvar Aalto, by Laura Berger, Aalto University publication series Doctoral Dissertations 127/2018.

25 ibid.

26 Marsio-Aalto, Aino. Fig 7. Travel diary, notes on the City Library, Viipuri, 1934–35, Stritzler-Levine, Nina. 'City Library, Viipuri, 1936,' in *Artek and the Aaltos: Creating a Modern World*. Bard Graduate Center, 2016, p.298.

27 Salingaros, Nikos. *Neuroscience, the Natural Environment, and Building Design, in Biophilic Design*, Wiley, 2008, p.63.

28 Passe, Ulrike. *Alvar Aalto's Open Plan Architecture as an Environmental Technology Device*. Working papers—Alvar Aalto Researchers' Network, 12–14 March 2012, Seinäjoki and Jyväskylä.

29 Stoakes, P., Passe, U., and Battaglia, F. 'Predicting Natural Ventilation Flows in Whole Buildings Part 1: The Viipuri Library,' *Building Simulation: An International Journal*, Volume 4, Number 3, 2011, Tsinghua University Press and Springer Press. Air flow simulations of the Viipuri Library were conducted to show how the spatial layout affected airflow for passive cooling and heating.

30 Pallasmaa, Juhani. A lecture entitled, *Mental and Existential Ecology*, Ljubljana, October 2009.

31 Patterson, Robert Earl, and Eggleston, Robert G. 'Intuitive Cognition,' *Journal of Cognitive Engineering and Decision Making*, Volume 11, Number 1, March 2017, pp.5–22.

32 Izaki, Christian Derix. *Empathic Space: The Computation of Human-Centric Architecture AD*. Wiley, 2014, 2nd Edition; Pallasmaa, Juhani. 'Empathic Imagination: Formal and Experiential Projection,' in *Empathic Space: The Computation of Human-Centric Architecture*. Ed. Derix, Christian and Izaki, Åsmund. Wiley E-Book, November 2014, pp.80–85.

33 ibid.

34 Goldhagen, Sarah Williams. *Welcome to Your World: How the Built Environment Shapes Our Lives*. HarperCollins Publishers, 2020, E-Book, p.101.

35 Colomina, Beatriz. *X-Ray Architecture*. Lars Müller Publishers, 2019.

36 Robinson, 'Nested Bodies,' p.151.

37  von Simson, Otto. *The Gothic Cathedral*, Princeton Architectural Press, 1988, 3rd Edition, p.4.

38  Louis Kahn, quoted in *In Praise of Shadows, Tanizaki, Jun'ichirō*. Vintage, 2001 (first edition 1933).

39  Robinson, 'Nested Bodies,' p.150.

40  Norberg Shultz, Christian. *Nightlands: Nordic Building*, trans. Thomas McQuillan. MIT Press, 1996, p.1.

41  McCarter, Robert. *Aalto*. Phaidon Press, 2014, p.216.

42  ibid., p.220.

43  Madsen, Merete. 'Light-zone(s): As Concept and Tool,' in *Enquiry The ARCC Journal for Architectural Research*, Volume 4, Number 1, 2007.

44  Stritzler-Levine, Nina. 'Lighting,' in *Artek and the Aaltos: Creating a Modern World*. Bard Graduate Center, 2016, p.679.

45  Aalto, 'Rationalism and Man,' p.92.

46  Aalto, 'Influence of Structure and Material on Contemporary Architecture,' p.99.

47  Aalto, 'The Humanizing of Architecture,' p.103.

48  Moe, Kiel. *Insulating Modernism: Isolated and Non-isolated Thermodynamics in Architecture*. Walter de Gruyter GmbH, 2014, p.189.

49  Olgyay, Victor, and Olgyay, Aladar. *Solar Control & Shading Devices*. Princeton University Press, 1957, p.5.

50  https://www.epa.gov/indoor-air-quality-iaq/introduction-indoor-air-quality#health (Accessed 05 March 2022).

51  Arbib, Michael. 'Toward a Neuroscience of the Design Process,' in *Mind in Architecture: Neuroscience, Embodiment, and the Future of Design*. MIT Press, 2017. p.84.

52  Arbib, Michael. 'Brains, Machines, and Buildings: Towards a Neuromorphic Architecture,' *Intelligent Buildings International*, Volume 4, 2012, pp.147–168.

53  Pallasmaa, 'Empathic Imagination: Formal and Experiential Projection,' pp.81–84.

54  Pallasmaa, Juhani. 'Body, Mind, and Imagination,' in *Mind in Architecture: Neuroscience, Embodiment, and the Future of Design*. MIT Press, 2017, p.52.

55  Pallasmaa, *Lived Space*.

56  The Architectural Review Online, Typology: Bathhouse, 13 February 2018.

57  Arup. https://www.arup.com/projects/gifu-media-cosmos (Accessed 05 March 2022).

# INDEX